FROM EMPIRE TO REPUBLIC

FROM EMPIRE TO REPUBLIC

An Austrian Editor Reviews Momentous Years

FRIEDRICH FUNDER

Albert Unger Publishing Co.

New York

Translated from the German
VOM GESTERN INS HEUTE
Aus dem Kaiserreich in die Republik
by Barbara Waldstein

English edition
by arrangement with the original publishers,
Verlag Herold, Wien

FOREWORD

Was it really yesterday and not two or three hundred years ago that we boys pored over our Caesar's *De bello Gallico* by candle-light; that a cyclist on a country road was a strange and unwelcome sight; that there was no such thing as an electric streetcar; that there were no films, no automobiles, no radio or television, and that flying was confined to characters in Greek mythology? As though the impact of revolutionary developments, the demands of progress and countless strange new experiences were not unsettling enough in themselves, we who stood between two epochs were called upon to face still further changes. We went through two world wars in rapid succession and we had to exchange our civic rights within an old and great empire for those of a small, troubled, but no less beloved Austria. And now we are facing another age, charged with new tensions and new problems, in which new forces are struggling to form the future.

Farewell and new beginning, crossroads of two eras. But today and tomorrow are inextricably bound up with yesterday, and it is our imperative task to carry over and preserve the essential values and traditions of the past for today and for the future. For was it not this very yesterday, its triumphs and failures, its accomplishments and omissions, indeed all its imperishable truths, which formed the heritage of the little Austria of today in the heart of Central Europe? It was to help the rising Austrian generation toward an understanding of this past that the original German edition of this book was published (by Verlag Herold) in Vienna in 1952. It has since been frequently suggested that the book could fulfill a similar task outside Austria, in fact even beyond the continent of Europe. Such suggestions, many of which have come from America, have led to the preparation of this abridged version, intended primarily for the Anglo-American reader.

Here, just as in the original version, is the voice of an old journalist, dedicated all his life to the ideals of a Christian reform of state and society. He was always ready to do battle when important issues were at stake, but he was ever conscious of his human limitations and increasingly concerned, in the light of experience, to respect the honest convictions of others—including his opponents. He hopes to find understanding, even beyond the frontiers of his own country.

It is seldom easy for the foreigner to be impartial, relying as he must upon the uncertain judgment of his own eye or his own ear, and indeed even on secondhand information, not always free from prejudice and resentment. It is scarcely surprising, therefore, that he is often confronted with a distorted picture of Austria, viewed in the light of inaccurate or ill-intentioned reportage and a biased interpretation of history. However, this book is not intended to be a historical record, but rather a simple contribution, drawn from personal experience, to the judgment of a significant era. God alone can judge the sum of goodwill and human weakness, error recognized too late, and genuine patriotism in those who influenced the turn of history in those fateful days. God alone knows, too, the effect of the disastrous flood of uncurbed passionate emotions upon events in public life and its threat of destruction to state and society.

It is the aim of this edition to deepen understanding of these facts, especially among those who, despite an unreserved admiration for the cultural achievements of the Danube Empire, view its later political developments with a certain sense of discomfort and mistrust.

It is hoped that in its own small way this book may serve to promote international harmony, for it is essentially concerned, not with hatred but with understanding and reconciliation.

DR. FRIEDRICH FUNDER

Vienna,
Spring, 1956

TABLE OF CONTENTS

Chapter I
YOUTHFUL JOURNEY

The gas lamp in the courtyard of a house in the Josefstadt in Vienna cast its feeble light through the high, dusty window of the cellar. The room smelled dankly of benzine and printer's ink. It was cold in the iron bed under the thin blanket, and I tried in vain to get to sleep after the events of the day. In the half-light I saw the outline of the table at which I was to study, and, beside it, the paper-cutting machine, its shining blade like the knife of a guillotine. A solitary chair completed the furnishing. This was to be the future lodging of Friedrich Funder, journalist and student of law at Vienna University, born in Graz[1] on November 1, 1872. In an adjoining cellar stood the few poor-looking machines which were to produce the *Reichspost*, the newly established independent daily newspaper for the Christian peoples of Austria-Hungary—a couple of proof presses and the printing press.

In the mornings I would be able to wash in water run off from the cooling water cistern of one of the machines. Would there be sufficient light down here during the day by which to read and work? I was to earn my living correcting proofs in the little printing office. Would there be enough time left over for those all-important studies? I was already nearly twenty-two and time was precious.

These were the problems of my immediate future which were keeping me awake. Only a fortnight ago I had still been a student of theology in Graz, a second-year seminarist, and now here I was in Vienna! I was poor and alone, without my parents, who had enough worries of their own in Graz. I possessed little else than a single shabby suit of clothes. Yet it was somehow impossible to feel discouraged, for everything had come about in such a wonderful way. A series of images passed before my eyes, the strange chain

[1] Graz is the capital of Styria, formerly a crown province and today a federal province. It lies approximately 130 miles south of Vienna.

of circumstances which had formed my young destiny, until at last sleep came and the events became part of my dreams.

I could remember little of my early childhood. My parents had a baker's shop near Graz. In 1878 my father was invited to join the Dresden chocolate firm Lobeck & Co. and introduce the production of a special type of biscuit known as Graz wafers in their factory in Löbtau near Dresden.

This offer of a post in Dresden came at an opportune moment for my father and seemed a way out of the financial worries and business difficulties of past years. My father was to go to Saxony for an initial trial year, and he left my mother behind in Judenburg with me and my three-year-old sister. Some months after his departure a new sister was born, a fat-cheeked baby whom I dearly loved. But my mother looked pale and worried. Money was short, for my father had to equip himself, at least with bare necessities, in far-off Dresden. Sad weeks followed. Both my little sisters died of scarlet fever within a short time of one another.

When at last the probation year in the Löbtau factory was over, my father summoned us to join him, and in November, 1879, my mother set out with me for Saxony. The industrial town of Löbtau, with its ten thousand inhabitants, had not yet at that time become part of the municipality of the adjoining city of Dresden. Even as a seven-year-old boy I very soon became conscious, in these grim surroundings, of the meaning of a working-class existence. The veneer of the big city had not yet covered the sordid town with its poor shops, the handful of dirty taverns and gin shops and the barber who did double duty as dentist. There was also somewhere an unpretentious Protestant church.

Long columns of pale-faced workers tramped to the factories every morning and home again in the evening. Once I watched them at work in the great fire-glowing workshop of the Siemens glass factory, gazing in terrified amazement as they blew bottles out of the red-hot molten glass. Food was very simple for these workers— a basic diet of herrings and potatoes. There was no public park or garden to break the monotony of the grim mass of industrial buildings, and the playground of the working-class children was the bed of a grimy stream which flowed between two sloping stone walls.

Here I soon learned from my contemporaries to dam up pools for the poor feeble little fish that had somehow contrived to escape death in the poisoned waters poured into the stream from the factories.

My parents had long planned to return home to Styria, and toward the end of 1886 they began to make serious preparations.

On a sunny day in April, 1887, we left Dresden station, a family of five with a modest collection of luggage. The train puffed its way along the banks of the Elbe and past the stony crags of the mountains of Saxony toward the Bohemian plains. It was a long day.

Vienna was veiled in mist, its towers and steeples rising out of the gray morning haze like castles in a fairy tale. Indeed this whole lovely city, with its white buildings and their shining windows on the hills of the Kahlenberg and Leopoldsberg, had a unique magic quality. Smoke curled over the Danube from the funnels of the steamers as our train hurtled over the bridge of the Nordbahn. I soon had my first sight of the Tegetthoff monument (how well I knew the story of Lissa!)[2] and then suddenly the spire of St. Stephen's cathedral rose above the Prater Street, miracle of silver-gray stone tracery against the morning sky. I remember the quiet moments of prayer and recollection inside the cathedral, the soft, warm accent of the friendly people who were ready to answer our questions and show us our way. As we passed down the Graben the young housemaids in their white caps were airing featherbeds in the sun from the windows of the tall, imposing houses (in Dresden the police would certainly have forbidden such a thing!). I was filled with a new, indefinable feeling of inner hilarity: I felt deliciously carefree and content with the world. My pleased astonishment increased as we crossed the Kohlmarkt and the courtyard of the Emperor's Palace to the Ring, whence a troop of the imperial guard came marching past in full array.

These first impressions of old imperial Vienna have always remained in my memory, like the pensive smile of a lovely graceful woman.

[2] Lissa is an island in the Adriatic and was an Austrian naval base. The Italian fleet which attacked this base on July 20, 1866, was defeated by the Austrian naval forces under Admiral Tegetthoff.

Home again in Graz, it was not long before I entered the seminary. It was a completely new world for me but I was happy. Fortunately a pleasant, friendly relationship soon grew up between myself and both my superiors and fellow pupils, who were much amused by my Saxon accent.

The Austrian school demanded hard work and we learned a great deal, but, despite the full curriculum, we were never over-burdened and, with a little planning, there was always time left over for reading, games and sport. In the fifth class I became one of the founders of a literary society called *Der Eichenbund* (The Oak League).

Events in the outside world began to make their first serious impression upon us boys during our last years at school. We began to take a special interest in events at the University of Graz, where we ourselves would shortly be students. The German-Austrian[3] universities throughout the monarchy were characterized at that time by their atmosphere of seething agitation, and many of the students were caught up in a kind of spiritual crisis, the causes of which were as serious as the effects were dangerous. The roots of this strange state of unrest lay deep in national political affairs.

It is difficult today fully to appreciate the many complex problems that faced the Austrian Empire at that time. Yet such problems laid the foundation for the subsequent events which for decades confused the political thinking of countless German-Austrians, seriously hindered the open discussion of vital questions of future state policy so necessary for the welfare of the Empire as a whole, and caused the ideological digression of many intellectuals of the younger generation. Without some attempt at a psychological analysis of events at the time, it is hardly possible to understand how so much high idealism and energy could have been misused to the detriment of the German population in Austria, and indeed

---

[3] The expression "German" or "German-Austrian" used refers to the German-speaking population of the Dual Monarchy, comprising 23.3 per cent of the total population. The remainder was made up of Magyars, Czechs, Slovakians, Serbians, Croatians, Poles, Ukranians, Romanians, Slovenians, Italians and Ladinians. The Germans in Austria should in no way be confused with the nationals of the district political unit of Germany proper.

the state as a whole, culminating disastrously in a highly cultivated form of chauvinism.

During the eighteen-fifties, when the first attemps were made to form an Austrian constitution, only a small minority broke away from the traditional national concept of the German-Austrians, the *grossdeutsch* political idea of a Germany under Austrian-Habsburg leadership, and advocated a new Germany under the primacy of Prussia, into which the German-speaking provinces of Austria should somehow be incorporated. Beyond a comparatively small group of the middle-class intelligentsia, little support was to be found for this new *kleindeutsch* solution of the problem. It was indeed significant that, when Emperor Franz Josef returned from the Assembly of Princes in Frankfurt, the Viennese *Burschenschaften*[4] turned out to greet him in full gala uniform.

An anonymous writer, apparently German-Austrian, said in his brochure *Das Deutschtum in Österreich*, published in Leipzig in 1871 by Otto Wigand:

> In addition to the existing "German concept" based on the traditional Austrian principle, there already existed at this time (before 1866), both in individuals and in groups formed to discuss political matters, that genuine national conviction which, despite all prejudices, recognized in Prussia the true leader of Germany. North Germans were very often the first to stimulate the acceptance of the *kleindeutsch* idea, as expressed by the Gotha Program, by the informaiton they spread about north German affairs, with special reference to Prussia. The skepticism with which they were met at first was soon turned into a genuine admiration for their foresight, as the events of 1866 confirmed the hopes they had held for Prussia.

The year 1866[5] brought about a drastic change for Austria and

---

[4] Students' associations professing political or ideological principles and distinguished by the wearing of colors or, on special occasions, by a gala uniform. These unions also were characterized for the most part by their special drinking and duelling practices.

[5] The year 1866 decided the destiny of the German Confederation. Prussia, allied with the smaller states of North Germany, defeated Austria and the troops of the Central German states at the battle of Königgratz. The old German Confederation ceased to exist when Bismarck formed the North German Confederation, which excluded Austria. The term *grossdeutsch*

one which was to have tragic results. The old Empire had not only lost a bloody war and its place within the German Confederation and in Italy, but also suffered the weakening of its position as primary Central European power, bound with the west and southeast by its history, its culture, its very organism and its economic implications. Nine million German-Austrians all at once found themselves cut off by law from their kindred German neighbors, confronted by a new and strange political way of life, alienated from the former *grossdeutsch* concept. Nor was there any apparent substitute for this concept, no fundamental patriotic ideal so essential for the development of the spiritual resources of any nation in the service of the community. Furthermore, it had been these very nine million who had formerly been the leaders among the nations of Austria, not merely on the grounds of tradition and the role they had played in history, but by their natural endowments and merits.

A few years later came the great German victory over France.[6] Bismarck won further distinction as a statesman and a new era began for Prussian Germany.

Where, in this situation, was the man capable of piloting the great ship of the Habsburg Empire on her new course, renewing shattered confidence and restoring lost hopes, repairing wounded pride and inspiring a new patriotic ideal? Faced with reality, it was clear that after such a blow a renewed sense of confidence and well-being within the monarchy itself must first be achieved in order for it to meet the new situation united in strength.

The primary step toward this aim was the Austrian Constitution and the creation of the Dual Constitution, the Austro-Hungarian settlement, or compromise, for the Empire. The measure was, however, only an emergency solution of the problem as a whole, for the dualism thus achieved was inadequate and indeed in part ambiguous: it was by no means a perfect long-term solution. The new

---

represents the solution to the German problem which included Austria. The solution excluding Austria (as successfully imposed in 1866) is known as *kleindeutsch*.

[6] In 1870-71 Bismarck defeated France and proclaimed the German Empire in Versailles on January 18, 1871.

order did, however, provide the Germans in Austria with a significant political "mission." Rightly interpreted, this mission could have led them to a satisfying conviction of their own responsibilities toward the Austrian state, and at the same time, despite the partition, provided them with the sense of fulfilling a high task in the interests of the German-speaking peoples as a whole, and indeed for the peace of Europe. It was Bismarck himself, in fact, who consistently reminded the Germans in Austria of their unique mission, not only in the Treaty of Berlin and in the international mandate for Bosnia-Herzegovina, but also in renewed clear appeals to his devotees in Austria. It was evident that a great European mission still existed for the Danube Empire in the Near East. For this very reason it was vital to remove all obstacles within the Empire itself to an evolutionary new order for the small nations within the monarchy, a development which, by its example, could prepare a peaceable new order for the Balkan states.

In this task, a task for a leading political party, the part representing the German liberalism[7] of the 'seventies failed. This party had long been all-powerful and, since the beginning of the constitutional era in Austria, produced some able men. Here too the state school system, created by that same German liberalism, failed. This anemic system, devoid of all drive and vitality, only instilled in the young people a kind of tepid local patriotism. It gave them no sense of their national responsibilities as Austrians, needed to enable them boldly to face the great changes in Europe itself and within their own

[7] Readers are reminded throughout the book of the fundamental difference between the term "liberal" as used in America and the same term as used in Europe. European liberalism has its roots in the philosophy of the French and German Enlightenment (Descartes and Kant), the aim of which was the *liberation* of the individual from all restrictions. We can differentiate among political liberalism (aimed against feudalism and absolutism), economic liberalism (aimed against the mercantile system, as seen in the physiocratic doctrine of Quesnay and the classic national economy of Adam Smith and David Ricardo), and an ideological liberalism aimed against dogma and the Church.

Political liberalism: The primary and certainly laudable aim, in addition to its demands for the division of legislative and executive power, was the securing of rights for the individual free from state interference. This aim has been embodied by constitutional law in the civil codes of almost all

community. The new Austrian generation which emerged from this school system was listless and resigned, except when the family atmosphere, the personalities of certain outstanding pedagogues, the milieu of imperial Vienna and the school autonomy of certain of the crown provinces (notably the Tyrol and Vorarlberg) succeeded in counteracting to some extent this widespread apathy. It was, however, small wonder that many of the more active elements of this generation felt drawn by the new flourishing Prussian German empire which fired their latent idealism and caught their imagination.

Up to the time of World War I secret societies were growing up among many of the German *Gymnasien* in Austria, starting among young people of fourteen and fifteen and fostering their enthusiasm for an idealized Prussian Germany. These societies were modeled on the students' associations at the universities and imitated their drinking practices and strongly political character. The doctrine of Georg von Schönerer, leader of the pan-German movement, flourished in most of the high schools and universities during the 'eighties. Supporters of the movement wore a cornflower (Bismarck's favorite flower) in their buttonhole, and if possible a Bismarck medal on their watch chain (surreptitiously of course so long as they were still at high school), and they sang "The Watch on the Rhine" in the wine houses. These secret societies were strictly forbidden by the school authorities, and heavy penalties followed their discovery. Though the membership of these societies was not very great, it sufficed to impregnate the various classes. Even certain private schools run by Catholic teaching orders were not entirely free from these influences. At the universities the various students' unions

---

modern states. The system of political liberalism ceased to be effective, however, when it limited representation in public life to the middle classes and it only reluctantly adapted itself to the demands of the approaching democratic age. It was marred in Austria especially by the tragically mistaken nationalities policy with the results of which this book is closely concerned.

Economic liberalism: This doctrine lay behind the developments of the new industrial era, with its well-known advances in production but none the less well-known social misery, especially among the working classes—a source of conflict between Christian and Socialist social reformers.

Ideological liberalism: Although it stimulated art and science, it very often encouraged a blind faith in science and progress alone, resulting in conflict between science and revealed religion.

and associations, distinguished by their individual official badges, openly acknowledged their pan-German tendencies.

As we graduated from the seminary in 1892, each of us realized that no easy path lay before him. Combat ahead? I relished the prospect, for all that I was to be a student of theology.

Chapter 2
ON THE WAY TO A NEW VOCATION

My parents had saved up for the traditional trip to celebrate my matriculation. I looked forward eagerly to this, for I was to visit Linz, the capital of Upper Austria, for the occasion of the third Austrian *Katholikentag*. As long as Catholics in Austria and Germany had still formed a common group, questions of religious and cultural-political importance were discussed at the official general assemblies of German Catholics—*Deutsche Katholikentage*—established in 1848. Six such congresses took place in Austria itself. The last congress in which the Austrians still featured as central figures was held in 1867 in Innsbruck, the capital of the Tyrol. It was not easy after this for the Austrians to organize independent congresses.

At last in 1877 the first such Austrian *Katholikentag*, in which representatives from all the Austrian nations participated, was arranged in Vienna. It took twelve years, however, before the next congress was held. On both occasions the lamentable problem of the press was raised and the lack of a responsible Catholic daily newspaper for all classes of the population was loudly deplored. Despite all the outcry, however, no action was taken to establish such a newspaper, but the tension was growing and Linz would clearly be the scene of repercussions.

Indeed there was every evidence that the congress in Linz would be revolutionary. A new movement had grown up among the German Catholics in Austria, the Christian Social movement emanating from Vienna. New names, new catchwords were to be heard, and people began talking about a "sharper tone." The Catholic press displayed its disapproval of the opinions and methods of the new movement, decrying its religion as hypocrisy and branding its leaders as rowdies and anarchists.

Since representatives of the "sharper tone" movement had already announced in advance their intention of attending the Linz

congress, it was clear from the outset that conflict lay ahead. Young
and old were conscious of the accumulated tension. Young people
waited in eager anticipation, among them myself and the two theological students, Eduard Gürtler and Karl Schwechler, who had
accompanied me to Linz.

There was a tremendous attendance at the *Katholikentag* which
was opened on August 8, 1892, in the building placed at its disposal
by the municipal authorities. Every conference room was packed to
capacity. The division of the two groups was accentuated by the pat-
ent identification of certain well-known public figures with the two
distinct movements, the old and the new.

In order to gain an over-all view of the various subjects which
were to be discussed simultaneously, we three friends agreed each
to take over a different field of activity. Gürtler assumed the press
section, social questions were allotted to Schwechler, and I undertook the school section. I found about sixty people assembled. The
speaker was from Vienna, Dr. Caspar Schwarz, founder and president of the Catholic School Association of Austria, which had been
formed in 1866. He was a versatile speaker. It was high time, he said,
for Catholics to take action against existing conditions in the schools.
Attempts to amend the liberal interdenominational school laws had
proved of no avail. Were the children of Catholic parents to continue to attend these interdenominational schools, which threatened
to destroy all Christian life in Austria? It would only be foolish to
expect any change in this state of affairs from a Liberal state! Catholics must take the matter into their own hands and, by means of a
mass movement, raise the funds from among themselves for the
establishment of private Catholic schools and Catholic teachers'
training colleges. Our age called for action, action to free the
Catholic conscience.

The speech was received with a storm of applause. Monsignor
Zapletal, the white-haired speaker for the opposition, was editor of
the *Graz Volksblatt*. The dignified old gentleman rose to read aloud
a long-winded resolution opposing the proposals of Dr. Schwarz:

"In view of the fact that the Catholic population in Austria is
much too weak to organize such a 'self-help' movement through
the whole monarchy with any measure of success . . . In view of

the fact that the episcopate itself had declared in a joint pastoral letter that Catholics could hardly be asked to *shoulder this extra burden*...In view of the fact that the right of the people to send their children to state schools should not be questioned..."

Opposition, nothing but opposition, but no practical action. The meeting heard the speaker's objections in silence and Dr. Caspar Schwarz's resolution was carried unanimously. I had the impression that judgment was being passed on far more than a mere resolution. It seemed to me that the majority vote was the affirmation of a positive form of Christian action which recognized no national frontiers. It was a protest against the ineffectual methods of an outworn system.

In the corridor outside the press section I met Eduard Gürtler, his face red with excitement. He could hardly wait to describe the heated proceedings in the conference room. The press section, led by the Viennese university professor Prälat Dr. Franz Schindler, had been the scene of a violent clash between the two groups. Before the enthusiastic audience of five hundred or six hundred which had thronged to hear him, the Redemptorist Father Bauchinger had spared no words in his criticism of the state of the existing Catholic press. He declared that there was a real need for a large-scale daily newspaper, published in Vienna in the heart of the Empire, the center of all cultural, economic and public life. Such a newspaper, he said, must be independent and national, conscious of its high Catholic responsibilities and uninfluenced by class or government considerations. The *Vaterland*, although it was the episcopal organ, he pointed out, made no appeal to the broad mass of the people, for in reality it merely served the interests of the aristocracy and feudal landowners who were its proprietors, and was unduly influenced by the government.

The speech drew tumultuous applause and the turbulent proceedings came to an end with the adoption of a resolution proposed by Ambros Opitz, editor of the *Österreichische Volkszeitung*, which appeared in Warnsdorf in Bohemia and was known for its Christian-Social tendencies. The resolution called for immediate steps toward the establishment of a modern "independent newspaper for the Christian peoples of Austria," with a double edition in Vienna.

In his closing speech the chairman did his best to pour oil on the troubled waters of the stormy proceedings. The small minority of old conservatives drew back in a corner to lick their wounds and the riotous atmosphere of the press section infected the entire *Katholikentag*.

We had been present at the birth of the *Reichspost*.

In the autumn of 1892 I received the silk girdle to my black student's soutane. The first crossroads had been passed. Now began the serious inner conflict: much that was normal and natural for a young man in the world had to be discarded. This needed courage and inner strength. I filled notebooks with poems fervently inspired by faith and hope and the spirit of sacrifice and abandonment to the will of God.

The reading room of the college included many Catholic newspapers and, in addition to the conservative periodicals, also one or two Christian-Social weeklies. Their size, news service and list of contributors were proof of their limited technical and financial resources. This was the press which had to compete with the large-scale liberal newspapers with their varied contents, efficient news service, specialist columnists for literature, art, technology and the sciences. There were wealthy newspapers of this kind in every big city, exercising a magnetic attraction, at any rate for the intellectuals. Despite the exertions of really excellent men, the Catholic press was unable, on account of its dire lack of funds, to compete in any way with such opponents, nor to assert itself in vital questions of principle. Commentary on important events was often omitted in the few Catholic daily papers or was clearly not the work of specialists. The daily news from both town and country often appeared late or even not at all. There was no special regular staff of correspondents. It was impossible for such a press to assert itself alongside the liberal press, or in any way to challenge its power.

My friends and I were obsessed by the idea of the new daily paper. If we could not help the Catholic press out of our own pockets, we decided to do our best with our pens. My friend Franz Puchas began reporting on events in Graz for the *Salzburger Chronik* and I undertook the same for the *Linzer Volksblatt*.

I increasingly felt the urge to take up a journalistic career, but there seemed no way in which I could support myself while I was studying.

It was almost Easter. I went to the director of studies, Prälat Dr. Griessl, and asked him to exempt me from the first vows, as I was uncertain of my vocation. The taciturn old man drew his bushy eyebrows together and scrutinized me, with his bright blue eyes. "Do your best to come to a decision soon," he said kindly.

It was indeed high time to come to a decision. The day soon came.

On April 17 I found a letter with a Viennese postmark on my desk. I did not recognize the delicate handwriting on the envelope: apart from two university students, I knew no one in Vienna. Who could have written to me? The form of address was unexpected:

Dear Friend,
I have heard that you intend to leave the seminary. The reason I am writing this letter is in no way to influence you, but rather to invite you to confide in me. At such a time one is in need of good counsel, and this I would like to place at your disposal, together with any help I can give you. Write frankly to me at my Viennese address: Augustinerstrasse 4.
Your sincere friend,
Dr. Carl Weiss

Who could this be? None of my friends recognized the name. Finally I learned that an imperial court chaplain of that name lived at the address given in the letter. Who could have told the writer about me? I have never been able to discover. The letter was a welcome message. In my reply I stated my personal situation quite frankly and declared my ambition to be a journalist. A few days later my unknown well-wisher replied. He wrote that he had discussed the matter with various influential people and asked me to come to Vienna and study law; a good journalist must have a good academic foundation. Preliminary arrangements had been made—the rest would follow.

This letter, which also enclosed a ten-gulden note for my fare to Vienna, followed a note from Ambros Optiz, the speaker at the Linz *Katholikentag* whose resolution for the foundation of a new Catholic daily newspaper had been so enthusiastically adopted. In the meantime he had gone ahead with the establishment of this newspaper, which had been appearing for the last few months under the title *Reichspost.* He asked me to visit him in Vienna. He said he had work for me if, as he had heard from Dr. Weiss, I wanted to be a journalist.

I was the happiest man in the world.

My mother wept bitterly as she gave me her blessing. My father was serious and kind and pressed a few gulden into my hand on parting. He could ill spare the money.

A slow night train bore me away to the capital.

There it was again, this beautiful city which I had loved ever since that day when I first fell under the spell of its enchantment. I walked through the city, conducted by my friends, and our first visit was to the Capuchin church, crowded with worshipers for early Mass. My heart was beating fast as afterward I climbed the steps of the house in the Augustinerstrasse in which Dr. Carl Weiss lived.

A great warmth and kindness radiated from this priest. It was as though I had known him all my life. He and his friends had already raised the money for the entrance fee at the university and for my primary needs. Letters of recommendation had been prepared by means of which I was to receive a scholarship. The most important thing now was to get started with my studies, and I learned that, despite the fact that the term had already begun, it would still be possible for me to be enrolled at the university. I would be able to live in the printing house of the *Reichspost.*

An interview had been arranged for the first Wednesday with Ambros Opitz of the *Reichspost.*[1] He was, however, unable to be

[1] When the *Reichspost* was first founded, the word "Austria" was used in the subtitle of the newspaper, indicating the unity of both states of the monarchy, still constitutionally recognized until 1868 by the use of the term "Austrian Monarchy." By means of the unconstitutional decree of November 14, 1868, this term was replaced by "Austro-Hungarian Monarchy" (Friedrich Tezner. *Die Wandlungen der österreichisch-ungarischen Reichsidee;* Verlag Manz, 1905). The inclusion of "Austria" in the subtitle therefore implied reaffirmation of the former constitutional expression *in the sense of a united Empire.* Dr. Stefan V. Rakovsky, a leading deputy of the Hungarian Catholic People's Party at that time in close touch with Vienna, called the attention of the editor of the *Reichspost* to the consequences of

there and so I was introduced to the editor in chief of the newspaper, Anton Weimar, who received me warmly. He had taken over the organization of the newspaper. He immediately offered me his legal notes, lithographed records of lectures in all the important branches. This was indeed a valuable gift.

Much as I liked the editor, I was not much impressed by what I saw of the newly-founded paper, launched with so much acclamation at the Linz *Katholikentag* as the "independent daily newspaper for the Christian peoples of Austria." Although I understood nothing of the press system as such, the working conditions seemed to me very poor. The wooden cubicles behind which the editors worked all day by lamplight—because the windows faced a dark passage —bore no resemblance to the pleasant editorial offices of the Graz Catholic daily. Wherever one looked in the compositors' workrooms and in the machine room, there was the same state of poverty, so different from the imposing exterior and ample equipment of the Styrian newspaper office. Such surroundings were to be the background for the new great modern Catholic paper with a circulation throughout the whole monarchy! In the little office of the head of the printing department they showed me the brush proof of a brochure, and I was instructed in the art of proofreading. From now on this was to be my daily work.

I would be able to have cheap meals in a little *Gasthaus* nearby and I was shown my sleeping quarters in the cellar adjoining the machine room of the newspaper.

It was here that once again the past and the strange set of circumstances which had brought me to Vienna passed like a procession before my eyes.

I reached for my rosary.

One morning I met the court chaplain, Dr. Weiss, and told him how I was faring in my new surroundings.

---

the use of such a subtitle. Much to the regret of his party, which had counted on the support of the *Reichspost* in combating the militant liberalism of the ruling party, this contradiction of the valid Hungarian constitutional term would hinder the widespread circulation of the newspaper in Hungary. In recognition of the objections raised by their Hungarian friends, the editorial authorities immediately took steps to change the wording of the subtitle: "...for the Christian peoples of Austria-Hungary."

"This won't do," he declared decisively. "Your studies are the most important thing at the moment—they must come first." With the help of one of his friends he found a pleasant, simply-furnished little room for me. With careful management, the sum of my scholarship, together with an allowance from a private benefactor, would cover my personal needs and expenses at the university until the summer.

I soon found my feet in Vienna.

My situation improved out of all recognition in the summer of 1894 when, through the intervention of another kind friend, I was offered the post of tutor in the family of the president of the Vienna High Court, Count Karl Chorinsky. In addition to my board and lodgings, I received a salary which relieved me of all financial worries. I learned much in the Chorinsky household which was to be of value to me all my life. It was a real Catholic family with a genuine faith, practical ideas of Christian charity and a strongly-developed sense of duty. Furthermore, my mind was broadened and my store of knowledge increased by contact with many of the leading figures of the day.

Working as clerks in the local election offices of the United Christians, we young students took an enthusiastic part in the great campaign for the Vienna municipal elections during which the stronghold of liberalism in the city was stormed from May to November, 1895.

As we saw it, the conquest of Vienna was only the prelude to something greater: the Christian-Social ideal must reform the whole nation by means of a great popular movement in which, irrespective of nationality, all Christians would join forces toward creating a constructive new order for society, the economy and the state itself. Each of us young Catholic students would have his part to play, however small this might be.

We held "debating evenings," often attended by Dr. Schindler, his friend Ambros Opitz or the deputy, Dr. Gessmann. We founded the Academic Christian Reading Association as counterpart to the pan-German organized German Reading Room at the university as a meeting center for Catholic students.

Our debates were concerned with topical problems which we

endeavored to analyze scientifically, problems such as electoral rights, corporative constitution, legislation for the protection of labor and land reform.

On one of these evenings I had to deal with the theme "The effects of universal franchise in the United States," a subject on which there was plenty of literature available. The notorious Tammany Hall affair and the Panama scandal had been causing a great stir at the time, and we felt that graft and political corruption were inseparably connected with universal equal suffrage. We came to the conclusion that a purely mechanical extension of the franchise must be opposed, and were in favor of parliamentary representation based on the corporate system. Christian sociologists had, in fact, already been closely concerned since the beginning of the 1890's with the idea of the introduction of a corporate order for society as a whole, to include also the legislative bodies.

As far as my own studies were concerned, I felt I had now reached the stage where I could take on some newspaper work. Provided I could still study for six hours every day, I reckoned that I would be through with my studies within two years.

The *Reichspost* had moved, at the end of 1894, from the Josefstädter Strasse to the nearby Strozzigasse where Baron von Vittinghoff-Schell had bought a house for the newspaper concern. It was here that I went to see Ambros Opitz, who had now taken over the editorship from Weimar, and asked him whether he could take me on. He heard my petition in silence and gazed thoughtfully out of the window for a moment before answering.

"Yes, but you'll have to come soon," he answered gruffly. "I'll pay you fifty gulden a month. Agreed?"

I did some rapid mental arithmetic; I would just be able to manage.

At the end of the summer term I gave up my post with the Chorinsky family, and on July 15, 1896, I climbed for the first time as editorial apprentice the worn stairs of the house in the Strozzigasse 41. My heart was beating fast.

Chapter 3
HISTORICAL SITUATION

An old world was crumbling in Austria as the century neared its end. Established concepts, handed down for generations as unwritten law, conflicted with new ideas. Class privilege and feudal traditions were threatened by the innovations of democracy. The Social Democrats had been rapidly gaining ground. There were violent flare-ups by radical nationalist elements who scorned the policy of moderation and the genuine good-will toward mutual understanding of those urging national conciliation. The radical Young Czechs appeared in Parliament after their victory over the Old Czechs with whom it was possible to come to terms. They struck a shrill note in the concert of nations. The two fundamentally different political concepts, federalism and centralism, vied with one another as never before. The ministry of Taafe was succeeded in 1893 by that of Windischgrätz, and this was followed in June, 1895, by the short-lived Kielmannsegg administration. In September, 1895, Count Badeni assumed office. Following their defeat in the municipal elections in Vienna, the Liberals' camp was like a swarm of angry hornets. In addition to this, the German Catholics in Austria split into two camps, and the resulting contrast between the old Conservatives and the young Christian-Social movement was often so pronounced that it bordered on the grotesque.

I was faced with these differences above all in my own work. Some five years ago Prince Alois Liechtenstein had left the Conservative Catholics and joined the ranks of the Christian-Socials, a fact which had foreshadowed a far-reaching crisis. The Prince, unquestionably the most distinguished figure among the Conservative German Catholics, renounced his mandate as deputy in 1890 as an expression of his lack of confidence in the policy of the Catholic Conservatives. It had been the hope of these Conservatives to enforce the primary demands of their program—the establishment of denominational schools and the securing of religious education for young people—with the help of the Slav Right-wing party in the parliament and by their own representation in the coalition government. Prince Liechtenstein saw the end of this hope with the appearance of the Young Czechs on the Right in the House of Deputies. These Slav, anti-clerical Liberals would certainly side with the German Liberals in such issues as the Catholic school question. If nothing further could be achieved in such vital fundamental demands, what had the representatives of the German Catholics to hope for by further participation in a government coalition,[1] a participation which in fact demanded so much sacrifice of principle?

Prince Alois Liechtenstein answered this question by accepting a Christian-Social mandate in Vienna-Hernals in 1891. The Christian-Socials were unencumbered by the commitments of the Conservative Catholics: in fact they stood in opposition to the government. Although they were prepared to recognize authority as such, they held no brief for the traditional Conservative sense of obligation toward a governmental authority based on what they considered to be an unethical coalition system.

But in addition to these tactical differences, there were still more profound essential differences of principle between the Conservative Catholics and the Christian-Socials. Such differences were concerned with that fateful and unique problem of the old Danube Empire which, even after its disintegration in 1918, was to remain the *key-problem of Central Europe*.

Ever since the old Austria made its first move toward the creation of a constitutional state in 1848, right through the absolutist period under Bach, to the attempts to form a constitution which began in 1860, the aim had always been to organize the various constitutive powers of the state toward the building up of a Habsburg common state. But the prerequisites were quite different and immeas-

---

[1] In contrast to the United States system of government, it is usual on the continent to form coalition governments. The reason for this lies in the fact that more than two parties are usually represented, neither of them possessing an absolute majority. By the formation of such coalitions of two or more parties, the government ensures the necessary parliamentary support without which—again in contrast to the United States—it would be unable to function.

urably more complex than those of the constitutional states of the West. The Empire was made up of twelve nations, comprising as a whole some fifty million people, but not one of these nations constituted even an approximate majority. The Germans represented 23.3 per cent within the monarchy, followed by the Magyars with 19.5 per cent and the Czechs and Slovaks with 16.5 per cent; next came the Serbs and Croats with 10.7 per cent, the Poles with 9.7 per cent, the Ukrainians with 7.8 per cent, the Romanians with 6.2 per cent, the Slovenians with 2.7 per cent and the Italians and Ladinians with 1.9 per cent. Even when considered alone, without Hungary, the Germans still only held 35.6 per cent and the Czechs 23 per cent: no absolute majority was to be found here either. Only Lower Austria, Upper Austria, Salzburg and Vorarlberg could be termed German-Austrian, for in all the other crown provinces there were considerable settlements of the various national minorities.

The vast body of nations divided itself within Austria-Hungary equally into nineteen provinces, differing in historical and constitutional background. Furthermore, Hungary demanded for herself a special privileged position, and Bohemia was seeking the recognition of similar rights.

The very persistence of these individual nations in their demands within the framework of the common state, and indeed the complex national structure of the monarchy in itself, pointed against a centralistic solution for the constitution.

A federal solution, on the other hand, which foresaw only the "historic" provinces as basic elements in its structure, ran contrary to the interests of the smaller nations, which feared for the rights of their own minorities within the self-governing provinces. Such minorities were, for example, the Germans of the Sudetenland, the Ruthenians (Ukrainians) in Galicia and the Italians in the Tyrol and Dalmatia. These various opposing interests clearly influenced the history of the constitution from 1848 to 1867, a record full of contradictions and vacillations. The Bohemian Charter of April 8, 1848, the imperial decree which granted Bohemia certain central administrative departments for herself; the recommendations of the Kremsier Imperial Diet for the formation of a federal multi-national state; the October Diploma of 1861 which attempted to form a unified

common state with autonomies for the various participant nations
—these were always followed again by centralistic constitutional
measures. The most lasting and yet inconsequential was the dualistic
constitutional legislation of 1867 which divided the Empire into two
states, the mutual vital interests of which were supposedly protected
by measures not only insufficient in themselves but often unclear and
ambiguous.

This constitution, which was clearly intended to assign the government of Hungary to the Magyars and that of Austria to the German-Austrians, created two centralistic states, both facing the same
problem. In neither case was the power in the hands of a true national majority, and it could therefore be maintained in these circumstances only by great dexterity or by dangerous artificial means,
if at all.

A further natural defect marred this new construction: efforts
by one or the other of the partners in this dualistic system to introduce some change, perhaps even some reasonable modification of its
artificial powers, were inevitably met by attempted though unlawful interference by one or the other partner, apprehensive of the repercussions such possible concessions might have within his own state.
But worse was to follow. Goaded by the recognition of the Hungarian constitutional law by the 1867 Constitution, the federalists of
Bohemia began to demand similar recognition of their own equally
ancient constitutional laws with which the powerful feudal Bohemian aristocracy felt their own rights to be bound up.

What at this juncture was the mission of the German Austrians?

The reputation of the Germans in Austria had been founded,
down the centuries, on their achievements in the national economy,
in public life, in the sciences and culture generally, as well as on the
field of battle and in the state administration. It was a justly honorable reputation and one which was not too difficult to maintain so
long as Austria was still a member of the German Confederation and
the Austrian Slavs had not yet reached full national stature. From
then on, however, their position as the acknowledged leaders among
the nations of the Empire was no longer to be regarded as a preroga-
tive, but could only be held by a careful policy of wisdom combined
with moderation.

At the very dawn of the constitutional era, many important figures among the German Austrians raised their voices in warning against losing sight of this vital fact. Even when German liberalism stood at the peak of its power and foresaw the fulfillment of its own political tenets and the guarantee of its own authority within the centralistic state, similar warnings had come from their own camp. Dr. Mühlfeld, one of the most outstanding German Austrians of the last century, was among the first to publish his views. Already in March, 1849, as a member of the German National Assembly, he was responsible, together with Dr. Egger, for the pamphlet published in Frankfurt, *Draft of a Charter of the Constitution for the Imperial State of Austria,* in which he advocated the organization of the state along autonomic lines and equal rights for all the nations as "fundamental state principles." In 1850 Baron Viktor von Andrian, Vice-President of the German National Assembly, wrote the following truly prophetic words:

Centralization in Austria is both anti-historical and revolutionary. Should it succeed, it will never induce an Austrian patriotism but rather a state of universal political indifference in which the state is viewed as something unfamiliar, distant and impersonal. Should, however, the experiment fail, this can only bring about the disintegration of the state.

But the 1867 experiment remained irrevocable and the state disintegrated. . . . In his classic book *Österreich und die Bürgschaften seines Bestandes* (Vienna, 1869, Wallishauser) the well-known scholar Dr. Adolf Fischhof wrote:

Inasmuch as it is the object of the modern form of constitution to preserve for nations their right of self-determination, there can hardly be a more flagrant breach of the constitutional principle than the transfer of a centralistic constitution from the national state to the multi-national state. Centralization in Austria is an anachronism, a sin against the spirit of the age. What is more, the German Austrian needs to commit no such sin. He needs no pedestal of special privileges, for he already stands above his fellow nations; his own moral strength offers him more lasting guarantees than a parliamentary majority gained by artificial means. He should no longer stand as the guardian of the other nations, but rather as their model and example. . . . In attempting to fulfil his cultural mission by Germanization, the German can only succeed in rousing the hatred of the other nations and furthering the aims of Russia. He can only serve the interests of Germany, and indeed of Europe as a whole, by smoothing the path to self-development for the Slavs of the south and west.

Now is the moment for the German Austrian guardian to declare that the peoples he has reared as his wards have come of age. He must henceforth allow them to take charge of their own affairs. The best guardian would but ill repay the gratitude of his charges by a further attempt to exercise his authority. For only the Slav fully aware of his race will be fully conscious of his Austrian citizenship. As Smolka said in the 1848 Imperial Diet: "Allow us first to be Poles and Czechs and then we will be the best Austrians; but you want to force us into being good Austrians and we still remain Poles and Czechs . . ."

Fischhof drafted in his book, in the light of these considerations, a federal constitution based on the Swiss model, in which the autonomous crown provinces would guarantee a recognized *Lebensraum* for the various national minorities.

Fischhof's appeal to his German Austrian contemporaries met with little response. The German Liberal and pan-German party leaders of the nineteenth century believed implicitly in their absolute German trusteeship and resented any criticism of their policy. History has since confirmed Fischhof's warnings. Long after the German Liberals had lost their position in the state, the concept of the centralistically-organized national state still hovered over the barren fields of pan-German politics. There were many, however, who called for a state reform which would provide autonomies for the individual nations and guarantee effective rights for the various minorities in their midst. Advocates of such a reform included men from various political camps, among them the Social Democrat Dr. Renner, the German Liberal Dr. Charmatz, the pan-German Dr. Schüssler, and that great Christian-Social statesman Dr. Seipel. In Seipel's opinion both centralism and federalism could have been acceptable, even to their respective opponents, provided either of these systems had granted self-administration to the individual nations.

Just as the German Liberals and their pan-German successors

clung obstinately to a narrow centralism, the Czechs and the Catholic Conservatives supported equally stubbornly a policy of federalism. The attitude of the Catholic Conservatives of the German Alpine provinces in their insistence on old provincial rights was based on both constitutional and ideological grounds. In opposing centralism they were at the same time opposing the liberalism identified with all centralistic institutions and which served such institutions to further its own ends. Liberalism had overthrown the denominational schools and, as for the provision of religious instruction in the state schools, they had taken care of this question, as Alois Liechtenstein expressed it in his highly controversial speech on the schools question in 1888; "like a family for an unwanted orphan." Liberalism had infiltrated into the administration and the universities and infected the literature of the day. Not content with the influence it wielded in politics, it strove still further to subjugate the religious outlook of the people.

There were countless signs which showed which way the wind was blowing during the 'seventies. People wishing to demonstrate their contempt of the clergy and their supporters would blatantly stroll through St. Stephen's Cathedral, top hats ostentatiously on their heads. A leading Vienna Liberal daily newspaper seized the occasion of the storming of the Porta Pia in 1870 to break out in triumph over the imminent downfall of the Pope. The Graz Municipal Council demanded from the government an exceptional law for the Catholic clergy, and the Graz Liberal daily paper recommended the establishment of special "asylums" for apostate priests, "mostly men of character and energy."

The Provincial Diets still represented for the Catholic population of the Alpine territories a strong bastion against the wave of militant liberalism from Vienna, the seat of the centralistic administration.

The Christian-Social movement in Vienna and Lower Austria, which since the beginning of the 'nineties had been winning the increased support of the younger generation, represented at the outset *a demonstration of a broad section of the population against the deplorable economic and social conditions* which Liberalism had created in the city. As yet uncertain of its aims, it gained its first foothold among the urban lower middle classes and the have-nots. Whole groups of craftsmen and workers in Vienna had already been ruined by the ruthless competition of wholesale industry. Others were nearing the same fate. Even after an official rise in pay, the average weekly wages of 80 per cent of Vienna's shoemakers amounted to between 6 and 10 kronen. Such salaries were barely enough for one person to live on, let alone a family. Circumstances were no different in the tailoring trade. Housing conditions were bad and tuberculosis was rife. The ravages of death and disease among the exploited working classes grew from year to year. In 1895 an investigation by the government office responsible for the compilation of labor statistics established that among those registered as sick in the Vienna tailoring trade, 10.66 per cent were tubercular. Among the shoemakers too 10.96 per cent were found to have tuberculosis. Taking into consideration the treatment for the disease at that time, one man in eleven seemed destined for an early death.

Out of this poverty and misery the working classes turned hopefully to the leaders of the movement which had pledged itself to do battle with their old enemy Liberalism, their economic and social oppressor. "Salvation from Social Misery!" This battle cry, which was loudly proclaimed at countless political meetings in Vienna and Lower Austria, was the title of a pamphlet brought out by its author, Dr. Ludwig Psenner, a Tyrolese living in Vienna. Together with the Viennese priest Father Adam Latschka, he founded the Christian-Social Union (March 7, 1887), thus creating the first meeting place for the people under the designation "Christian-Social" for the interchange of ideas within the new movement.

The United Christians Party made no secret of the many and varied elements within its ranks, nor did it seek to deny this fact in its choice of title. Criticism and attack of the existing social and economic conditions served as a common bond to link these elements together. All kinds were represented: men who had been through a hard school as Liberals, pan-German anti-Semites, Catholics from the Viennese political clubs, and countless others who had not been inside a church for years; workers from the lower middle classes, such as shoemakers, amber workers, bakers, artisans and railway workers, aware now, perhaps for the first time, that they too were Christians. The movement developed a program aimed at economic and social reform.

From the very beginning, however, the United Christians Party kept a safe distance from Georg von Schönerer, leader of the pan-German racial anti-Semites. In his Prussian ardor for a Hohenzollern empire, the Austrian Schönerer wildly encouraged the doctrine of "Protestantism for the Ostmark" among his followers, but remained himself a Catholic. The Vienna Christian-Socials were fortunate indeed in having Baron Carl von Vogelsang from the very beginning as their mentor and guide; Prince Alois Liechtenstein also belonged to the group, as did Dr. Gessmann. Karl Lueger and young Leopold Kunschak were in close touch with the movement, which made good use of their counsel and support. Another figure who shared in consolidating the inner stability and forming the fundamental principles of the Christian-Social movement was the Vienna University professor Dr. Franz Martin Schindler, a man who, perhaps due to his own personal modesty, has never really received the credit due him for the special part he played in defining the political concepts of the Christian-Social party.

On May 15, 1891, just at a decisive juncture, the Encyclical Letter "Rerum Novarum" of Leo XIII was published. This epoch-making Magna Carta of Christian social reform established the dogma of the Christian-Social movement in Austria.

The significant Social Program of 1891 was undoubtedly linked with the Encyclical. This remarkable—and, as far as I know hitherto unpublished—document, was far in advance of its time and reflected the theories of many social reformers of the age. The section dealing with landed property, for example, contained demands for "the legal restriction of the parceling out of land in cases of the compulsory sale of farms; the legal restriction of the amalgamation of peasant property to form large estates; the revision of the land tax over shorter regular periods and related to the yield of land and market prices." The paragraph on small-scale trades demanded the further development of trade reform by the extension of the system of co-operative societies and facilitation of the formation of co-operative concerns for the manufacture and distribution of goods. Paragraph IV of the Program "concerning workers in large-scale industry" sets out the following points:

1. The strict enforcement of legislation for the protection of labor, especially in respect of fixed maximum hours, the prohibition of the truck system and the setting up and observance of factory regulations.

2. The extension of labor legislation, especially by the universal compulsory introduction of trade union courts of arbitration; the granting and regulation of the right for the workers themselves to share in controlling the observance of the laws for the protection of labor by means of a representative elected from among themselves; the extension of regulations for maximum hours of work to employees of the transport and communications industry; the legal restriction of the granting by the administration of exemption from laws governing work on Sunday.

Up to the middle of the 1890's, no one political party had emerged as the recognized outward expression of the movement; its name was as yet uncertain. In 1890 the vanguard of the movement, led by Dr. Lueger, who had already been a member of the House of Deputies since 1885, had penetrated not only to the Vienna Municipal Council (following the first electoral successes) but also to the Provincial Diet of Lower Austria. In March, 1891, Lueger had already established in the House of Deputies the Free Union for Economic Reform, based on Christian principles, with a membership already of twelve. Two months later he was able to claim a new breach in the Liberal stronghold in the capital to his credit: the Vienna municipal elections had brought him a great victory. Forty-seven newly elected councilors of the great capital city, so rich in property and influence, appointed Dr. Karl Lueger as chairman of an anti-Semitic party within the Vienna Municipal Council.

Lueger had succeeded in his first task: despite the economic and political power of his opponents, he had consolidated his many and scattered forces—a victory over an apparently almost invincible enemy. It now remained to be seen whether the second move would succeed: to create a real united organization out of this somewhat loosely-bound conglomeration. The Catholic-thinking sections of the population formed a dependable backbone, and the determination and enthusiasm with which the Viennese Catholics in particular followed the movement naturally encouraged its development. Men around whom such Catholics were grouped included such figures as Baron Max von Vittinghoff-Schell, Father Heinrich Abel, the Redemptorist Father Freund, the writers and poets Richard von Kralick, Trabert and Eichert, Canon Himmelbauer, the religion instructor Stauracz, and others.

Hundreds of thousands of Christian-thinking people of all nations within the old Empire breathed a sigh of relief. The Christian-Social doctrine which came from Vienna, the heart of the Empire, brought good tidings indeed. It proclaimed a new Christian era, an era of social justice, economic progress, of common effort toward a spiritual and material reform. Christian peoples of all nations, so long senselessly divided, would unite to retrieve Austria's greatness. Patriotic sentiments began to be roused.

The Christian-Social movement was fortunate in having Dr. Lueger at its head, a man whose gifts of leadership were unprecedented among the German-Austrians of the constitutional era. The first decade of his public activity revealed his outstanding capabilities in achievements which were to be remembered in history.

In 1875, at the age of thirty, he was elected to the Vienna Municipal Council. In the economic party which he himself founded he sought to form a basis from which to combat the deplorable conditions in economic life brought about by the influence of Liberalism. Liberalism was once again his target when, on March 8, 1882, he presented before the Erdberg electorate his "Democratic Program" declaring a policy of economic protection for the underdog. In 1893, together with Dr. Albert Gessmann, official of the Vienna University Library and Christian-Social journalist, he faced fearlessly the storm of mockery and abuse from the Liberal press which met his own daring attack upon the Liberal potentates of high finance, the exponents of "Manchesterism" and the newspaper magnates.

It was the small fry, the so-called "five gulden men" (who had at last in 1885 gained the right to vote by the reduction of the annual tax from 10 to 5 gulden) who sent him, "the democrat," to the

Imperial Diet. At this time Lueger's connection with Vogelsang began; he became a regular member of the Social Studies Circle run by the Vienna University professor Dr. Franz Schindler, and on January 10, 1889, he appeared in Dr. Ludwig Psenner's Christian-Social Union for the first time as speaker under the Christian-Social flag. He confronted the pan-German challenge to the Austrian state with a vigorous affirmation of his own patriotic views: "I shall always be black and gold to the core!" On the occasion of the *Katholikentag* in 1889 he made a special appeal to the Austrian Catholics: "This *Katholikentag* is our meeting place; let the seed take root here in our hearts, and let us realize here that we are all brothers, whether we come from the town or the country, whether we are Germans, Slavs or Italians. Let us unite from now on, brothers in Austria, brothers in Christ."

In 1891 he declared before his Margareten constituency in Vienna: "My goal is clear: the rivival of the greatness of my fatherland Austria." He already began to speak of "the Christian-Social movement" and "the Christian-Social party," for, since those days of the election to the Imperial Diet in early March, he was standing among the ranks of men elected on the Christian-Social vote and already united in a parliamentary group. Dr. Albert Gessmann, Jax, Prince Alois Liechtenstein, Professor Schlesinger, Muth and Walther von Troll were the first; others were to follow.

I first heard Lueger speak in Vienna in 1894. The broadshouldered handsome man, a typical dark Viennese, could have been a model for one of Altdorfer's drawings. He was sparing in his gestures while speaking, retaining such devices to accentuate some special point of rhetoric. His clear voice could penetrate the most deafening tumult. He kept to the point and used short clear phrases. He possessed the gift of finding just the right words, so that his meaning was immediately clear to the simplest of his audience. He did not concern himself with long explanations, legal definitions and long-winded arguments. But he could hold his audience and convince them of his point in a few simple sentences.

One of the most controversial issues in the contention between Austria and Hungary and a favorite examination question for the degree of doctor of law was the determination of the "quota," the material contribution of both states in relation to their common expenditure. Lueger, wishing to explain to a political meeting the difficulties involved in the critical negotiations just taking place, simply said: "We Austrians and Hungary own a house together. Each of us must contribute his share to the housekeeping costs. But the Hungarians would like to give the orders and leave the others to foot the bill!" In defending his criticism of the abusive practices common in commercial life at that time he said: "The Jews have no right to be so touchy when someone complains about their race. If the Jew is a good Jew, then it's no affair of his anyway. If he's a bad Jew, then it serves him right!" Then again, when he was accused of being a state socialist for condemning the exploitation by capital: "I'm going by what is in the Bible," he answered his critics. " 'Render to Caesar the things that are Caesar's. There's no mention anywhere of 'Render to the Rothschilds what belongs to the Rothschilds'!"

Hair-splitting pedants took exception to such popular phraseology, but Lueger's voice found an echo among the people. Typically Viennese, Lueger loved to spice his speeches with humor and puns. The force of his personality was not due to his gift of oratory alone, for Lueger was above all a real Viennese, and as such he appealed to his fellow citizens in their common love of his city and its great traditions. He shared their kindliness and gaiety, their friendliness and sense of humor, but he also shared their tendency to skepticism and ability to laugh at themselves and their own affairs. He understood perfectly the musical and artistic traits in the Viennese character, even when these sometimes appeared superficial and frivolous. It was this Viennese Lueger, with his passionate love of his city, his Austria and his Empire, his masculine candor, unselfishness and integrity, who won the hearts of the people and was accepted by millions throughout the Empire as the prototype of the genuine Austrian.

Dr. Lueger publicly reaffirmed his attitude to Catholic Christendom in his opening speech at the Lower Austria *Katholikentag* in Vienna in November, 1894. This speech was the most outstanding event of the day. The Christian declaration of the Vienna people's leader is memorable as one of the noblest examples of Catholic rhetoric of our time. Lueger began:

"I am addressing you neither as borough councilor nor as town councilor, neither as a member of the Provincial Diet of Lower Austria nor as a deputy of the Imperial Diet. I am here as the representative of no official body. No, I am speaking simply as a man with insight into the hearts of his fellow men and as such I can say to all of you assembled here: the Vienna Municipal Council does not as yet come to greet you—it does not as yet dare. Nor is the Provincial Diet of Lower Austria here to bid you welcome—it has not the courage either. No mayor, no provincial marshal, no governor and no minister stands here to receive you. Your greeting comes from the Catholics of Vienna and Lower Austria!"

And Lueger ended with the words:

"By your presence you have shown that you are not content to stand by and see the Catholic faith treated as the servant of the state, whose sole function it would be to support the state police force so that the cries for help of the oppressed should not be heard. No, it is not the Church which has need of the state's assistance, for the Church is eternal and invulnerable. It is the state which has need of Christianity. Mankind lies bleeding to death from a thousand wounds. Eyes are raised in entreaty to Him who was scourged and crowned with thorns, to Him who died on the Cross for the Salvation of humanity. Mankind recognized once again the rebellion of love, justice and mercy in contrast to the theories and embittered domination of the powerful over the weak. They acknowledged once again the rebellion of the poor and oppressed. Once again men found comfort and once again their lips uttered that greeting which their mothers had taught them in their childhood—that same greeting with which the Social Democrats thought to mock me, that same greeting which I believe will be the victory cry for the whole of mankind: 'Praised be Jesus Christ!'"

There had been a breathless silence in the audience while Lueger was speaking. Then suddenly a tumultuous shout of jubilation broke loose. I witnessed with my own eyes the unforgettable scene. Men stood pale with emotion, with tears in their eyes, women waved scarves and handkerchiefs from the stands and galleries, leaning over the railings to acclaim the speaker. The applause seemed endless.

In order fully to understand this reaction, it must be remembered that the Christian conscience had long been subjected to the deepest humiliations by the Liberal domination and suffered constant indignities through the contemptuous attitude of the all-powerful anti-clerical press. When had such words been heard before from a layman, a leader in public life?

Shortly after I arrived in Vienna, the whole city was reverberating with the echo of the *Kulturkampf* which had broken out in Hungary. Wekerle's Liberal administration had already started the attack in 1892 in order to divert the unruly chauvinists who were clamoring for a separate Hungarian army and for Hungarian independence. In this way Wekerle succeeded in achieving a brief Indian summer for Hungarian Liberalism which had lost much of its former power. The aim of the Hungarian Liberals was the abolition of the church marriage register and the introduction of compulsory civil marriage. Church marriage would no longer be recognized as valid by the state.

There still existed at that time a strong consciousness of the bond between the fellow Catholics of Hungary and Austria. The Viennese viewed with indignation the noisy challenge of Hungarian Liberalism in the *Kulturkampf*, a challenge from the same Liberal opponent whose domination in their own city they had vowed to overthrow. They sent encouraging messages of sympathy to their fellow Catholics in Hungary, attacked by these same Liberal forces. Father Abel, S.J., called upon the Catholic men to join in common prayer for the Hungarian Catholic cause. St. Stephen's Cathedral was filled to overflowing. People thronged the side chapels, crowded the altar steps, pressed against the altar itself; they packed the choir stalls and lined the aisles. Father Abel was in the pulpit. Clearly and convincingly he described the plight of the Catholics of Hungary and the aim of the instigators of the attacks: the depriving of the Habsburg Empire of its most solid foundation, the unity of its peoples in the Catholic faith. The whole cathedral was roused by the preacher's words. Father Abel led the vast congregation in prayer for the oppressed Catholics and for the Emperor, that he might be given the strength to withstand the assault upon his ancient house. The voices of the men rose in a mighty shout which was taken up by the crowds outside who had found no place inside the cathedral.

I was present on this occasion. I could well understand why Father Abel was called "the *men's* apostle of Vienna."

Beginning in 1889, a group of interesting figures in the Christian-Social movement used to meet every Tuesday evening for the purpose of "the mutual discussion of important topics of the day" under the chairmanship of the university professor Dr. Franz Schindler. The evenings were more or less a kind of schooling in social questions for most of those present. In contrast to the three leaders, Lueger, Liechtenstein and Father Abel, who stood constantly in the public limelight, whether on the political platform or in the pulpit, Schindler remained in the background and took no active part in the noisy political arena. Contemporary literature barely mentions his name. Yet Schindler was one of the most remarkable men in the Christian-Social movement. Not only did he render invaluable service in laying the foundations of the Christian-Social doctrine in Austria, but he was the faithful guide and mentor of the party, directing its course through innumerable perils. Unassuming, selfless and ever vigilant, he secured the Christian-Social principles by means often more effective than political rhetoric.

Born in Bohemia in 1847, Dr. Franz Schindler was appointed professor of moral theology at Vienna University in 1887. He had an unusually wide range of knowledge and, in addition to his academic activities, he began at an early age to write on a variety of subjects. He was constantly preoccupied with moral and social problems affecting community life and the broadening of the Christian social order. Shortly before he was called to Vienna, he was associated with the Union of Catholic Sociologists directed by the Swiss deputy Dr. Decurtins, in Fribourg. Schindler thus shared in the valuable preliminary work contributed by this group and by the German Free Association of Catholic Sociologists toward the Encyclical "Rerum Novarum."

The year 1885 saw the first evidence of compulsory social insurance which had begun to be introduced by law in various countries. In the German study group the Prussian member, Droste, raised certain scruples against this institution of social insurance on grounds of Christian ethics and natural law. Schindler answered for the moral justification of compulsory insurance in eight theses of the greatest clarity in which he so defined the right of the state in the important field of social order as to render further discussion of the matter superfluous. The further he advanced in his sociological studies, and the more his findings were crystallized in organic planning, the more he favored the reconstruction of society on a corporative basis.

In 1888, at the express wish of the Cardinal Prince Archbishop Ganglbauer, Schindler drew up a comprehensive memorandum on social questions for the Austrian episcopate, in which he indicated the various ways in which the clergy is called upon to participate in the solution of social problems. He suggested in this memorandum that young priests gifted for this work should be sent to study social welfare among the workers of the industrial region of the Rhineland, and that in every diocese a priest should be made responsible for the special task of furthering and supervising the work of social welfare. He also suggested to the bishops the value of cooperation with influential members of the aristocracy, landowners and industrialists in the development of Christian social reform. He emphasized—already in 1888—the importance of the united efforts of the bishops and the Catholic laity toward the establishment of a large-scale modern Catholic daily paper in Vienna, which should be the standard-bearer among all Catholics in the great crusade for Christian social reform.

Schindler's *Manual of Moral Theology* is regarded as his most mature theological work, a book in which all the results of important research in the field of philosophical-theological speculation are discussed.

But remarkable as are all these various single achievements, perhaps Schindler's most enduring contribution to the intellectual history of Austria lay in his ability to co-ordinate the forces of the educated Catholic laity, scattered in their various callings, and organize them in a united body. Above all, it was he who, after Vogelsang's death, took over the latter's task in the systematic formation and extension of the doctrine and political program of the Christian-Social movement. His work *The Present-day Social Question in the Light of Christianity*, which appeared in four editions during the first decade of this century, became a recognized guide for many, especially for the younger members of the clergy. The "social courses" which were held under his direction were invaluable in stimulating the Christian-Social idea and promoting practical Christian-Social activity. The very first of these courses claimed the somewhat anxious attention of the Liberal press. *Die Neue Freie Presse*, which always had its ear to the ground when it sensed Catholic activity, in fact devoted a leading article to the subject:

> It must be admitted that the instigators of this agitation, modeled apparently on the Jesuit missions, spare themselves no pains to keep the pot boiling. For them there is no vacation, no peace, no recreation. Perhaps no other party agitation in Austria has ever been pursued with such assiduity, such intense perseverance, indeed with such self-sacrifice. What other explanation could there be for the astonishing success achieved, considering the lack of talent and knowledge among the members of the movement?"

Those who had participated in this course in Vienna went home full of enthusiasm. The hundreds of Catholic workers' associations which sprang up all over the Empire were ample proof of the success of the course. As a result a second course was organized in Vienna in 1899. No man could have been better fitted than Schindler to undertake such a large-scale educational mission. Wise and scholarly, the unpretentious man never sought public recognition. Again and again, however, he was elected dean of his faculty and on one occasion also rector of the university. He received papal honors as a Prothonotary Apostolic, and the Emperor conferred a decoration upon him and appointed him to the Upper House, the first chamber of the Parliament. Lawyers and priests, university professors and higher civil servants, young parliamentarians, scholars and writers, all gathered regularly to discuss topical problems under his stimulating leadership. It was always a pleasure to hear Schindler speak on such occasions, for he was a past master in the lucid summing-up of a controversial debate.

But these discussion evenings represented only one facet of the Christian-Social movement. Universal harmony by no means prevailed throughout the new movement, particularly in the press sector. Ernst Vergani, editor of the *Deutsche Volksblatt*, a newspaper founded in 1888 which had gained rapid popular recognition through its association with the movement, was endeavoring through his newspaper to direct the course of the United Christians party along more pan-German lines. Vergani, who himself had had close associations with Georg von Schönerer, was a self-assured and autocratic personality. He had broken with Schönerer on the grounds of incompatibility, but he had nevertheless assumed many of Schönerer's anti-clerical and anti-Semitic views and these formed the basis of his whole ideological concept. The newspaper often conflicted in its views with Christian principles. It was clearly highly undesirable that the paper should continue as the organ of the Vienna movement and that the leaders of the movement should identify themselves in any way with the policy dictated by the publication and by its editor.

Lueger in no way condoned Vergani's Schönerer views and heartily disliked his highly-developed turn for business and his autocratic pretensions, but he nevertheless accepted the invitations to the social evenings which Vergani arranged with such deliberation at his house: he could not afford at this juncture to break entirely with the *Deutsche Volksblatt*, for he had as yet the support of no other Vienna newspaper with the same range. The *Reichspost* was still in its infancy, and the *Vaterland*, the organ of the Catholic conservative aristocracy and the episcopate, was openly opposed to the new people's movement. In view of these circumstances the press clearly represented a serious threat to the position of the movement. The Liberal press seized its chance in attempts to compromise its opponent in accusations of anti-Semitism. Although no responsible leader of the Christian-Social party was involved in any way in racial anti-Semitism, in their striving for social reform they were often concerned with certain unsound facts which undoubtedly called for open criticism. Such censure was often interpreted, both falsely and superficially, as an expression of anti-Semitism, with the conscious or unconscious intention of casting a slur upon the Christian-Social attitude.

There can be no doubt of the important and influential position of the Jewish minority in the intellectual and commercial life of Vienna at the turn of the century. The Jews at that time constituted 9 per cent of the total population of the city. Their quick intelligence, business ability and diligence brought them success. The fashionable streets of the city were lined with shops owned by Jews. Many of these firms, with their valuable overseas business connections, were renowned for the quality and impeccable good taste of their merchandise and also for the correctness of their business transactions. They furthered the reputation of the Vienna market and increased home production. The worldwide reputation of Viennese *haute couture*, jewelry and leather goods is in no small measure due to the achievements of reputable Jewish firms. Above all, in banking circles the commercial flair of the Jewish minority was most pronounced. All the Viennese banking houses, including the Bodenkreditanstalt, the bank of the imperial family and of the conservative landowners, were in Jewish hands. In the center of Vienna there was only one solitary exchange office the proprietors of which were Christians. Jewish capital controlled the great transport concerns and 75 per cent of industry.

But there was another, darker, side to this impressive picture of Jewish achievement and power. The Vienna streetcar monopoly, for instance, with its old horse-drawn trams, was a public disgrace to the city, not only on account of its out-of-date technical equipment but especially because of the notoriously bad social conditions among its employees. "Mushroom firms" sprang up for the mass-production of shoddy goods and organized a widespread hawking and peddling system which hit local industry and was detrimental to the honest shopkeeper. The clothing industry set up an army of pieceworkers and subjected them to sweated labor conditions. Such exploitation was evident in many different forms and was not confined to the towns. Large-scale speculation in housing property and land followed, with evil results. In comparison with the 4 or 5 per cent which represented normal mortgage rates of interest at that time, figures produced by the Vienna Statistical Office revealed mortgages of 10 per cent in the working-class districts of the city. In the center of the capital the value of the square klafter of ground was raised in the interval between 1888 and 1895 from 1200 to 2600 gulden at the instigation of Dr. Paul Schwarz, director of the mortgage department of the *I. Österreichische Sparkasse*.

It was clear that this ruthless drive for monetary gain pursued out of all proportion by a certain section of the Jewish population threatened to destroy many fundamental values, both moral and material. This fact largely explained the rising tide of indignation and the tendency of many to resort to an unfair generalization in holding all Jews responsible for these evils.

Far-sighted Jews deplored the fateful turn of events. I remember a conversation I had one day with a Viennese wholesale merchant, a Jew held in the highest esteem for his personal character and culture. "I can't understand," I said, "why you, the great majority of decent, honest Jews, won't openly disassociate yourselves from these others who are not only enemies to society as a whole, but also to your own community. Why continue to take personal offense yourselves at criticism directed against offenders who are known to you?" I received the following reply: "The fateful history of our race follows us inexorably. The attitude you question is founded on the endless suffering and oppression which our race has endured down the centuries, right up to recent times. Again and again new catastrophes have been brought upon us by the actions of a minority, heaping new sufferings on guilty and innocent alike. If one of our race is attacked, we all feel instinctively that we must hold together. That is why we can never disassociate ourselves from the others." The argument was understandable, but it was to end in disaster.

The same reasoning may have influenced the Liberal press, which could not see that the justifiable combat of deplorable social and economic conditions could not be condemned wholesale as racial hostility. It is certainly extremely difficult now, after half a century and after the terrible interlude of the concentration camp of Auschwitz-Maydanek, to find the right yardstick for the fundamentally different conditions in economic, political and social life which gave rise to the term "anti-Semitism." It is, however, significant that not once during the whole Lueger period did the phrases of heated speakers or journalists give rise to any formidable demonstration against the Jews, and that the propaganda popular at that time urging the public to "buy from the Christians" in no way succeeded in deflecting the stream of people in the Vienna streets from their old accustomed shops. It is no less significant that, right up to his death, one of Lueger's most trusted friends and collaborators was the Deputy Mayor, Dr. Josef Porzer, a recognized authority both in legal matters and in city administration. He had come from the Vienna Catholic camp. Everyone knew that Dr. Porzer was part Jewish, yet none of the anti-Semites would have dared to use this fact as argument against him with Lueger. It was imperative at this critical point for the young reform movement to keep its distance from the anti-Semites. In the field of journalism it was the particular aim of the *Reichspost* openly to stress the fundamental separation between itself and Vergani's publication.

Had any doubts existed of the expediency of such a policy of isolation from the anti-Semites, these would have been quickly dispelled by an unforeseen turn of events. Early in 1894 strange tidings came from Rome. It appeared that certain charges had been raised in the Vatican against the Christian-Social movement in Vienna, charges which called for ecclesiastical censure. The Prince Archbishop of Prague, Cardinal Franz Schönborn, was named as having delivered these charges in person. Ernst Plener, acknowledged political authority of the Liberals at that time, mentions in his *Memoirs* (Volume 3, Page 219) the "steps taken against the Christian-Socials" in Rome, and writes: "Not uninteresting was the episode concerning our attempt to enlighten the Holy See on the Christian-Social movement and to protest against any support given to these anti-Semites." This action, as Plener further explains, was taken at the instigation of the Minister for Culture and Education, Dr. von Medejsky, who, with the agreement of the Prime Minister, Fürst Windischgrätz, prepared a memorandum "on the dubious aspects of the agitation of this party . . . its attacks against conservative circles . . ." declaring further:

Under the high-sounding name of "Christian-Social reform," a group of persons motivated either by ambition or extreme radical tendencies, some indeed holding office in various representative bodies—the Imperial Diet, the Provincial Diets and the Vienna Municipal Council—have joined together to launch a campaign in a manner lacking in all propriety and discretion. Any sign of a strongly radical trend against authority in the Imperial Diet can certainly be attributed in good measure to the confederates of the Christian-Social movement . . . In this way these anti-Semitic Christian-Socials are thrusting their rebellious way to the forefront of public life, challenging secular and ecclesiastical authority. . . . Whatever they represent or with which they are concerned runs the risk of being discredited in the eyes of the respectable section of the community. . . . It was, therefore, all the more distressing to all serious-thinking people in Austria to learn that their most formidable opponents had shared in the special Papal Blessing for the Linz enterprise (the convocation of an assembly by Dr. Lueger in Linz, despite the refusal of the bishops to participate) and furthermore that the *Reichspost*, the journalistic organ of the movement and a newspaper justifiably forbidden by the Bishop of Linz to be read in his priests' seminary, should similarly have been honored with the blessing of the Holy Father."

The memorandum quoted above was delivered by Cardinal Schönborn, as Plener mentions, "to the Congregation for Extraordinary Affairs." "The whole action in Rome met with no success," writes Plener. The Christian-Social movement was apparently viewed not without favor in Rome on account of its connection with the young clergy and for the part it played in the revival in church life and the increase in the membership of clerical associations due to its influence. Plener makes the final judgment: "The intervention of our government in Rome was certainly well-intentioned but, in view of the attitude of the Papal Nuncio in Vienna and of the Vatican itself, it proved to be of no avail." So much for the commentary of Austria's most distinguished Liberal leader. It was true that the Christian-Socials had some good friends among the Austrian bishops, such as the Bishop of St. Pölten, Dr. Rössler, the former rector of Prague University, the suffragan bishop, Dr. Frind, and the military bishop, Dr. Belopototzky, all men of great distinction and highly esteemed. But the majority of the bishops were uneasy; they saw that the new movement divided the Catholics into two camps, and feared that this "Vienna hotch-potch" would only serve to dissipate their forces. Moreover, several attacks had been made on the episcopal authority, and certain church dignitaries, among them Cardinal Grusha, viewed this as a personal insult. A universal pastoral letter of exhortation to the clergy was even considered.

Commentators of the Liberal press in Rome reported the imminent condemnation of the Christian-Social doctrine by the Supreme Pontiff. Such censure from Pope Leo XIII would put an end once and for all to those troublesome innovators, those anarchists who had dared to penetrate into the most sacred precincts of Austrian Liberalism. With the Catholics out of the way in the United Christians party, it would be easy enough to deal with the others.

Facing indictment in Rome, the Christian-Socials prepared their defense. At the request of Dr. Lueger, a group of prominent men of the Christian-Social movement, among them Prince Alois Liechtenstein, met in February, 1894, under the chairmanship of Dr. Schindler to lay down their fundamental doctrine and aims. They had finished their work by the end of February. The result was a memorandum drafted by Schindler, incorporating the various reforms held to be essential for the welfare of the working classes. The program revealed the far-reaching force of the spirit of reform which animated this group of intellectual leaders of the Christian-Social movement.

Since this historically interesting document, entitled "Social and Economic Program," was never published, the sections concerned with social reform are reproduced below, taken from Schindler's original Latin manuscript:

"3. We desire that every member of society should receive

his due from common goods and that all be granted and rendered in fairness and justice that which they are legitimately entitled to claim and possess as their own. We wish to see the establishment of a system of public order whereby every member of society can obtain without difficulty and according to his circumstances and station in life the necessities for a reasonable material and spiritual existence.

"4. As far as those classes of society are concerned whose members are in our view unduly oppressed and exploited such as the peasants, craftsmen and artisans, we desire to see above all the setting up as soon as possible of appropriate organized corporations for all trades. Such organizations would not only be advantageous for the individual classes themselves, but would unquestionably benefit society as a whole. To enforce this order it is further essential that such corporations should be empowered with all just rights and privileges, without which they cannot function effectively.

"5. In regard especially to the peasants, we desire to see the legal restriction of the sale and parceling out of peasant-owned land and the merging of such to form large estates; to prevent the excessive mortgaging of such properties, a fixed mortgage limit should be imposed; the heavy burden of debt on agricultural properties, to the ruin of our good peasant stock, must be relieved in justice and equity with the assistance of the state. The vital welfare of the peasant population should be considered in the setting up of tax regulations and in the tax collection system, in tax legislation and in the laws governing the export and import of agricultural products.

"6. In regard to the manual worker and artisan, we desire to see the trade corporations recently established in Austria further extended and developed, so that these craftsmen may have the satisfaction of combining their forces under the guidance and control of the state in preventive measures against the competition of large-scale industry; that they should have the right freely to decide all questions affecting the training of apprentices and their admission to trade corporations; that disputes between masters and workmen should be settled by arbiters nominated by the corporation; furthermore, that the interests of craftsmen and workers should be protected in customs legislation and export and import regulations.

"7. In regard to large-scale industry, we demand the restriction of the ruthless competition practised by manufacturers and merchants by legislation regulating home production and limiting imports. In our opinion such regulation of production and imports can best be achieved by means of trade corporations comprising employers and workers. Such corporations could, under the auspices of the government, determine measures meeting the demands of the consumer, protecting the monopoly of certain manufacturers and merchants and determining fair prices for all goods.

"Workers in industry must receive a wage adequate for a reasonable and proper existence, provided sufficient profit is shown as a result of their working capacity. The idea should be encouraged that workers should in time become partners in the business or factory where they are employed, or that at least their wages should be increased and their status raised according to the duration of their employment. Provision should be made for old age and illness and, in the event of death, for the care of widows and orphans. The employment of women and children in factories is to be discouraged. Night work is permissible only in exceptional cases and then only for adult male workers. Working hours during the day must be fixed at a maximum, varying according to the type of work undertaken. Day and night shifts should cease on Sundays and holidays when this can be arranged without causing undue loss to production. Religion and morality, especially of women and children working in factories, must be respected.

"Workers should have the right to participate by means of their own representatives in the inspection of factories and in the control of working contracts with employers and in seeing that no action on the part of such employers should be permitted which could endanger the life or good health of the workers or violate the principles of justice. Disputes between employers and workers should be settled by courts of arbitration under the chairmanship of an impartial third party."

Many of these demands were born ahead of their time; many

of them were realized a full generation later; some have been newly-phrased in the meantime, and some have been proved to be impracticable. The most remarkable feature of this reform program, however, is that it represents the first real attempt by any one political party to constitute a corporative order of society, with its appropriate organizations including both employers and workers.

But essential though it was to formulate the Christian-Social aims in social reform, the open censure of anti-Semitism and anarchist tendencies demanded first and foremost a decisive answer. For this reason, therefore, the declaration is particularly concerned with these charges, and the following paragraph—in no way connected with the actual social program as such—is placed deliberately at the beginning:

"Love, in the Catholic sense, must, as we see it, be translated into deeds, not merely words. We in no way hold the view that our Jewish fellow citizens should be excluded from our love. On the contrary, it is our earnest wish that they should come to recognize the Christian truths and share in the benefits of legitimately acquired privileges and possessions in peace and prosperity. Should we appear to be engaged in active combat against the Jews, this is only because we are in fact concerned in protecting the rights of the Christians. These rights are threatened and spiritual and material values are endangered by all those aiming to undermine the Christian faith and the high principles of the Catholic population. In the ruthless pursuit of material gain, the unprotected classes of our people are exposed to oppression and exploitation. Since it is the Jews who are primarily responsible for such oppression and exploitation, there are some among us who call themselves 'anti-Semites' as an open demonstration of their abhorrence of the capitalist outlook and atheist materialism of which, in their view, the Jews are the chief exponents.

"Should it occur that certain Catholics have exceeded the bounds of moderation in their opposition to such evils, their excuse lies in the heat and long duration of the conflict and in the misery of the oppressed. Not hatred but rather love is the force which drives them to such lengths. Furthermore, many of those especially concerned with the mission of freeing the exploited classes from their present state have only recently found their way to join us from the ranks of the so-called Liberals: it may be that they have not yet learned to appreciate to the full the Catholic spirit—essentially a spirit of charity—and have on occasions attacked their opponents in outbursts of reproach arising less from hatred and envy than from genuine distress and compassion.

"Love is our guiding principle, a love which exacts that very justice which is an intrinsic part of itself, tempering severity, urging the fulfillment of duty and banishing forever the undisciplined egotism which lies for the most part at the root of all injustice."

So much for the program. It bore the signatures of Schindler and Prince Liechtenstein in the name of the commission, and was sent (as Schindler himself testifies) "at the express wish of the Vienna Nuncio Agliardi" through the latter's mediation to the Secretary of State at the Vatican, Cardinal Rampolla, and to the Union for Social Studies in Italy, an association of sociologists of high standing.

Agliardi, the nobleman from Lombardy, had succeeded a long line of illustrious papal diplomats in imperial Vienna. With remarkable perspicacity he soon summed up the situation as far as the Catholics in Austria were concerned. This energetic, courageous man unhesitatingly took the part of the much-maligned Christian-Socials. He became their friend, counselor and intermediary in Rome. And so the program was drawn up.

Detailed replies were received from both authorities to whom the program had been submitted. It is significant of the importance of the document that that great man the Secretary of State, Cardinal Rampolla, should have dealt in such detail with every point of the program in his letter to Agliardi, the letter which Schindler describes as "*sequens rescriptum.*"

In view of its historical importance, Rampolla's hitherto unpublished document is given here, taken from the original Italian text:

"I find nothing in this [the program submitted] contradictory either to the highest principles of the Christian religion or to the doctrines evolved in that memorable Encyclical 'Rerum no-varum.' On the contrary, I am surprised that, since the program is based on the very principles, maxims and provisions contained in that solemn document, specific mention is not made of this fact. Moreover, for the very reason that the program is inspired (*s'ispira*) by the pure, noble and universally binding teachings of Christian ethics, I hold it more fitting that the combat against the opponents of these values should not be tempered by an openly anti-Semitic trait, more especially since such a tendency can add nothing new to the value of the proposals, to the efficacy of the means suggested of attaining these aims, nor indeed to the significance of the combat in itself.

"Having defined the most important obligations of every citizen, the program goes on to demand a system of public order enabling all members of society to obtain without difficulty (*comodamente* underlined in the Italian text) and according to his circumstances and station in life the necessities for a reasonable material and spiritual existence. While this is a highly commendable ideal and one toward which we must always strive, I have my doubts as to whether it can ever be realized here on earth (*quaggiù*). To mention only one of the many prerequisites of social life, namely that of human freedom, it seems to me that the abuses, excesses and lack of discipline of freedom will always threaten to disturb the social order, not only in the moral and legislative sense, but extending over the economic and financial sector and affecting not only the sphere of civil law, but covering the far more extensive range of public law and international relations.

"As for the measures contained in the program designed to improve the conditions of the peasants, craftsmen and workers, these seem to me in general to be just and proper. Some are, however, too generalized in their formulation and the expressions used are not sufficiently clear; in the last case I resorted to my own interpretation of the meaning of the original text. Other expressions used are concerned with material which is highly controversial, not only among economists of the various and opposing schools, but also among Catholic economists. For example, the program repeatedly advocates the intervention of the state. But is such intervention always justifiable, beneficial or even desirable? This is a difficult and delicate question. It is extremely difficult to draw the line, to the advantage of a sound economic and social life, between those who would prefer to leave almost everything to private initiative and those who expect everything from the state. Furthermore, one must bear in mind the precept that legislation carries little weight when private and public moral values have been discredited and destroyed.

"The program proposes that legislative measures be taken in fairness and justice to relieve the over-heavy mortgages on peasant property inasmuch as these are detrimental to the peasant class as such. A measure of the greatest consequence. But in which way and through whom could such encumbrances be discharged? No information is given on this point.

"In its demands for the legal restriction of free trade, the program shows certain protectionist tendencies. This again is a controversial subject and it seems to me that we have not heard the last word here either. The program demands a wage for the worker sufficient to ensure him a fair and fitting existence, but does not specify whether this applies to the worker alone or also to his dependents.

"The program urges that workers be made partners in the business and industrial concerns in which they are employed. This is not at all a bad idea in so far as it is concerned with the sharing of profits earned in commercial and industrial concerns in which the worker is employed. Such profits are, however, highly disputable, and in practice their determination is beset by difficulties which would seem to me in many cases to be insuperable. But it appears to me that here one is going still further and aiming for co-partnership for workers in the actual commercial and industrial firms themselves. How, and by what means? There is no mention of this.

"The program advocates that provision be made for old age and cases of illness among workers, but no mention is made of the accidents among workmen which so frequently occur, nor of the insurance schemes which normally provide for such cases.

"Moreover, I feel it my duty to say that it would be impossible to form an accurate opinion of many of the measures suggested in the program without an exact knowledge of the particular conditions in agriculture, industry and commerce, as well as the situation of the peasants, craftsmen and workers in the various sectors covered by the program. In addition I would need a detailed knowledge of the economic and financial taxation system in Austria-Hungary, a knowledge which I do not possess.

"In conclusion, I feel that the program submitted can be approved and encouraged (*approvare e incorraggiare*), but such approval and encouragement refers rather to the noble and beneficent intentions expressed in the program than to the methods proposed for achieving these aims. Furthermore, it is recommended that, when allusions are made to these various methods and means, very general terms should be used, for the points in question are of a highly delicate and controversial nature."

This was the letter sent to the Vienna Nuncio by Pope Leo XIII's Secretary of State and valued collaborator in the preparation of the Encyclical "Rerum novarum." As far as the moral legitimacy of the Christian-Social aims is concerned, the letter constitutes the approval of the Church; as far as the economic and social proposals of the program are concerned, it constitutes an opinion and a counsel of the greatest importance.

The opinion of the *Unione cattolica per gli studii social d'Italia* was received by Agliardi from Pisa, dated May 28, 1894. It was signed by the president, Professor Toniolo, and by the vice-president, St. Medolago-Albani, Bergamo.

This interesting document, hitherto unpublished, declares at the outset that "in appreciation not only of the different circumstances but also of the diverse national characteristics of a foreign state," the Union for Social Studies in Italy must allow great latitude in forming its opinion of the program submitted since this was concerned with "practical institutions and preventive measures of an economic and legislative nature which should operate within the framework of another nation." "For this reason," continues the report, "it would appear to be sufficient if complete agreement is reached on the fundamental principles and the most important points, especially those in which Catholic values are involved."

In four detailed expositions the Union states its approval of the proposals contained in the program for the setting up of trade corporations: "the organization of society according to trade or profession by the means of individual corporations furnished with judicial powers, their own common means and the capacity to regulate the moral and civil conditions essential to the life of their members." The Union further approved the proposals contained in the program for the improvement of conditions for the peasants and small-holders —without commenting upon the freeing of land from encumbrance through the state—and also the paragraphs covering workers' rights, and comments: "We recommend that every type of industry should aim toward a profit-sharing scheme for its workers, provided this is feasible and allowing the maximum scope in the execution of the plant. This matter has already been discussed in Italy at the General Congress in April of last year."

The presidents of the Union comment upon a point in paragraph 7 of the Austrian program concerning the proposal to entrust the trade corporations referred to with the power of controlling the production of all types of goods and fixing price limits. In their opinion this would not only be extremely difficult but could also be dangerous: the associations, while incorporating both employers and workers, nevertheless represented the interests of the producer class and, as such, could easily be inclined to draw up regulations to their own advantage but detrimental to the consumer. The report closes with a cordial and significant phrase in which the Union expresses the belief that the questions raised by the Austrians had been answered "sharing the same ideals and sentiments."

The point of the submission of the program to the authorities concerned, as initiated by the Nuncio, was to provide the Christian-Socials with a cover in the event of an attack which could prove dangerous. So much had been achieved. In case of need it would now be possible to refer to these documents. But in the meantime they remained confidential.

On February 17, 1895, the newspapers reported that Cardinal

Prince Archbishop Schönborn, this time together with the Bishop of Brunn, Dr. Bauer, and accompanied by the Dominican Father Albert Maria Weiss, had arrived in Rome. The purpose of the visit, so the press reported, was to submit a formal indictment of the Christian-Social movement to Pope Leo XIII and to obtain the public condemnation of the movement by the Holy See. The Papal Nuncio Agliardi had been informed that this action had also the full support of the Cardinal Prince Archbishop of Vienna.

The distinguished Austrian delegation presented its four-point indictment to the Holy Father at a special audience.

The indictment was transmitted, as copied by the office of the Papal Secretary of State, through Cardinal Rampolla to the Papal Nuncio in Vienna. The latter had the document sent to Dr. Schindler for answer. The original Italian text was retained in the copy which Dr. Schindler made in his own hand.

The note from the Papal Secretary of State ran as follows:

A reply is requested to the following observations (*osservazioni*):

1. The Christian-Socials are charged with harboring in their ranks certain harmful and undesirable elements whose tendencies and purposes are not Catholic, but anarchist and socialist. Such elements, which on the one hand exploit and on the other hand discredit their Catholic adherents, will end by overthrowing the whole party and making themselves its masters.

2. The Christian-Socials are charged with taking action independently of the bishops (*agire*), even at times in opposition to them, thereby inciting insubordination among the lower clergy and stirring up discontent among the Catholic population.

3. The Christian-Socials are charged with failing to acknowledge existing legitimate rights and of furthering class hatred and the overthrow of the present social order.

4. The Christian-Socials are charged with a want of moderation in their language (*nei modi*), whether on the platform, in the press or at public meetings. Such immoderate language is designed to incite unhealthy emotion among the people, encourage base desires for gain and stimulate anti-Semitism.

Once again it fell to Schindler to act as mediator for the Christian-Socials. I found the draft of his answer to the note of censure among his papers after his death. He repeatedly admits in his arguments that "in the heat of the battle it has sometimes occurred that, in both the spoken and written word, the language used has exceeded the bounds of moderation and expressions have been used which could offend the Catholic attitude." But what political party is faultless? Every man-made institution has also its human frailties. But such faults still cannot detract from certain positive facts, facts which in themselves disprove censure.

In answer to the four charges, Schindler points out that the Christian-Social idea in Austria originated from just such men as Baron Vogelsang and Prince Alois Liechtenstein. He stated that in Vienna, and indeed the whole of Austria at present, there were signs of a vigorous new religious life which owed its impulse to the Christian-Social movement. The Christian-Socials' point of view was shared by clergy, both secular and regular, men highly esteemed for their personal qualities and for their pastoral work. The Christian-Socials were so bitterly attacked by the Social Democrats for the very reason that they upheld the existing legitimate order, aiming to make peace between the proletariat and the upper classes of society and establish a just and proper civic order. As for the reproach that the Christian-Socials "stirred up the people and encouraged base desires," "it is astonishing," continues the reply to the accusation, that a Catholic could brand in such a way efforts to achieve the re-establishment of a social and economic order based on those very principles of Christian justice discussed in detail by the Pope himself in the Encyclical "Rerum novarum." It would thus appear that those who aimed for the practical application of the principles of Christian justice in private and public affairs "incited the people and encouraged base desires."

Against the charge of anti-Semitism, the answer was similar to that contained in the program prepared for Cardinal Rampolla, with the additional emphasis:

"We do not identify ourselves with that radical anti-Semitism directed against the Jewish race as such, and with which our party, as is evident from our program already submitted, is in no way concerned."

This declaration bore the date February 24, 1895, and was signed by Schindler and by Prince Alois Liechtenstein.

Since the plaintiffs themselves had gone to Rome, Schindler considered it right and proper that he should follow in their footsteps and appear personally before Pope Leo XIII. He found on his arrival that the Nuncio in Vienna had paved the way for him in the Vatican, and any doubts or worries he might have had were quickly dispelled by the cordial reception of the Holy Father. Leo XIII, who showed himself to be acquainted with every detail of the Christian-Social controversy, displayed with all the warmth of his vital personality a real interest in the ideas of the Christian-Social movement and in the results it had achieved. He accepted the program giving his approval and encouragement. The audience, which afforded the defender of the Christian-Social cause the privilege of a detailed discussion with the Holy Father, ended with Leo XIII's message to Dr. Lueger: the leader of the Christian-Socials should know that he had in the Pope a warm friend who sent him his blessing. The Pope sympathized with the Christian-Social endeavors and had the greatest understanding for certain difficulties, "but these will be overcome."

In his great wisdom the Pope had, by this intervention, determined the development of the Christian-Social movement in Austria. The Austrian Catholics were now on sure ground.

Just at this time the *Civiltá Cattolica*, whose publications rated as authoritative, printed an article in praise of the work of the Christian-Socials which could be considered as expressing the official Vatican viewpoint. Had the Pope seen fit to pass judgment against the Christian-Socials, the party, once robbed of its Catholic backbone, would most certainly have disintegrated; as it was, its position was assured. Shortly afterward the Papal Nuncio Agliardi was recalled to Rome where he was honored by Leo XIII, who appointed him to the high office of Cardinal of the Curia. But for months after the departure of the Nuncio Vienna was in a state of fever caused by an unusual turn of events.

The Vienna municipal elections in April and May, 1895, were a severe blow to the Liberals in their stronghold of the Vienna *Ra-*

thaus, for, as a result of these elections, the Christian-Socials almost gained a majority. Dr. Lueger in fact, gained 70 out of 135 votes in the elections for the office of mayor on May 29. He declined to accept, however, knowing that, supported only by a pseudo-majority whose existence largely depended upon his opponents' votes, he was certain to be overthrown at the submission of his first large-scale political plan. New elections were held, which it was hoped would clarify the situation.

The citizens of Vienna were called to the polls in the second half of September. Lueger's desperate opponents resorted to appeals to patriotism and the devotion of the Viennese to their old Emperor. All who loved their city and were loyal to their Habsburg ruler were called upon to "prevent the triumph of this anarchist." This, so they declared, was the Emperor's own wish. Should Lueger be elected, the Emperor would refuse to sanction his appointment. Was Vienna to be reduced to chaos?

This last life-saving device by the former overlords at the expense of imperial authority failed utterly. It only served to increase the bitterness with which the mass of the population rallied to dislodge the enemy from his entrenchments. The funds for the election campaign grew from the small coins of tens of thousands of the lower classes. Volunteers went canvassing from house to house. We students reported for duty in the polling booths of the Christian-Social party.

On September 17 all 46 mandates of the third *Wahlkörper*[1] had been gained by the Christian-Socials. On September 23, election day for the second *Wahlkörper*, that of the middle classes and intelligentsia, 32 were secured from 46, and on September 26, even in the first *Wahlkörper* among the noblest and richest of the population, 14 out of 46.

---

[1] At that time in Austria the so-called census electoral system was in force. Electors were grouped together according to the taxation census in various *Wahlkörper*, or electoral classes. Each *Wahlkörper* voted for the same number of deputies. In addition to the four *Wahlkörper* (landowners, commerce, town and country) a fifth class was introduced in 1897, comprising a larger section of the population. Since the tax payable by one landowner of large estates represented approximately as much as that of a large number of the urban population put together, his vote carried disproportionate weight.

On the evening of the last election day a total of 92 representatives of the United Christians party confronted the 46 remaining
Liberals. Vienna had thus the right to claim a Christian-Social mayor.
There was no doubt as to who was to be chosen to hold this office
from among the 92 Christian-Socials elected.

The power of the Liberals had been broken. It was something
which could scarcely have been imagined a few years before. The
central stronghold of the Liberals had been stormed, in the imperial
capital itself, and by an assailant who had the high financiers and
the Stock Exchange, as well as the united Liberal press, the Liberal
bureaucracy and an influential circle at court against him.

The citizens of Vienna celebrated the victory in the streets.
People who had never met before fell on each other's necks. Many
were weeping for joy. It seemed to them as though a miracle had
happened.

But the end of the Liberal domination in the Vienna *Rathaus*
as a result of the September elections by no means brought about
a return to peaceful conditions in the city. The new conflict which
ensued was unparalleled in Austrian constitutional history. The
Hungarian Prime Minister, Baron Bánffy de Losoncz, joined the
Austrian opponents of the Christian-Socials and added the weight
of the whole Hungarian government to the protest against the appointment of Lueger as mayor of Vienna. The Emperor was as-
sailed from all sides: Lueger was a demagogue, a dangerous innovator, a disturber of the peace in Church affairs. Bánffy and his Budapest newspapers declared that "this enemy of Hungary" who attacked the leader of the Hungarian state in his speeches was a men-
ace to the monarchy and unacceptable to the Hungarian government as mayor of the Austrian capital. The new Austrian Prime
Minister, Count Badeni, who had only just left Galicia where he had
held the high office of governor, decided on his arrival in Vienna
that the best course in the circumstances was to join the majority,
and, as spokesman for the Council of Ministers, advise the Emperor
to refuse to endorse the appointment of Dr. Lueger as mayor.

Unabashed by the clamor of their opponents, the 93 members
of the Vienna Municipal Council (more than a two-thirds majority)

elected Dr. Karl Lueger as mayor of the imperial capital. The Liberal minority refrained from voting.

The Emperor withheld his sanction. On November 13 the Vienna Municipal Council met again for a new ballot, and once again Lueger was elected. The Council remained adamant, insisting upon its rights, whereupon the Imperial Commissioner produced from his pocket a decree providing for the dissolution of the Council and the holding of new elections.

On this November evening the loyal citizens of Vienna thronged in thousands to the Rathausplatz, crowding the high stone staircase and the arcades of the old palace to await the election results. It was an unruly crowd, and the many bitter calls swelled to a storm of protest as the proceedings in the council chamber above were made known. And again and again the shout rose in affection, anger and disillusionment: "Lueger! Lueger! We want Lueger!"

In bitter determination the Christian-Socials of Vienna embarked upon the new election campaign. On April 18, 1896, 96 instead of the previous 93 voted Christian-Social, and once again Dr. Karl Lueger was elected mayor of Vienna.

This time the Emperor summoned the Vienna people's leader in audience. While he acknowledged his personal integrity, his ability and his genuine loyalty to his Emperor and fatherland, he made it clear that "in the interests of the re-establishment of normal conditions in the autonomous administration of the city of Vienna" he expected Lueger voluntarily to renounce his claim to office.

Lueger would not have been true to himself had he not deferred, in honor, to his Emperor's wishes.

The interlude only served to draw the ranks of the Christian-Socials closer together. Twenty-five Catholic Conservatives from the Alpine provinces resigned from the Conservative Club, a pillar of the government coalition, in protest against the attitude of the government in the handling of the election question in Vienna. They formed the Catholic People's Party, and as such constituted the first political party to draw nearer to the Christian-Socials. Indeed the events in Vienna brought the Christian-Socials new friends from all nations within the monarchy. Lueger became the most popular man in the whole Empire. But in the depths of the nation's consciousness, hidden away and barely perceptible, there was a flaw—a small crack as yet and presenting no immediate danger, but a crack none the less. It had not been the Christian-Social "rebels" but the originators of the events in Vienna who had damaged the prestige of the crown and the state itself.

Chapter 4
A DIFFICULT BEGINNING

The atmosphere in Vienna was still vibrating with the repercussions of the recent events in Vienna as I took up my post as journalistic apprentice on the staff of the *Reichspost* in mid-July, 1896. I had no idea at that time how a newspaper was run, but it was obvious to me that, with such a small editorial staff, the production of a daily paper must demand a high standard of work and efficiency from every individual concerned. I was curious and at the same time full of admiration. The shabby clothes of the various editors were in keeping with the old house with its dusty, poorly-furnished rooms. A framed reproduction of a portrait of Leo XIII was the only decoration on the bare walls. I liked this Franciscan poverty, and found it fitting for the mission of the *Reichspost* as champion of the poor and oppressed and herald of a new and better social order.

Ambros Opitz led me back to his own office in which I was also to work.

"I must now tell you how we stand, so that you'll know how you've to think and to work here."

I was already conversant with the outlines of the history of the newly-founded paper which, as had been declared at the Linz *Katholikentag*, was to be the modern, popular Catholic daily, with a double edition, for the whole of Austria-Hungary.

At the end of May, 1893, a leaflet was published announcing the new paper, the *Reichspost*. The name was significant: the newspaper was to fulfill a mission for the Empire throughout all its nations. Its watchword was a vigorous affirmation of the state ideal of the Habsburg Empire in the face of all separatists and nationalist eccentrics.

The Christian-Social point of view was made quite clear.

The first official number of the *Reichspost* appeared on January 2, 1894. The leading article ended with the fine words: "Our heart and our strength for the Christian nation and the Christian nation for us!" On its front page, like a shield against misinterpretation and malevolence, the first number bore the declaration that Leo XIII had bestowed the Apostolic Blessing on the chairman of the editorial committee for the success of the new undertaking.

By the end of the first year the *Reichspost* had reached a circulation of 5,000 on Sundays and some 800 less on weekdays. The newspaper came out at four o'clock in the afternoon, a most unfavorable hour but one dictated by technical, or rather financial, reasons. On the premises in the Strozzigasse we were short of everything. Only one telephone was available for the use of the editorial office, the administration and the printers. The reference books for the editorial staff consisted of an old directory of Vienna, a still-more-out-of-date official gazette and a few clerical manuals. We possessed in addition an encyclopedia—Volumes A to H.

Of course we could barely afford to pay fees to contributors, and, since I had been made responsible for the *feuilleton* section, it was up to me to procure unpaid articles. As a result I began to write myself, and was soon turning out articles on every conceivable subject, ranging from "The Man in the Moon" to "Hieroglyphs in Philae." Besides this I still had to devote six hours each day to my studies.

Shortly before the opening of the autumn sitting of the Imperial Diet, a new job was added to my work on the *feuilletons*: I was appointed parliamentary reporter. Only the shortage of editorial staff could have accounted for entrusting of this responsible task to an inexperienced novice like myself, for the parliamentary reportage was one of the most important sections of a political daily newspaper and upon it depended its prestige.

It is practically impossible for the layman to realize how difficult it is to condense a long, important speech into a tenth or a twentieth of the space that a full report would take up, without losing the essence and the effect of the original version. What is more, this must be done with the utmost speed. The work demands a comprehension of the material involved, the ability quickly to grasp the salient points and the style, and to paraphrase long passages in a few short words.

The *Reichspost*, with its eight pages, was the smallest in volume of the Vienna newspapers and for this reason its parliamentary reports necessitated the greatest condensation. It seemed a hopeless task for the beginner. Even today, when I look back on my early days in journalism, I have a sense of uneasiness about those first parliamentary reports. Those months were a hard schooling for me.

The Liberal newspapers were the overlords in Parliament. Their correspondents represented a united front, and in the eyes of the parliamentary officials they and they only counted. It was they who distributed the seats in the press gallery and determined, according to the interests of their own papers, the issue of the official parliamentary gazette. The *Neue Freie Presse* had the right to its own private telephone line in the House of Deputies, for "the government could not function without the *Neue Freie Presse*," as a minister once remarked.

The press in Vienna at the turn of the century was a remarkable structure. It had been formed and developed by a series of influential men over several decades with studied art and calculation, so that it finally represented a dictatorial power. Its sway extended not only over the political sphere, but also covered the economy, the world of science and the arts, and included the *salons* of society. It was in its commercial interests to cater to the needs of the various classes of the population. It knew just how to attract the attention of its readers, to stimulate their desire for knowledge, to rouse their latent passions and to lull the solid citizen into a state of comfortable complacency. It made itself invaluable to the financier as a source of information, to the scholar and artist as patron, and to the politician as champion of his reputation. It could bestow praise and honors, but also censure and abuse, and above all it influenced the masses to believe exactly what it wanted them to believe—an art which the Vienna press at that time had brought to the point of virtuosity.

Much could be learned from this press in Vienna. I diligently studied their leading articles, masterpieces in their command of history and knowledge of literature as well as in their style. We Austrian Catholics could claim no such schooling. Our leading men, for the most part clerics, were still struggling against unequal odds in a press hampered by a lack of many vital necessities. They could barely afford to pay their contributors and could rarely hope to gain the permanent collaboration of well-known writers. For this reason the Liberal press was far ahead of its Catholic rivals in its cultivation of literature, the fine arts and the sciences, and exercised an influence upon the public and upon intellectual achievements well beyond that of the Catholics.

It was indeed from these seemingly neutral zones of journalism, rather than from its political maneuvers, that the Liberal press drew its vast circulation, its prestige and its widespread influence among the intelligentsia. The enormous circulation of the Liberal press accounted, furthermore, for its virtual monopoly of the newspaper advertising market, a most valuable source of income.

The sixteen months between the fall of 1896 and January, 1898, were decisive for the destiny of the Christian-Social movement. The election to the Imperial Diet in the winter of 1897 brought fresh proof of the increased support of the masses. For the first time, on March 9, 1897, the newly-established *V. Kurie*, an addition to the four existing *Wahlkörper*, or electoral corporations, extended the franchise to the masses of the population, irrespective of tax considerations and property. Although members of the other four *Wahlkörper* participated in the voting within the new *V. Kurie*, the vote of the masses made itself felt, and in Vienna-Lower Austria every seat of the new *Kurie* was gained by the Christian-Socials.

In Vienna a total of 117,003 Christian-Social votes had been counted—approximately 29,000 more than the Socialists'. The Liberal candidates could raise only a total of 10,000 in the city of a million inhabitants and the pan-German vote was a paltry 2,530. Many of the former Liberal supporters had pinned their hopes on the Social Democrats and their votes remained with this party, then and in subsequent electoral campaigns. These middle-class adherents did the Social Democrats no good.[1]

---

[1] Subsequent developments showed that although the political successors of the middle-class Liberals in the First Republic followed the dictates of common sense and amalgamated with the Christian-Socials to form a

From the 593,090 votes of the *V. Kurie*, 262,712 (44.5 per cent) were Christian-Social; they exceeded the Socialist vote by 31,000 (39 per cent) and came for the most part from the German electoral districts, while the Socialist vote was spread among the German, Czech, Polish and Italian regions.

The Christian-Socials had, by this election, penetrated victoriously into the Alpine provinces. The designation "a Vienna party" so often used against them was no longer appropriate.

When, therefore, in April the majority vote of the Municipal Council elected Dr. Lueger for the fifth time as mayor of Vienna and shortly afterward the Emperor's approval of this appointment was finally received, this constituted the recognition of the overwhelming will of the people, as demonstrated throughout the whole of Austria by the vote of the *V. Kurie*.

But the electoral results were significant also from another point of view. Unmistakably a large number of workers had voted Christian-Social within the *V. Kurie*. For the first time a worker belonged to the Christian-Social Club in the Parliament. Already some years before, a group of young working-class people had formed around Leopold Kunschak, a young upholsterer in the Westbahn works. From this circle developed the Christian-Social Workers' Union for Lower Austria, formed on December 4, 1892, under Kunschak's leadership. It was the first political rallying-point and instructional center under Christian-Social auspices. Legally the nineteen-year-old founder was not yet eligible for membership in a political organization. For this reason, Leopold Bischof, a carpenter's apprentice, was entrusted with the chairmanship. In the face of many attacks from outside and various internal crises, the new movement steered its precarious way through the first five years. At the end of this period Bishof, worn out in the heat of battle, re-

---

government, their antipathy to the latter's "clerical" tendencies resulted in an ever increasing reserve. Various elections during the Second Republic indicated the decided leaning of the Liberal middle classes toward the equally anti-clerical Socialists. For all that, particularly during the Second Republic, they actually had fewer ideological ties with this party than with the Christian political party. This reveals anew the emotionally deep-seated anti-religious attitude of certain middle-class hitherto Liberal circles.

linquished his office to Kunschak, who was destined to preside over the Christian-Social Workers' Union for the next half-century.[2]

The hour had come in which, by the integration of the Christian-Social workers into the body of the Christian-Social movement, it had achieved the structural realization of its program: the harmonious unification of all classes. Primarily of lower-middle-class origin and formed with the ideal of combating the rampant power of capitalism and the evils of social injustice and exploitation, the movement was closely bound up with the interests of the workers. Toward the end of the 'nineties the now state-controlled Vienna public transport concern and the city gas works demonstrated to their workers, to a degree previously unknown, the practical meaning of social welfare. The result was that not only did thousands of workers of the state-controlled works join the Christian-Socials, but the movement penetrated into the co-operative organizations representing the apprentices in Vienna. By the further gain of the support of an organization for railroad workers, the movement achieved a strength which even surpassed for a short time that of its Socialist rivals in one of the most tenaciously held of their own class strongholds.

The Socialists used every means in their power to combat "the Christians." They recognized a rival who rejected their own Marxist doctrine. For this very reason they saw in this rival the cat's-paw of the capitalist class and the enemy of the proletariat, the Christian-Social concept of the state and society being so fundamentally opposed to that of Marxism. The Social Democratic workers' movement had from the outset to fight every inch of its way against the hostility and prejudice of the Liberal bureaucrats and capitalists.

Already in 1873, in addition to various types of workers' unions, there existed 152 associations comparable to trade unions with a membership of 32,853. These organizations were subsequently almost completely exterminated when a radical faction broke away from the Social Democrats and resorted to anarchist methods, using

[2] (45 *Jahre Christlichsoziale Arbeiterverein*, by Leopold Kunschak, September 1937, Typographische Anstalt, Vienna. *Festschrift zum 60. Geburtstag Leopold Kunschaks*, by Dr. Franz Hemala, 1931, Typographische Anstalt, Vienna).

robbery and violence, which not only provoked the introduction of severe preventive measures by the state, but gave rise to active protests on the part of all those hostile to the workers as such. Of the 23 delegates from the Bohemian mining industry sent to the Miners' Congress in Vienna in October, 1890, 21 were summarily dismissed; similarly, of the 18 delegates from Moravia-Silesia, 17 were thrown out, and in another mining concern 200 workers were given notice for having participated in collecting funds to cover the traveling expenses of their delegates.

The Marxist workers had not yet developed an effective means of self-protection. When their party congress was held in Mainfeld in 1889 the Social Democrats had raised only 15,500 members from their 104 party organizations; two years later at the party congress held at the end of June, 1891, the Social Democratic trade union organization had already established 300 branch organizations with a total membership of approximately 16,000.

This was the victorious body which now encountered the new Christian workers' movement. The backbone of the Christian body was formed primarily of the Catholic workers' organizations and the local branches of the Christian-Social Workers' Union, generally ideologically and politically well-informed groups. A worker who was a member of a Catholic workers' union or a similar Christian-Social body would often stand isolated at his work, confronted by the closed ranks of the trade unionists whose "non-political" organization was run on Marxist principles. In many cases no other course was open to the worker thus isolated than to capitulate before the trade union, whose concepts ran contrary to his own but which wore down his resistance with a relentless pressure. The Christian-Socials sought to lessen the dangers of this situation by the establishment of trade unions run on Christian principles. These efforts, begun at the turn of the century, were praiseworthy and courageous, but the Socialists were a whole decade ahead in their extensive work in this field. At the Extraordinary Congress of Independent Trade Unions held in December, 1905, already 293 trade union organizations had been established with a membership of 283,892, a figure which rose to 415,195 in 1913.

Once again Leopold Kunschak came to the fore. Already in 1897 he had campaigned for the Christian trade union ideal among the workers. On September 7, 1902, ten years after the foundation of the Christian-Social Workers' Union, the Imperial Association of Non-political Unions of Christian Workers in Austria was formed, the first central integration of all Christian workers' organizations: this formed a broad basis from which the planned construction of a Christian trade union organization could be undertaken. By the middle of the first decade of the new century there already existed such Christian unions for bakers, textile workers, builders and masons and for tailors. When the first Congress of Christian Trade Unions in Austria was held in 1907, the chairman could already refer to 13 central organizations with 481 branches and a membership of 27,018. Two Czech Christian trade unions also existed with 21,100 members, in addition to various local German organizations comprising 11,609 members as yet not incorporated into any association. As is confirmed by official figures published in 1919, the new Austrian Republic was able to retrieve 25,933 members of Christian trade unions from the chaos of World War I and the disintegration of the Empire. From then on a new era began for the Christian trade unions, as a result of which five years later the membership had risen to over 80,000. The independent Socialist trade unions could register a figure ten times as great, but the Christian trade unions had achieved their commendable position in the face of tremendous odds. They had fought tenaciously, not only for every strategic position, but for every single man, not only outnumbered, but exposed to the terror campaign of an enemy with all the advantages on his side.

The *V. Kurie* election results had already shown that the German-Nationals could not free themselves from their old Liberal ties. Moreover Schönerer and his radical pan-German adherents were hot on the trail of their German-National rivals, declaring to the electorate that they and they alone were the true German representatives. As a result of the ensuing rivalry in national radicalism, there were certain inevitable estrangements from the Christian-Socials in the crown provinces.

The situation in Vienna was, however, less clear. The German-National group in the *Bürgerklub* in Parliament maintained a reasonably good relationship with the Christian-Socials. The attitude of the *Deutsche Volksblatt* gave cause for concern: the newspaper could not be relied upon to uphold the Christian standpoint on vital issues and was moreover possessed by an incurable "clerical phobia." The newspaper could be compared to a typical Viennese *Bürger* who had only recently left the home comforts of Liberal domesticity. The father had probably participated as a member of the National Guard in the 1848 Vienna revolution; the atmosphere in the home had been Liberal. One had been sent to the interdenominational schools of the *Kulturkampf* era, had learned a little of this and a little of that, but precious little catechism, and emerged as an enlightened citizen who had read Liberal newspapers and voted Liberal (with a certain skepticism and with growing doubts)—until Lueger appeared on the scene. Needless to say, one had always been what is termed "a good Christian": one went to church on the principal festivals and always contributed something toward the Corpus Christi procession. One would of course receive the Last Sacraments (but not too soon), for this made a better impression in the obituary notice. One was by no means a "holy Joe," and the parish priest was held in esteem for his aptitude as a taroc partner. Otherwise it was better not to have too much to do with the clergy.

This represented the Christianity of thousands of worthy Viennese citizens—those left over from the influence of Josephinism and *Freisinn*. For a long time many did not even realize of how much they had been bereft.

In this lukewarm atmosphere such hybrid specimens as Vergani's newspaper throve. The inevitable crisis eventually came and was dearly paid for.

The *Reichspost* had repeatedly declared its desire for the maintenance of good relations with other newspapers representing a kindred standpoint. When, however, fundamental principles became involved, the *Reichspost* felt in conscience bound clearly to voice its opinion. Again and again it was forced to protest against the racial anti-Semitism proclaimed by the *Deutsche Volksblatt*. It knew that in this matter Dr. Lueger would in no way be opposed to its attitude, for, much as Lueger deplored and opposed the detrimental influence exercised by some of the Jewish minority in public affairs and the economy, he held no brief for racial or religious prejudice and gave proof of this often in his own actions. It was after all Lueger himself who had summoned Dr. Porzer, a most able man and a devout Catholic, to the Vienna Municipal Council, for all that his origins were not purely Ayrian. It was certainly something of a feat in those stormy days, when political catchwords were being bandied about and feelings were running high, for the *Reichspost* to counter this racial anti-Semitic trend and at the same time to voice its legitimate protest against the various evils resulting from the Jewish predominance in public affairs.

On April 5 and 25, 1897, the Badeni language ordinances for Bohemia and Moravia were issued. They cast the ship of state into a stormy sea and it took many years before it found its way into more peaceful waters—having suffered irreparable damage in the meantime. A political body so fundamentally Austrian in its ideals as was the Christian-Social party must of necessity have become actively involved in the events of those stormy years when the Austrian state concept was threatened and impassioned political elements sprang up, hostile to the Imperial dynasty.

One day Baron Dipauli, chairman of the Catholic People's party,

³ The Badeni language ordinances superseded the former Stremayr ordinances of April 19, 1880, which had determined the *external* administrative language to be used by officials: in their direct relations with the public, political and judicial authorities were obliged to use the same language as that in which the verbal or written application, etc., had been submitted; general regulations, proclamations and the like had to be formulated in both the national languages, when these were not directly concerned with individual districts and municipalities. These ordinances were further supplemented by the Badeni decree which declared that also *within* the administration itself all correspondence, etc., concerned with a verbal or written application or case must be conducted in the original language in which it had been presented, and not exclusively in German as had previously been the rule. It was furthermore declared that in future all officials of the administration must be bi-lingual and that as of July, 1901—after four years—only such candidates for official positions would be accepted as wholly fulfilled these demands.

informed me that the Liberals had at long last declared themselves prepared to agree to the transfer of the school legislation from the central government in Vienna to the individual crown provinces. This would mean the realization of the long-cherished hope of the German Catholics: the establishment of Catholic schools in the Alpine provinces. In return, so Dipauli told me, the Conservatives were to vote with the government on the language ordinances issue, and the Christian-Socials had apparently no objection to participation in such a course. Ambros Opitz, to whom I told this news, hurried to the Parliament and, in an impassioned speech of intervention on behalf of his three and a half million German compatriots in Bohemia, he succeeded in turning the Christian-Socials from their course.

The practical implications of the ordinances lay in the fact that the double language would in effect be introduced in all offices of the state administration in Bohemia and Moravia. This applied also to the 72 out of the 219 judicial districts in Bohemia which, in an enclosed German-speaking region, could claim very small, if any, Czech minorities. Since the Sudeten Germans, in contrast to their Czech compatriots, had far too few officials conversant with the second national language, the new regulations would mean the pensioning off of many German officials and their replacement by Czechs—in fact the "planting" of the exclusively German-speaking region with Czech officials of every rank and grade. Grave errors committed in the past had contributed in no small measure to the unfavorable prospects facing the national minorities concerned. From the very beginning of the constitutional era, young people at the *Gymnasien* had been given a bi-lingual education. The legislation which, even before the introduction of the Stremayr decree, put an end to this, drastically reduced the numbers of the German rising generation with a knowledge of both languages.

Ambros Opitz, well aware of the delicate national-political structure of his homeland, summed up the situation immediately. The Sudeten Germans would protest in desperation against the measure and appeal for help to their German racial *confrères* within Austria. Whoever took the side of the Government and its Slav parties in the coalition would invite the most violent national indictment. Were the Christian-Socials to take this step, it could only bring about their ruin in Bohemia and Moravia and irreparable damage to their prestige in other quarters.

The bitter tide of national hatred and discontent rose to the point of frenzy during the months that followed. The House of Deputies echoed and re-echoed with the deafening noise of the so-called "technical obstructionists" who, under the leadership of the radical pan-Germans, demolished massive oak desks and chairs and emptied inkpots over the heads of ministers. Solid Viennese confectioners, shopkeepers, journalists, bank officials and even conventional landowners drummed and whistled or gave vent to some other ear-splitting din. The Christian-Socials demonstrated their rejection of the ordinances in line with the other left-wing German parties, but protested strongly against this violent obstructionism which degraded the parliamentary tradition in Austria to an extent never previously known.

I was one of those who heaved a sigh of relief when, after two chaotic months, the witches' Sabbath was finally brought to an end by the summer parliamentary recess. The days were over when, during endless obstructionist speeches, I had done my best to digest the principles of civil and penal law. On July 8, 1897, I passed successfully the second and third of my six legal examinations.

That same evening I took the night train to Graz. It was dawn as I threw the three roses against the window in a house in the Klosterwiesgasse, the secret sign that I had passed the examinations. In that room slept the young girl I loved and whose parents had agreed to our engagement, provided I passed the examination.

We became engaged on July 10.

In this lost Eden of ours true love is a foretaste of paradise.

Chapter 5
IN THE HEAT OF BATTLE

It was November 26, 1897. A vast unruly mob thrust its way from the Burgring to the University. Wild shouts and cries rose to the lowering sky, cloud-hung, dark and threatening. Riots had broken out. From the direction of the Parliament came the clatter of hoofs and the clank of steel and a squadron of dragoons, riding in a broad front right across from pavement to pavement, drove the crowds toward the Schottentor. In the vicinity of the Parliament I was myself caught up in the tide of the mob and borne along hopelessly with it. All around me rose shrill cries and whistles; clenched fists and sticks were raised and insults and threats were flung against the troops. The sharp commands of the officers cut through the tumult like the lash of a whip. The crowd was brought to a standstill, but the commotion only increased. People with faces like madmen grabbed for the bridles of the horses in an attempt to draw the soldiers from their saddles. Sword blades clattered menacingly. New crowds had gathered round the University and the police had forced their way into the building. Students were wrestling furiously with them, hand to hand, in the aula and in the lecture halls above.

A turbulent stream rose against the Alser Strasse. Would the mob storm the building of the Provincial Law Courts where the pan-German deputy Karl Hermann Wolf had been brought for custody? Inflammatory calls rose from the crowd. Some began to sing "The Watch on the Rhine": it was not to the taste of the mob.

The aspect of a great city in revolt is totally changed. It seemed as though new fanatical citizens had suddenly taken the place of the old-accustomed Viennese.

Something strangely sinister and menacing hung over the reputedly light-hearted city on that sullen November day, but the dark tide receded toward evening with arrival of the news that Lueger had come from the Emperor and had proclaimed from the balustrade of the Rathaus the resignation of Badeni's government.

Vienna was thrown into chaos on that 26th of November. In the House of Deputies the pan-Germans had, under the pretext of obstructionism, wrecked everything they could lay their hands on. In the ear-splitting din we journalists could barely hear the hailstorm of invective which broke loose against the government, the President of the House and the coalition party. I had often experienced the disruption of Christian-Social political meetings by the Socialist hecklers, but the tumult in Parliament was a hundred times worse.

"We shall come tomorrow with revolvers and shoot you down like dogs!" the deputy Wolf had cried, and a well-known Prague university professor had chased about with a long knife in his hand and threatened some Czech or other that he would "slit his belly." It was hardly surprising, therefore, that a precautionary measure was introduced by the deputy Count Falkenhayn, empowering the President of the House to suspend from three sessions any deputy who refused to comply with his second call to order. As the order was read aloud utter confusion broke loose. The deputy Wolf, raving like a madman, had to be carried out by the police and taken to the Law Courts buildings.

Force is a strange thing. Even when it is legally exercised in the interests of law and order, it is almost as though it thereby demands proof of its justification. Universal public opinion tends always to be directed against it. This would seem to constitute a warning which has its roots in the natural order that just force should only be imposed in cases of extreme necessity, and a token that force used contrary to justice will finally turn against its originators. The force which was used in the House of Deputies on the grounds of a legitimate decree for the maintenance of parliamentary order, perhaps even for the protection of personal security, would have been accepted in less turbulent times, even if with some protest. As it was, however, in the fever of nationalist emotion the obstructionist deputies were hailed as national champions and those seized by the police suddenly became helpless victims surrounded by an aura of sacrifice. The pan-Germans had hitherto found little support in Vienna, least of all among the broad masses of the people. Now all at once their fortunes changed. The Socialists, always quick to sense popular feeling and jealous if anyone else claimed popularity, rushed into the fray. They accordingly added their voice to the demonstrations in the streets on November 26.

The pan-German agitators now started another uproar. On December 11, during a meeting of several thousand young and exuberant students in the courtyard of the University, a medical student called Foedisch ended a fiery speech with the cry: "Away from Rome!" At the pan-German party congress which took place a few days later a student called Rakus from the "Ostmark," the most radical of all the pan-German students' unions, took up this call amid thunderous applause as a new battle cry. All the other points of the congress shriveled into insignificance in the heat of the new slogan, which was adopted as the party resolution. The worst had happened: the political conflict had penetrated into the sphere of religion.

German Liberal *Freisinn* had already paved the way during the 'sixties and 'seventies in warping the minds of the intelligentsia and the semi-educated. Oswald Spengler writes bitterly in his book *Jahre der Entscheidung* ("Years of Decision"), published in 1933, of a "bleak intelligence" and "the weeds of the city pavements which spring up in incredible profusion." "This is no longer the thrifty, age-old wisdom of the peasants which maintains its truths as long as the generations themselves endure, but the naked spirit of the day— the daily newspapers, the current literature and the public meetings, the spirit without blood which gnaws away in negative criticism on what remains of a genuine culture."

Among the students and young people, the unfortunate victims of a biased or at any rate inadequate historical education, the hostile propaganda against the Catholic Church fell on fertile ground.

Openly subversive propaganda against the state was mingled with the pan-German anti-clerical propaganda. The formula which was proclaimed so often at pan-German rallies during the 'nineties was the demand for "a constitutionally created Greater Germany."

This was the fertile soil upon which the seeds of discontent following the Badeni language ordinances had fallen. The designation "Away from Rome Movement" was in fact inaccurate, for a movement as such had actually never existed. Movement in the life of a nation requires first and foremost an impetus springing from the heart of the people themselves. The superimposed "Away from Rome" doctrine of the pan-Germans found adherents only among a thin upper stratum of Liberal origins in the cities and small provincial towns, above all in the German border regions of the Sudetenland, Styria and Carinthia. The so-called movement had no success worth mentioning in Vienna; it was decisively rejected by the German peasants in Austria and met with cold indifference among the workers.

It was evident from the beginning that the pan-German movement was misusing religion as a subterfuge. Its leaders were concerned with the policy "Protestantism for the peoples of the Ostmark" only as a preliminary step toward *the unification of Austria with the German Empire.*

The "Away from Rome" agitation drew into the fray the contentious Evangelical Union from the German Empire, not the official representatives of the German Protestants but an openly belligerent organization. Two publishing houses closely connected with the Evangelical Union started an action with leaflets and brochures against the Catholic Church, against the Austrian state (although this was allied with the German Empire) and against the Habsburgs. A large-scale pamphlet smuggling racket began, particularly around Asch and Jägerndorf. Parcels of "Silesian linen" and "fancy goods" concealed batches of propaganda leaflets. The instigators of this propaganda, ruthless and audacious, boasted later to have distributed three million leaflets in Austria up to 1910. A pamphlet published by I. F. Lehrmann in Munich in 1899 and entitled *Austria's Collapse and Reconstruction* already divided up the Austrian state. The pamphlet declares:

The Austro-Hungarian Empire is on the verge of collapse. Many things are responsible for this state of affairs. First and foremost, however, are the dynasty, the oligarchy of families who rule the state, the Jesuits and the "half and half" policy which has been adopted as a state principle. . . . This imminent collapse of the Danube Empire is certainly no welcome occurrence for the German Empire, as yet still concerned with its own internal constructional problems. But German diplomacy must be content with an adequate preparation of the German Empire both militarily and by alliance with other powers. *A continuation of the war of 1866 will then be unavoidable.* Then at last the Danube nations must be delivered from the curse of half-and-halfness (*Fluch der Halbheit*). There must be a constitutional break with the past.

War is the best basis for the creation of a new state system. . . . This half-German Austria must become a wholly German member of the new German racial Empire.

This product of the lowest form of "pot-house politics" is quoted only in order to give some idea of the morbid attitude of those connected with the "Away from Rome" campaign. They were paving the way for Hitlerism. . . .

Similar views were held by Pastor Bräunlich of the Evangelical Union, as expressed in his leaflet *The German Faith*: "As soon as our people comprehend and respond enthusiastically to this great ideal [Protestantism for Austria], the task of the evangelization of Austria will achieve its victorious goal: *one nation, one Emperor, one God.*"

The tremendous expenditure involved in the efforts to accomplish this aim was perhaps the most sobering feature of this pathetic campaign. According to the *Magdeburger Zeitung*, during the period 1897 to 1901 nine million marks were dispensed for the "Away from Rome" propaganda in Austria.

There were doubtless some people in the German Empire who felt they were supporting a worthy Protestant cause in contributing funds toward the action in Austria. There were also pastors who came across to Austria, full of religious ardor, in the genuine belief that a new Reformation era had dawned for Austria. The pan-German spokesman must be given credit for having done everything to dispel such delusions. Already in December, 1898, the *Ostdeutsche Rundschau* impressed upon the pan-German adherents that "the German racial slogan 'Away from Rome!' arose purely from political considerations. A racial German party could *never* consent to serve the religious interests of any one denomination."

Some weeks after this, at a rally designed to rouse the somewhat apathetic hangers-on, the "fundamental resolution" was proclaimed that the break with the Catholic Church is foreseen *for racial reasons only*, "and then only when at least 10,000 have left the Church."

Pastors who had come to Austria in the good faith that a great missionary task lay ahead of them learned from the *Unverfälschte Deutsche Worte* (April, 1899) that the Lutheran and the Old Catholic churches were only intended as "stopgaps" over the transition period before the establishment of a German racial religion. According to the *Unverfälschte Deutsche Worte* of January, 1903, both these denominations represented the "lesser evil" between which the choice rested if one did not prefer to belong to no specific religion. The *Freie Deutsche Schule* (No. 20, 1898) talked about the aim for a "religion of the development era" and the *Unverfälschte Deutsche Worte* further declared: "This is the final goal, and it is our task to realize it: the fostering and manifestation of the German ideal as the essence of every virtue, *every religion.*"

Protestants of high standing raised their voices against the pan-German action and warned against this "evangelization" of Austria. The Viennese pastor Dr. Johanny declared before a large congregation at the consecration of the new Währing Protestant Church on December 2, 1898, that "the evangelical church had no sympathy with those who under the device 'Away from Rome!' propagate the conversion to Protestantism as a political demonstration." He added that it was a Christian duty "formally to protest against every abuse of our precious faith to serve disloyal and anti-patriotic ends."

Pastor Thümen in Friesach, one of the disillusioned who had come across from Germany cherishing different hopes, observed in an article in the Stuttgart *Evangelisches Sonntagsblatt* that the paper brought out by the most radical of the pan-German "Away from Rome" spokesmen, Deputy Wolf, "not only displayed little clear understanding of evangelicalism, but indeed—astonishing though this might seem—an open hostility to it." He declared further that opinions were expressed in the newspaper which "consigned not only Rome but every other religion to the rubbish heap." Finally the Evangelical Union received its due for the part it played in the "Away from Rome" campaign. In May, 1901, the *Deutsche Adelsblatt*, the organ of the official association comprising the aristocracy of the German Empire, voiced its strong attitude against the antireligious campaign of the Union. Speaking on behalf of "a very great number of our members," the writer denounced the tactics used by the Union as "neither Christian, nor Protestant nor noble." The Union, so he declared further, represented an "unclear and negative form of Protestantism" and was "in no way a suitable organ for the propagation of the evangelical faith in Catholic countries."

The action inspired by the *Kulturkampf* ended as a bitter satire upon its instigators. The hollow falsity of the whole campaign finally came to light. Already in 1901—three years after its pretentious beginning—one discreditable revelation followed another. Karl Hermann Wolf, the *Reichsrat* deputy, was the first to be stripped of his former glory as a national hero and the founder of a new German racial religion. As the result of a serious lapse of conduct in connection with the family of a party friend, he was expelled from the pan-German parliamentary club. Next came the pan-German deputy Herzog, who was convicted of blackmail, libel and various other offenses. Finally Habermann, the editor of a radically anti-Catholic paper, was found guilty of procuring and of slander and infamous conduct.

A veritable Pandora's box filled with an inexhaustible content of new and repulsive scandals seemed to have been opened. The opponents of the Catholic Church now turned upon one another in condemnation. Their enterprise was thus itself reduced to the mockery of the masses and roused the mistrust of many pan-German supporters and the ridicule of those who saw through its devices. According to the report published by the official Imperial Church Council of the Augsburg and Helvetian denominations, 14,835 of the nine million German Catholics in the Austrian Empire joined these communities during the four years of the heated pan-German propaganda from 1898 to 1901. The figures produced by the Protestant churches were also so low that an article in the *Unverfälschte Deutsche Worte* admitted: "We need make no secret of the fact that, despite undeniable results, the number to date who have seceded from the Church of Rome has fallen far short of the expectations and hopes justifiably cherished by their friends of the "Away from Rome" movement, that truly liberating movement which paves the way for a Greater Germany."

This slow trickle only began to increase in 1904 when the Social Democrats, allied with the middle-class "German Radicals" in the election campaign against the Christian-Socials, started their campaign among the workers, urging them to leave the Church. By 1909 the Catholic Church had lost approximately 50,000 of its members, largely due to the Socialist *Freisinn* propaganda.[1] It became increasingly difficult from year to year to establish an accurate figure, however, for these secessions were counterbalanced by a constant stream of returns to the fold of the Church.

Here was a mission for the *Reichspost*. The paper was free from all external considerations, its only obligation being to the Christian conscience. It became the leading publicistic opponent of the "Away from Rome" press and its political wire-pullers. The pan-German anti-clericalists were bitterly conscious of the enemy which hounded them day after day. Against no other of their antagonists did they fight so furiously as against the *Reichspost*.

Public speakers lent their support to the journalists in the counterattack. On Sundays I would go off to attend the public meetings held in nearly all the German crown provinces.

It was the pan-German campaign which finally served to clarify the political position of the Christian-Social movement. The real

[1] The Austrian Socialists have been unable to overcome this anti-religious "complex" even up to the present day. This revealed itself during the period of the violent political struggles between the Social Democrats and the Christian-Socials of the First Republic and, despite certain gratifying improvements in this respect after World War II (Catholics and Socialists were often together in the same Hitler prisons), the same anti-clerical view persists among Socialists of the old school. For this reason it is still hardly possible for the conscientious Catholic to vote for the Socialist party, even when this state of affairs is gradually improving.

object behind the pan-German attack was after all the Austrian state and its instigators made no secret of their treasonous intentions. In officially recorded speeches in Parliament Schönerer and his group of deputies gave vent to unprecedented outbursts of abuse against the Austrian state.

"I declare aloud: we want to join the German Empire!" cried Deputy Stein on February 28, 1901. On March 18, 1902, Schönerer made his notorious speech in the House of Deputies in which he declared that he must oppose every government which did not view a federal state integration with Germany as its primary aim. He ended his speech amidst the cheers and stormy applause of his party confederates with the cry: "Long live the Hohenzollerns!"[2] Confronted by this agitation, the German-Nationals stood by irresolutely, uncertain of their course. While they were prepared to stand for an Austrian state concept which would allow for a realistic German national policy, they were at the same time aiming to impress the electorate by an excessive show of nationalist sentiment. Such German-Nationals as were close to Lueger in Vienna from the beginning of the anti-Liberal movement and had no desire to participate in this new form of "national" politics now turned to Lueger and joined the Christian-Socials.

Although the group centered round Vergani and his *Deutsches Volksblatt* maintained a certain distinct course of their own and liked to be known as the "left wing" of the Christian-Social party, they kept a safe distance from the German-Nationals both in Parliament and in the provinces who had been caught up in the wake of the radical agitators. Despite the link of the Christian-Socials with the left-wing German parties within the so-called German National *Verband* (Deutschen Gemeinbürgschaft), a parliamentary roof organization for widely divergent German parties, the rift between the Christian-Socials and these German-Nationals was nevertheless great. This was much to be regretted since it would have been the destiny of the German-Nationals as a "middle party" to form a bridge between the Christian-Socials and the German Conservatives on the one side and the German Liberals on the other: the binding

---

[2] The Hohenzollerns were the ruling dynasty in the German Empire.

element between the German Austrian state parties against the radical pan-German negationists of the state.

But the pan-German renegades with their seditious propaganda against the dynasty and the state had reckoned without that great Austrian Karl Lueger. No other of his antagonists was subjected to the expressions of anger and furious biting contempt which Lueger reserved for Schönerer and Wolf. Whether he was speaking on the pan-German agitation in Parliament or from the platform of a public political meeting, his eyes would blaze furiously and he would raise his right fist accusingly; his voice took on a hard metallic ring, his words falling like sword thrusts. At that time Lueger became the standard-bearer for countless thousands, even far beyond the bounds of the German regions within Austria. In the fervent avowal of his own devotion to Austria he appealed to the hearts of the Viennese citizens and fired their latent patriotism, so often veiled by a mania for fault-finding and even sometimes by a certain frivolity but always emerging victoriously in the face of a serious crisis.

This decisive attitude of the Christian-Social leaders against the pan-German renegades emphasized in itself the importance of positive Christian and religious values in both public and private life. Those who had formerly stood apart, hesitant and mistrustful (among them the Catholics from the Conservative camp), felt their former prejudices and doubts as to the basic Christian aims of the movement being dispelled. The clear course indicated every day by the *Reichspost* began to win over the educated younger generation; many young graduates, for the most part Catholics, now joined the movement. In July, 1900, voices among the Conservative Catholics began to advocate closer co-operation with the Christian-Socials. It was the first sign that the bitter antagonism of the past two years would be overcome.

At midnight of July 8, 1900, the Prime Minister, Dr. von Koerber, handed the President the imperial decree dissolving the House of Deputies, since the Czechs were obstructing the legal settlement of the language question by the government. New general elections were to be held in the spring of 1901. In Vienna the electorate could see for itself the fine accomplishments of the new administration. The city had taken on a completely new aspect. The reform achievements were in themselves irrefutable arguments in favor of Lueger. Things looked less rosy for the Christian-Socials outside the capital.

Never before in its history had the Austrian nation gone to the polls to elect its highest legislative body so influenced by that worst evil of democracy—the empty phrase-mongering of seditious demagogues with their cheap invective against the state and their own compatriots. The nationalist strife and the exploitation of nationalist emotions to serve the election interests of the radicals overpowered the voices of the peace-lovers and those prepared to work. The situation in no way dismayed either the leaders of the *bourgeois* Liberal camp or the Social Democratic party chiefs, although the latter might well have feared for the safety of their own well-equipped house against the threat of the nationalist firebrands. Wherever Lueger's men were to be found, it seemed that the object of these elections was to bring about the ruin of the Christian-Social party. Christian-Social political meetings ended often in bloodshed and it became a dangerous mission to distribute Christian-Social propaganda leaflets or to deliver newspapers.

As was only to be feared, the elections, the real purpose of which should have been to constitute a new and able-bodied Parliament, ended more or less in a victory for the masters in chauvinistic hymns of hate and anarchist agitation, both German and Czech. Among the vanquished were all those who strove in the light of their own fundamental principles as embodied in their political program for a policy of moderation and conciliation in nationalist affairs. The Christian-Socials lost 8 of their 30 seats in the House of Deputies, the Catholic Conservatives were forced back from 41 to 37 and even the Social Democrats lost 4 of their 14 seats. The most serious and significant factor of the election results for the Christian-Social party was the drop in the number of votes it received within the general electoral body from 262,742 to 174,503. All along the line the nationalist radicals triumphed. Behind the irreconcilable attitude of these nationalists lay much more dangerous motives directed against the state itself. The pan-Germans increased their number of seats in a sudden spring from 5 to 21; among the Czechs,

Klofac and Fresl appeared on the scene for the first time as "National Socialists," surpassing all previous parliamentary furor.

Were these destructive elements to gain the upper hand? The Prime Minister, Dr. von Koerber, showed more skill in handling the situation than his predecessors. With his gold-framed economic program which foresaw an expenditure of about one billion kronen for its large-scale schemes, he succeeded in maintaining a working parliament over a period of a few years. Now, however, in addition to the constant nationalist problems, further constitutional dangers of the utmost gravity became evident.

In the midst of the turbulent events just described which had so disturbed the internal life of the state, I was able to snatch time to celebrate two great occasions of my own. On short leave from the front, so to speak—which was what my journalistic career had now come to be—I had succeeded in passing the last of my legal examinations. To the great joy of my parents I received the degree of Doctor of Law from the University of Vienna on July 18, 1898. A wonderful prize now awaited me. No emperor could have bestowed a greater reward upon me—the hand of my bride.

Despite inner conflict in the choice of a career, in the face of family opposition and countless external obstacles, I had been able to win her. My love for this pure being had shone for me like a star through the hardships of those first years as student-worker and through the manifold dangers of the metropolis. It had filled me with a happy assurance and strengthened my will to give of my best in my work and prove myself worthy of her love in return.

On October 8 Cäcilie and I were married by her uncle, Father Josef Strobl, the Dean from Steyr, in the Sacred Heart Church in Graz. The eight-day vacation which was all the editor of the *Reichspost* could spare me for our honeymoon and which was my first since joining the newspaper, was spent in a thanksgiving pilgrimage to Mariazell.[3]

---

[3] Mariazell is Austria's most famous pilgrims' shrine and lies 85 miles southwest of Vienna. Founded as a monastery in 1157, it was renowned already in 1330 as a place of pilgrimage for those specially devoted to Our Lady. The three-towered Gothic church was built in 1366, enlarged in 1644 and finally completed in baroque style in 1704. The image of the Madonna at

We moved into a tiny apartment in Vienna furnished with the barest necessities bought on a monthly payments system, for it had been impossible for me to save anything from my salary of 50 gulden (100 kronen). We could not even afford to buy a winter coat for my young wife. Although Ambros Opitz had increased my salary after our marriage to 125 gulden, this only barely covered the rent, the monthly payments on the furniture and our modest housekeeping expenses. Ever since I had gained my doctorate, my friends in Vienna who saw our situation had been urging me to give up journalism, arguing that the narrow financial scope of the Catholic newspaper virtually condemned us to starvation and that it was irresponsible to start a family in such circumstances. Various offers which I received of posts in the Salzburg provincial administration or in the service of the Vienna municipality fell through, partly through circumstances beyond my control, and partly because of my own unwillingness to give up a career which I had chosen from the very beginning out of real conviction.

When I once mentioned to Dr. Lueger that I had chosen to be a Catholic journalist because I was convinced that it was a genuine vocation, he looked at me penetratingly for a long time without saying a word. Throughout his life he showed me great kindness and gave me many proofs of his confidence. In spite of all the calls upon his time, he was always ready to receive me. He would sometimes entrust me with some special mission, the highest token of his confidence. It was through Lueger that I was admitted as a standing member of the Christian-Social Deputies' Club in Parliament. The sole non-deputy, I remained a member of this institution for thirty-five years, throughout the change in the state form in 1918, right up to the end of the Parliament of the Austrian Republic.

As a young man I had somehow contrived to put by something

Mariazell is certainly the oldest symbolically interesting carving in Austria. Mariazell has always been a special center for Hungarian pilgrims; kings and peasants have knelt at the altar steps. Still preserved today are the tower and nave of a Gothic church which was erected above the chapel by King Ludwig I.

On May 1, 1954, the Young Catholic Workers of Austria took over the custody of the altar of the Polish St. Ladislaus, as a token of their voluntary sponsorship of the persecuted church beyond the Iron Curtain.

from my meager earnings for the more extensive study trips which I knew would be of value to me in my journalistic work. Stimulated by the consular reports published monthly by the Austrian Mercantile Museum as information for businessmen and grossly undervalued by the Viennese newspaper editors, I began to take a special interest in the position of the Empire in regard to the sea and its economic and political connections with the Levant. I now began to realize how much the significance of the monarchy as a great power depended upon its prestige at sea, its coastal possessions and the importance of its relationship to the peoples of its own lands in the southeast and above all with the South Slavs.

These facts prompted me to spend my vacations on journeys and walking tours through Dalmatia, at that time a lonely country, its people characterized by a typical hilarious southern gaiety mingled with a haunting melancholy arising from dreams of their great past. This passive land brought in its taxes but slowly, and the funds for every new budget expenditure had to be extracted from some other source.

The more I penetrated into this strange South Slav region with its differentiating national characteristics and religions and unique political problems, the more I realized the fateful significance of this small South Slav world, understood by so few and half-forgotten in the midst of our own domestic political problems. They were an important but at the same highly dangerous possession, these Croat-Serbian regions between the Sava and the Drina, between the Gulf of Fiume and Lake Skutari, lying right at the juncture of Western and Eastern cultures, coastland of the Adriatic and threshold to Greece. Their position within the state as yet unclear, they were furthermore all the more susceptible to the dangerous processes of political fermentation.

The personal knowledge which I gained of these regions so increased my conviction of the vital importance of this question that I devoted much of my time to the study of relevant literature on the subject, both historical and political, and sought to widen my personal contact with many Slav personalities. For example one of my old friends in Sarajevo was General Emanuel Cvjetićanin. This old frontier soldier had founded the unique *gendarme* force known as the *Štrafuni*,[1] a crack troop of picked men of all nations within the imperial army who lived a kind of trapper existence and cleaned up the centuries-old tribes of bandits in the mountains of the occupation region. The *Štrafuni* were incidentally the first military troops in the world to carry the rucksack which has now been universally adopted by all armies. Many were the evenings when my wife and I would sit up till midnight listening enthralled to the reminiscences of the chivalrous old warrior and his blood-curdling anecdotes of his adventures with his *Štrafuni* in combat with the *Tscheten*.

One of the most fascinating figures in Bosnia was the Archbishop, Dr. Stadler, a pure-bred Croat with a German name. He was wonderfully generous to the poor, in the support of charitable institutions and in ecclesiastical foundations, and retained very little for his own modest needs. Despite his sizable income, it happened on occasion, for instance, that his personal medical advisor, Dr. Richter, would borrow money from him on the 20th of the month, only to be asked on the 25th of the same month to go halves with him in what still remained of the sum, as he had not even sufficient money to pay for his postage stamps. The Archbishop had a fiery character and was deeply devoted to the imperial house and to Austria. He was the personification of the old loyal Croatia, the Croatia which through generations had provided the Habsburgs with some of their best soldiers and great generals.

He was moreover a saint. Under his leadership the archdiocese, the foundation of which had only been made possible when Austria-Hungary occupied Bosnia, had flourished and developed. His authoritative personality secured him undisputed leadership in all ecclesiastical and cultural-political affairs among the episcopate of the whole coastal region of Croatia. It was he who gave the new reviving impetus to San Girolamo, the institute for the higher education of priests in Rome which resulted in the increased fervor of

---

[1] The Štrafuni were a strictly disciplined troop of adventurers wearing civilian clothes and equipped with tourist rucksacks. They had no fixed quarters or base and roved through the country, sometimes even spending the night in the treetops, in order to attack the robber bands which for centuries had had their hide-outs in the mountain regions.

the clergy in pastoral work. When the Habsburg monarchy came to an end and the nationalist waves broke over the church in Jugoslavia, it was the powerful figure of the Archbishop, hard as iron in all matters of principle, who resisted the violent attempts to supplant the Latin rite with the old Slav liturgy. The Suffragan Bishop, Dr. Saric, who worthily succeeded him, continued his good work at the gateway to the Christian Eastern Church.

I enriched my knowledge of the Near East in roving through Albania, Greece and Macedonia, down to the Black Sea. The more I concerned myself with the special problems of the eastern Adriatic countries, the more aware I became of the little rifts within the lute of the alliance relationship between Austria-Hungary and Italy. The claim laid to *"Mare nostro,"* to the complete domination of the Adriatic, was more than a cheap phrase coined by the newspapers: it represented the urge for expansion of a nation whose development through five decades had been favored by a series of fortunate contingencies and whose aspirations were now fixed on new goals. Furthermore, hundreds of small signs in the life of the Austrian Maritime countries were proof of an as yet cautious but none the less systematic Italian political propaganda.

Ten years before Italy's declaration of war against Austria, I wrote an article for the Munich *Allgemeine Rundschau* predicting that the withdrawal of Italy from the Triple Alliance and subsequent conflict with Austria was only a matter of time. No special prophetic gift accounted for this forecast of events, despite the official constructions put upon the existing alliance relationship in Vienna and more especially in Berlin.

Chapter 6
THE TURNING POINT

The Liberals had been seriously alarmed by the outcome of the elections in Vienna during the years 1895 to 1900 and the loss of their supreme leadership in the imperial capital. The lords of the Liberal press could least of all adjust themselves to the new situation. Their newspapers still wielded tremendous influence in the field of the arts and literature and in scientific circles, not to mention the special sphere of high finance. This influence had been built up not only on friendships, interrelationship and coteries, but undoubtedly also on the practical achievements of some excellent brains. There were some intelligent men among them who realized that their innumerable relations had gone too far, that the scales were turning the other way and that accordingly the political losses suffered were in fact an adjustment of the balance. Not that there was any threat of a pogrom in Vienna. Nevertheless too little moderation was to be found in the Liberal press at that time. Journalists were bitterly intent upon avenging the Liberal losses in personal attacks against their opponents.

Up to 1900 the journalists' and writers' association, Concordia, was the sole professional union of the Vienna press. Founded in 1859 on the anniversary of the birth of Schiller, the organization assembled in its midst throughout many decades not only the publicistic nonentities but also the celebrated journalists of the Liberal and anti-clerical camp. Its exclusive narrow-mindedness came to an end after World War I. The reputation of Viennese journalism which was recognized even abroad had been built up to a great extent by men from the Concordia. The union had the merit of being one of the few organizations which as early as 1870 was seriously concerned with the establishment of social institutions for its members. A pension insurance scheme was introduced and provision made for cases of unemployment and for a fund for widows and orphans, etc. Concordia raised its funds from the charity exhibitions arranged by the Viennese artists, which brought in substantial sums

86

each year. Concordia constituted a power to be reckoned with in Vienna. The reputation of deputies and ministers, of artists and writers, even of men of science, was at its mercy. It could determine success or failure by praise or criticism. Nor was there any appeal against its judgment. To receive the praise of Concordia was to be made a man, but those unfortunate enough to incur its censure were more or less damned if they could not fight back.

It was small wonder, therefore, that a young unknown journalist who had only just received his doctorate and was, moreover, employed on the staff of "the curates' little paper," the *Reichspost*, was unanimously blackballed on his application for membership in the sole existing professional association with its health insurance and old age pension schemes. Things were different in those days.

In December, 1902, at the suggestion of Ambros Opitz and upon the decision of the editorial committee, I was appointed editor in chief of the *Reichspost*. I had only some seven years of newspaper experience behind me, and my appointment at the age of thirty above the heads of deserving older colleagues caused no small stir and much disapproval in press circles. It was true that I was the only unversity graduate on the editorial staff and my academic training had been specially directed with a view to my work as a journalist. In the editorial office I had been entrusted with an increasing number of the most important spheres of activity. I was, however, the youngest member of the staff and the older men could not disguise their rancor. The faith in my capabilities which the editorial board had shown in their choice was in fact combined with a certain risk. My impetuous nature, my tendency to form rash judgments and my inadequate knowledge of human nature as yet unripened by experience were decided drawbacks for an editor.

Perhaps as a result of my seminary education I was furthermore handicapped by a certain shyness in society, a shyness which I have never been able to throw off throughout my career. I infinitely preferred working at my desk to frequenting the many government and diplomatic receptions and countless official representative events at which I was bound to be present as editor of a Vienna daily newspaper. This cost me many valuable contacts.

But perhaps there is something to be said occasionally for not appearing too often. The British Ambassador once declared to me: "Dr. Funder, one sees you so rarely that you have already become a sort of mystical figure!" Nevertheless I found much attention paid to me when I did come.

One of an editor's most difficult but at the same time most important tasks is to direct the controversial opinions of close collaborators into a single course, especially when these are concerned with significant events or matters of fundamental importance. Furthermore, this unification of outlook must be achieved with due consideration of the spiritual freedom of the members of the editorial staff and without surrendering one's own point of view. To fulfill this task more is needed than a mere specialist's knowledge of the matter concerned: it is a task which calls for patience, a virtue which it is difficult to practice in the rush and bustle of an editor's office when every minute is often of decisive importance. It would have been better had I possessed more of this virtue.

When in January, 1904, the *Reichspost* celebrated its tenth anniversary with a special issue, I had the satisfaction of seeing the first signs of the emergence of the newspaper from its hard beginnings and my own early reform achievements reflected in the aspect of the paper itself. The special number had a volume of 48 pages, a number never before attained, and contained contributions from all the leading Christian-Social parliamentarians, as well as an article by the subsequent Reichsrat deputy, Dr. Alcide De Gasperi, who was later to win fame as a statesman in his office of Prime Minister of Italy.

Chapter 7
THE EMPIRE IN DANGER

The twentieth century began in Austria with several auspicious omens. The economic appeasement action of the Koerber era with its broadly-planned railway and canal schemes had served to draw German, Czech, South Slav and Italian interests closer together. At the same time an enthusiastically creative municipal policy had miraculously transformed the face of the imperial capital. A new Vienna had grown up, with fine model buildings and splendid social institutions. This Vienna gave practical proof to friend and foe of the fulfillment of the Christian-Social promises. New hope and pride radiated from the great city at the heart of the Empire: hope and pride of millions of Austrians in their noble imperial capital, city of the great Congress of Vienna. It was no fanciful Utopian dream, therefore, which led Aurel Popovici, the Transylvanian Romanian, to write his sensational book in which he spoke of a new Austria, a "United States of Austria," of a peaceable new construction of the Empire based on a national-autonomic form of the Habsburg monarchy; it was he who kindled the enthusiasm of the younger generation especially to participate in a movement led by the Christian-Socials with the program contained in their manifesto at the Eggenburg[1] Party Congress.

This congress, which was held in the Eggenburg town square and which drew vast crowds, featured the resolution read by Deputy Axman protesting against "the deprivation of the rights of the non-Magyar nationalities in Hungary" which was unanimously accepted and enthusiastically acclaimed. The resolution declared that "the almost complete exclusion from public and parliamentary life of this section of the population so genuinely loyal to their Emperor, King, and the Empire itself signified an irreparable loss for the mon-

[1] Eggenburg is a little old town in Lower Austria, some 45 miles from Vienna.

archy as a whole, especially since just this section was the only one capable of offering effective resistance to the arrogant political clique dominating Hungary today." The resolution finally demanded that *"in place of the present decaying state form, the Empire should be re-founded on a unified, consolidated basis."* From then on, as long as the monarchy endured, the Eggenburg resolution determined in the constitutional discussions the policy followed by the Christian-Social party.

Viewed from Austria, the political situation might have given good cause for satisfaction, had it not been for a far-reaching political landslide in Hungary on January 27, 1905. The scene was the legislative body, the powerful Hungarian parliament in which, according to the traditional system, approximately four-fifths of the total number of seats were held by Magyars, although the Magyar nation (comprising not quite 40 per cent) in no way constituted a majority of the population. The destiny of Hungary lay in the hands of this national minority. The Liberal party, since 1867 the traditional mainstay of every government, had been bitterly defeated in the new elections held by the Prime Minister, Stephan Tisza, in the vain attempt to overthrow the cocksure opposition led by the Kossuth party. The Liberals retained only 159 of their approximately 250 seats. They were confronted by the triumphant Independence party, the strongest party with its 169 seats, headed by Franz Kossuth, son of Lajos Kossuth who had led the rebellion in 1848. Julius Andrássy's group held 27 seats, Desider Bánffy's faction gained 13, and the People's party 25—unreliable elements who soon formed a coalition with the Independence party. The Romanians, Slovaks and Transylvanian Saxons held a total of 12 seats.

With the victory of the Independence party the dam had burst which for nearly forty years had safeguarded the 1867 Constitution against the ideological forces of the Hungarian revolutionary years of 1848. The so-called 1867 Compromise was intended as a truce between the Habsburg dynasty and the Magyar nation, ending the state of unrest which had recurred within short intervals even after the victories of the imperial forces under Prince Eugene and the liberation of Hungary from Turkish rule. Throughout the eighteenth and the first half of the nineteenth century the politically dominant feudal landowners and nobility had persisted in their nationalist grievances against Vienna and the dynasty, grievances and demands directed toward the "corpus separatum" of a Magyar national state. The primary object of the Magyar demands, however, was the raising and training of the "exercitus hungaricus," the Hungarian-recruited army which had been incorporated into the imperial forces after the liquidation of the Hungarian army in 1715. These demands were motivated not only by the urge for proud domination based on constitutional rights, but arose also from the national-political recognition that, in view of the existing national composition of Hungary, made up of six national elements, the character of the Magyar state could be preserved in the long run only if the non-Magyar youth were put through a military training strongly impregnated by the Magyar national creed.

Nevertheless the military and national catastrophe of 1848/49 and the uncertain regrouping of European power brought home to the Hungarian nation that her security and her future lay in her bond with the vitality and prestige of the monarchy as a great power within the continental structure of nations, and laid the foundations for the 1867 Compromise. This compromise left several important questions open. From the very beginning, however, even in the discussions between the Austrian and Hungarian negotiators, the unity of the army of the common state was constitutionally anchored as a secure foundation and conceded to the royal prerogatives of the Emperor as a bulwark of the monarchy as a whole. There was no doubt as to the loyalty of the Hungarian participants in the agreement. The fire set alight by Lajos Kossuth in 1848 was, however, still smoldering.

The 1867 Compromise had not yet outlived the century before the same shrill cries could be heard from the at first so insignificant Hungarian Independence party; the same nationalist myths began to rouse the Hungarian people which had led to disaster a generation before.

The constitutional myth propagated by the Magyar nationalists remained unknown and uncomprehended in the widest public circles in Austria. Dr. Harold Steinacker, a professor at Innsbruck

closely connected with the question on account of his own Transylvanian origin, set out the convincing results of his thorough investigation of the history of Hungarian constitutional law in justification
of this concept. The study is contained in an article in *Mitteilungen
des Instituts für österreichische Geschichtsforschung*, 1907, p. 276,
and in an examination of "the legal nature of the common monarchy" published in *Österreichische Rundschau*, Vol. XXII, No. 5.
He finds the causes in strange class remnants, lacking a legal basis,
while Count Albert Apponyi, that champion in the army demands,
attempts to interpret these causes scientifically:

According to Apponyi, the Crown in Hungary had been
limited from the very beginning, despite its great power, by various
factors: the national assembly, the electoral rights of the nation, the
right of armed resistance, the two laws of 1231 and 1298 which
reveal the elements of a parliamentary system apparently earlier in
Hungary than in all other lands, and furthermore by the national
rights bound up in the very coronation itself. In his discussion
Steinacker follows up Apponyi's authority, Timon: "All these various guarantees of the constitution converge in the doctrine of the
Holy Crown by which the Magyars were the first among all other
nations to realize the modern concept—unknown in the Middle Ages
—of the state as a distinct being, as an organism. The state is embodied as an organic entity in the Holy Crown, which again is personified as the holder of public power deeply rooted in the nation
itself and vested jointly in King and people in the political sense.
Thus even earlier than in England the authority of the Crown is
regarded as a trust; earlier than in France, it must logically be noted,
the fundamental principle of national sovereignty is eastablished as
apparently contained in this doctrine." Apponyi at any rate deduces
from it for his day that in Hungary "*the nation is the source of all
rights, including the authority of the Crown.*"

On November 6, 1902 Minister of Defense Géza Fejérváry
presented before the House of Deputies a bill proposing the increase
of the annual "recruit contingent"—the military contribution to the
common imperial army—by 18,000 and the Hungarian militia
(Honvéd) by 2,500 men. A wave of nationalist feeling broke out

in demands for the use of the Hungarian language in the military commands, Hungarian national flags and emblems, exclusively Hungarian officers for Hungarian troops, interspersed by threats of a break-away from Austria, of a personal union.[2] The press joined in with a shrill chorus and there was obstruction in Parliament. Prime Minister Kolman von Szell resigned and his successor, Karl Khuen-Hederváry, was overthrown almost before he had set foot in the Prime Minister's residence on the Burghügel.

In vain Stephan Tisza next tried his luck. The so-called Nine Points Program was established under his ministry: he had been concerned himself with the drafting of the progrm while he was still a deputy and Liberal party leader and now presented it to the Emperor in his capacity as Prime Minister. The program in fact opened the way for all the knavery of the noisy nationalist agitators, and was of far greater consequence than Tisza seems to have realized in the first tumultuous uproar. As loyal adherent of the 1867 compromise with the Crown, Tisza stood for its vested rights and its obligations. The Liberal party still in power declared in this program that it upheld the authority of the King to determine the language to be used in service and command with the Hungarian army, as an integral part of the army as a whole, but also stated:

"The political responsibility of the ministry *extends—as in every action of the Crown—here also*, and the legitimate influence of the *Imperial Diet—*as in the case of every constitutional right—*remains valid also in this instance.* This situation can be changed in legislation *determined mutually by the Crown and the Imperial Diet.*

"The Liberal party, by emphasizing the rights of the nation, does not raise the question of the Hungarian command and service language, since it does not consider this desirable for important political reasons affecting the interests of the nation."

The program concedes all chauvinistic demands and declares the prerogatives of the Crown to be dependent upon the decision of

---

[2] The Austrian Dual Monarchy was constitutionally a real union, that is to say an alliance of two states according to international law with definite common functions. Personal union represents the alliance of two or more states solely in the person of the sovereign, without any of these common functions.

the Parliament, but by sec. 9 put aside what the others were demanding so loudly. Once again, he is lost who plays into the hands of the devil. Stephan Tisza and the Liberal party, unchallenged power since 1867, were defeated in the election of January, 1905.

The Liberal defeat left Hungary without a government, without law and order and in a state of parliamentary anarchy. The inability of the victors of the January election to form a government with a workable program prepared the ground for the "Civil Servant" ministry of Fejérváry-Kristoffy, which had the good will and confidence of the Emperor but which in the eyes of the public in general seemed to be more or less of an anemic creation without political roots which could command no respect—until a flash of lightning suddenly revealed the political landscape in a totally different light.

On this hot day in July, 1905, the Minister for the Interior, Josef Kristóffy, announced the plan for an electoral reform which promised the rise of a new Hungary, whereby the *petit bourgeois*, the small peasant and the artisan were called to participate in the affairs of state through universal suffrage and the secret ballot. The panic which broke out among the former privileged classes as a result of this proclamation was followed by a tumultuous agitation which lasted for several months under the slogan "The Constitution is in danger!" Nationalist passions were raised to white heat against the "traitors" of the "satellite government," and louder than ever came the cry for a break-away from Austria and the immediate establishment of an independent Hungarian customs region.

Feelings were already running high among the workers: thousands rose in stormy demonstrations for their promised electoral rights and against the adversaries who sought to protect their old privileges. The day finally came when the leaders of the electoral victors had to make the pilgrimage to Vienna, only to come away, after a memorable five-minute audience in the Hofburg, with the knowledge that they could not expect to enforce their demands all at once. The outcome for the time being was a form of agreement which provided for the establishment of a coalition government under that old master of the political gamble, the Transylvanian-Swabian Alexander Wekerle, but with the ominous *obligation to enforce the electoral reform.* The negotiations on concessions in the army question were relegated to a House of Deputies to be newly elected.

The new elections in April and May, 1906, resulted in 252 seats for Kossuth and the advocates of state independence for Hungary. The great Liberal party was scattered like chaff before the wind.

In this defiant spirit they challenged the Emperor and Austria. Was it to come to the final test? At all events everything was at stake, not only the unity of the imperial army, the monarchy, indeed the whole future, if the rebels were to gain the upper hand. This would be the end of everything. The army was the irreplacable pillar of the Empire. The parliamentary decay on both sides and the party disintegration had not yet been able to penetrate into its ranks.

The incalculable consequences were, however, not of a military-political nature only. The common army had up to now been a school of citizenship among the various nations. What the state school system on both sides of the Leitha had failed to provide was made up for as a matter of course by the army in the training of its troops, particularly in its courses for noncommissioned officers. The army imparted that bearing and polish and self-confidence evident in soldiers of the imperial army, whether peasants from the miserable hovels of the Galician latifundia, men from the mountain gorges of Transylvania, and the lonely regions of the Karsts and the Dalmatian islands, or easy-going proletarian town dwellers.

The army was the great impartial structure without political tendencies which integrated all nations, and nationalist jealousies and hostilities ceased within it. It preserved the national individuality of its personnel with such care that there were even regiments with four regimental languages, all of which the commanding officer had to know in order to communicate with the various national elements in his regiment. Thus many men in the army gained a supra-national, cosmopolitan point of view which gave them a noticeable advantage over those who came directly from the self-contained nationality states. Only the existence and the character of this army with its century-long influence upon the various nations can account for the Habsburg Empire having endured so long, in the face of the greatest trials, and despite the sins committed against her by her statesmen and political scholars.

This army was the guardian of the Empire of so many nations, the very nature and history of which were personified in its structure. If in Hungary this army were to be converted into a national Magyar-directed military force, it would be turned into the tool of an absolute Magyar dictatorship to be used against the simple peasant population who had settled on Hungarian soil. It would become a threat to the national existence of these people, only serving to drive them over the frontiers into the inviting arms of their racial kinsmen of the neighboring compact national states. This Magyar army could, therefore, only be an explosive unit which would shatter the whole monarchy.

Nothing could justify the risk of such a development.

The events in Hungary found the public in Austria unprepared, uninformed and helpless. It was one of the strangest features of the relationship between these two states ordained to form a common empire and to share a common destiny, that each partner lived its own life and was in no way concerned with the character, institutions or indeed the needs of the other. The Austrian schoolboy was far more conversant with the causes of the Roman wars against Carthage and the character of the people of Carthage than with the state institutions and opinions of the neighboring nation which formed with Austria the common Habsburg Empire. There was, furthermore, no readily accessible informative literature on Hungary which would have thrown light on the modern requirements of the dualistic Empire and schooled community thought. As for learning Hungarian, it was easier to learn Sanskrit than to master the national language of the partner state with whom the Germans of Austria held the joint balance within the Habsburg monarchy according to the dualistic agreement of 1867! Thus every cultural contact was lacking.

The two nations met together only in impassioned political conflict over the contributions to be made toward the cost of the common household—or to listen to Hungarian gypsy music. The Catholic Church provided a solitary bridge between the two partner states in the Pazmaneum, the Hungarian priests' seminary in Vienna, founded by that great Hungarian prince of the Church Pázmány, who for years was active as priest and professor of theology in Graz. The University of Budapest was also founded by him.

A raging fire had now broken out which was obviously threatening to burn down their common house, and yet even in this moment of danger neither of the neighbors could find the requisite constructive strength for mutual understanding. Despite the serious digressions on the Hungarian side from the imperial community, it is only right and logical in the interests of history also to establish the shortcomings and errors of the German-Austrians.

It was understandable in this severe crisis which hovered over them and which threatened to involve the whole Habsburg state, that public opinion in Austria was confused and divided in its reaction to the Magyar attacks against the common army, the customs union with Austria, indeed against every national bond with Austria. The bragging and blustering of Kossuth and his followers was obviously grist to the mill of the pan-Germans. Neither up to 1906 had the German-National camp yet been able to decide on its course in face of the excesses of the Budapest politicians. A parliamentary interpellation from the German People's party in June used inflammatory expressions such as "It is impossible to maintain a common existence with a country whose population is filled with such bitter hatred against its partner state. There can only be one decision: Away from Hungary!"

Influenced by Vergani's *Deutsches Volksblatt*, which lent itself to such devices, even the German-National faction of the Christian-Social party in the Vienna Municipal Council were on the point of joining in with the cries for "Away from Hungary!" Dr. Lueger called these thoughtless members to reason with the simple statement that the customs barriers against Hungary would mean the ruin of 84 per cent of the exports of the typically Viennese fine industries. The Vienna daily press, traditionally bound with the Budapest Liberalism, presented no better picture in its reportage and statements on the ever louder question of the continued existence of the Empire.

My small editorial staff, so deeply concerned with this issue, had closely followed the bitter conflict of Magyar power with the vital interest of the Empire from the very beginning, and were well aware of their responsibilities as Austrian journalists in the face of this crisis. The Vienna press as a whole either remained silent or was prejudiced by the influence of the many conciliant voices and the talk of the compromise which emanated from the ministries and from the various offices at court.

As a matter of course the *Reichspost* quickly took the lead in the heated controversy concerning the boisterous Magyar nationalism with its impending threat to the monarchy and all its basic institutions. We found many friends and helpers in our task. It was wonderful to be a journalist at this moment. Nevertheless there were some things which I would have done otherwise, had I known better at the time.

One day in early summer of 1905 a tall officer of the Imperial Guard came into our office. He had orders from the aide-de-camp of His Imperial Highness the Heir Apparent to collect three copies each of such and such a number of the *Reichspost* containing such and such a leading article. What was this? We had never had a visitor like this before in our little office.

Some days after this visit I was called personally to the Belvedere, the Vienna residence of the Heir Apparent. In an unpretentious room I was received by the Archduke's aide-de-camp, an officer of the General Staff, Major Alexander Brosch von Aarenau, a small, active man with a pleasant, open face and penetrating blue eyes. He summed up the situation for me with typical military brevity. His Imperial Highness followed with attention and great interest the course of the *Reichspost*. He was impressed by the courage with which the newspaper challenged the dominant political cliques both in Hungary and here in Austria, in no way intimidated by the counterattacks, while the rest of the Vienna daily press displayed indifference or even supported the assailants of the monarchy. Much, perhaps everything, was at stake in this fiery conflict. The Heir Apparent had confidence in me; he wished to encourage me in my task and to urge me to maintain my stand firmly in the face of the low standards of the others and all efforts of those in higher office to win me over to their side.

As I came out of the Belvedere I thought over the significance of this interview for me, the young journalist disregarded by the world in general. It was after all the future Emperor who had called me to the Belvedere, and the subsequent conversation had covered vital questions concerning the Empire itself; I had been entrusted with a high mission.

My contact with Brosch grew close. I was called several times in the week to the Belvedere and could telephone whenever I thought it necessary; I received special information and instructions for the information of the foreign press; I wrote articles for the *Kölnische Volkszeitung* and other such newspapers and for various English reviews. I was able to watch the play behind the scenes, which was hidden from the public eye, the ministerial and court intermezzo in the drama of the battle for power. The longer the crisis continued, the louder were the voices of those favoring a compromise, of those advocating an agreement with the chauvinistic Magyar gentry. What harm was there, after all, they argued, in a few Hungarian flags and Magyar national emblems for Hungarian troops, and exclusively Magyar officers for the Hungarian personnel of the common army?

In the strictest privacy a Council of Generals was held in the winter of 1906 under the chairmanship of Archduke Friedrich, the oldest ranking military dignitary after the Heir Apparent. Concrete measures were drawn up. Some days later Major Brosch handed me a bulky memorandum which Archduke Franz Ferdinand was to present to the Emperor in reference to the Pressburg Conference. I was to disclose the existence of the document to no one, to regard its contents as strictly confidential guiding principles and return it immediately the next day.

I returned home and read the document through behind locked doors. It lay under my pillow during the night, for I did not dare to leave it out of my reach. The memorandum contained such a ruthlessly sharp judgment of the prevailing power in Hungary and so described the consequences of a withdrawal in the face of this power and the necessity of the measures to be carried out for the protection of the Empire as a whole, that the very reading of the document filled me with a chill of apprehension. I had the feeling that were the secret of the existence of this top secret document to be revealed, a catastrophe would result in Hungary.

Brosch had given me—probably on the orders of his imperial chief—a proof of confidence which I regarded as the greatest distinction.

The relations of the Belvedere with the *Reichspost* could not long remain secret, all the more so since Franz Ferdinand himself took no trouble to conceal them. The Liberal press, however, which never bothered to hide its disapproval of the Archduke's personal convictions ever since he had taken over the patronage of the Catholic Schools Association in 1901, nevertheless regarded this singling out of the *Reichspost* as an infringement of the proper order of rank within the Vienna press, and reacted with half-hidden barks and increasingly sarcastic commentary.

In other circles too, from the spheres of Liberal bureaucracy and high finance, the confidential position which the Heir Apparent had accorded to the editor of the *Reichspost* and which extended, of course, to the newspaper itself, aroused much criticism. In their eyes the choice of this "clerical" newspaper was unfitting, a newspaper when all was said and done with a restricted circulation and modest pretensions and which had, moreover, the reputation of subscribing to troublesome democratic opinions.

This mood was to change, however, as the *Reichspost* grew from year to year in achievement, circulation and political import, in some quarters into affability, in others into hostile anger. This hostility was scarcely surprising, for the *Reichspost* was sharp in its censure of their attitude in the decisive matters of imperial policy. When in a verbal discussion with Foreign Minister Aehrenthal in the spring 1907 the Heir Apparent referred to an article in the *Reichspost*, the minister only growled: "I'd rather have the red-white-and-greens"—he meant here of course the Hungarian Independence party and its followers—"than those black-and-yellow fellows!" More serious, however, was an episode which followed a leading article in the *Reichspost* which severely criticized the Minister of War, General Schönaich, for his free-handed diplomacy in negotiations, a policy which he pursued at the cost of the army and against the interests of the state as a whole.

The consequences were far-reaching. Two days after the article appeared, Brosch called me up and we arranged to meet privately. In his brother-in-law's apartment he confided to me, that as a result of the article, which he incidentally found excellent and which had his full approval, he had been called up by General Schönaich and charged with having written the article himself. His military career was jeopardized. He asked me to testify in all truth that the article was not his work, but to enter into no further explanations. In point of fact the article had been written not by Brosch but by myself. The forthcoming written testimony to this effect in no way pacified the Minister of War, however, and Brosch was nevertheless summoned to appear before a military court.

The relations between the Heir Apparent and the *Reichspost* were widely known. If the officer in charge of the Archduke's personal military bureau was called up to answer a charge connected with the newspaper, then the Heir Apparent automatically became involved. At this level the conflict reached its climax. Franz Ferdinand appeared personally and declared unequivocally that, Major Brosch having already given his word of honor in the matter, if the persecution of his personal aide were to be continued, he himself would resign from his office as General Inspector in Chief of the Armed Forces. The military proceedings against Alexander von Brosch were subsequently withdrawn at the express command of the Emperor.

Only the isolated position of Franz Ferdinand at the Vienna court could account for this grotesque affront against this man who stood nearest to the imperial throne. An article clearly issuing from official channels of the Ministry of War even appeared in the *Wiener Journal* in 1910 openly attacking the military bureau and even the Heir Apparent himself.

These and other similar episodes had the quite unsought-for side effect of focusing public attention in the widest circles upon the *Reichspost*. The newspaper gained rapidly in prestige and circulation and outgrew the framework and functions of a mere organ of the Christian-Social party. Even before the days of its ties with the Belvedere, the *Reichspost* had established contact with leading figures of Dr. Frank's Croatian party and with the Slovaks in Hungary: it took up the cause of the Croats and the Slovaks and Romanians so harshly treated by the Budapest overlords. The parish priest of Rosenberg, Father Hlinka, was another who was championed by the *Reichspost*. The newspaper now went on to gain further ties with the leaders of the non-Magyar nationalities who in the last elections in January, 1905, had at long last penetrated into the Hungarian parliament as the first freely-elected, independent representatives of the Romanian and Slovakian nationalities. They pinned their hopes upon Franz Ferdinand, the future Emperor, who would build up a new Habsburg Empire, an Empire of united autonomic nations, an Empire of justice and freedom for all and which no longer tolerated the hegemony of a Magyar gentry drunk with their own power and a government composed of oppressors and rebels against the Empire and the dynasty. They lent their enthusiastic support to the Heir Apparent as the herald of a new era of freedom and of peace.

While in Budapest the sworn adherents of a Magyar national dictatorship were reveling in the first raptures of their electoral victories, a small group of men of widely differing national and political backgrounds gathered in the Belvedere around the Heir Apparent. The Bishop of Grosswardein, Dr. Lanyi, who had taught Hungarian to the Archduke, was responsible for making the preliminary contacts which led to the formation of this "Belvedere Group."

The first of the newly-elected Hungarian deputies representing the national minorities to visit the *Reichspost* personally via the Belvedere was the Transylvanian deputy Dr. Alexander Vajda von Vojvod, a Romanian doctor who had studied medicine in Vienna. I found him a charming and highly-educated man with a fine sensitive disposition; he had indeed much that was typically Viennese and was a lover of the fine arts and of literature. We soon became close friends. Alexander Vajda knew that I only got through most of my work around midnight, and would often come and sit with me at my desk about this time. We would talk for hours into the night, deeply absorbed in the many difficult problems with which the Empire was confronted at that time. It was sometimes dawn before he left me.

This friendship lasted throughout World War I, during the

first years of which Vajda worked as a doctor in the Vienna hospital, the Allgemeines Krankenhaus. Later in Romania he held office in successive governments. We remained in correspondence and he always came to see me when he was in Vienna. On these occasions it was sad to see from his own person and from what he had to tell me the disillusionment and yearning for the ideals which we had pursued together but which had come to nothing.

One day I received a letter from this man who, when the monarchy disintegrated, had turned his hope to the unification of the Romanian nation. "The people of this country deserve the greatest admiration for their incomparable magnanimity," he wrote. "In the face of the maladministration and corruption rife here at the moment, any other nation would have long since made short work of the dynasty and the smug potentates in this country."

During his first term of office as Minister of the Interior he was once in Vienna and paid me one of his night visits. We sat at my desk together as we had done in the old days. "I have a great deal to do," he told me with a hint of irony, "for my power does not extend beyond my anteroom. I have to give up a great deal of my time to receiving the people who fill my waiting room, for I am never quite sure what the official in the next room would make of the various cases."

Quite another type was Vajda's compatriot, the Deputy Julius Maniu, a lawyer by profession and a syndic of the Greek United Archbishopric of Blasendorf. This man, who must at that time have been in his early forties, was an impressive figure. He was as thin as a lath, with a sharply chiseled face which betrayed his firmness of purpose and relentless will, and a pair of steel-blue eyes. From the very beginning he was destined as a leader of his nation. His experience of human nature, complete disregard of personal interests, his great gift of oratory and his impeccable private life qualified him for his difficult task. For four decades he was able to maintain this position of leader, due in no small measure to his courage and inviolable integrity in a country in which abuse and corruption were rife in all strata of political life. The name of Julius Maniu was inseparably coupled with the Romanian Zaranist party, the political peasant movement of Transylvania and later the whole realm.

Together with his friend Aurel Popovici, already celebrated as the literary champion of the Romanians in Hungary, he worked on the broad draft of a program for the autonomic recasting of the state. It was a program drawn up quite without sentimental visions but with a hard, realistic approach. For his opponents he was by no means an easy man to deal with. He was not accustomed to beat about the bush and made his views clear from the start in any discussion. Victory looked near for Maniu during the Kristóffy era, but even when this hope was shattered and the position of the Romanians demanded even greater sacrifices, Maniu remained loyal to his trust as the champion of freedom for the Transylvanian Romanians.

Shortly before Christmas in 1937 he was in Vienna for a short time and invited me to come and see him at the Hotel Bristol. He spoke then of the vital necessity for mutual understanding between the Romanians and the Magyars, two small peoples like national islands in a stormy sea. "We have after all both learned our lesson from experience," he continued. "There can be no other workable solution for us than to say good-bye to the idea of a conglomeration of small states and to prepare our place together within an autonomically-organized Danube empire extending from the Sudetenland to the Black Sea. And you Austrian-Germans, unencumbered by other ties, would be the very people to co-operate in such a concept!"

In 1947 Julius Maniu, this hero of his people, was thrown into prison by the Romanian government.

Other representatives of the national minorities came to Vienna with Vajda and Maniu and found their way to the Belvedere. Among these was Dr. Milan Hodža, a Slovak and an exceptionally gifted journalist. Dr. Hodža was a Protestant with a clear logical brain, polyglot and nimble-minded. He was the personification of his own people which, wedged in between Czechs, Germans and Magyars, inclined least of all toward the racially kindred Czechs, just tolerated the Germans and openly fought with the Magyars, nevertheless sending them its most gifted men for the state administration and managing skillfully to escape Magyar domination by virtue of an inborn talent for politics and economics. Hodža loved Vienna: not even later in "Golden Prague" could he forget the old Imperial capital. Hodža was liberal in his opinions and seemed to me to have a stronger leaning toward achieving agreement than to doing battle. His true character was demonstrated later beside Beneš as Crechoslovakian minister; and later as Prime Minister he would have made peace with the Germans in Czechoslovakia had not Beneš been against him.

Hodža and Dr. Maniu were undoubtedly the greatest political thinkers of the "Belvedere Group." When the Danube monarchy disintegrated, Hodža, like his friends Vajda and Maniu, was called to take a leading position in setting up the new household within his own national state. He too, like Maniu, emerged from this experience more convinced than ever of the truth of the concept of "Mitteleuropa" as expressed by the "United States of Austria." He rose to the peak of power first as a minister and then as Prime Minister of the young Czechoslovakian nation so cosseted at first by the Western powers and then abandoned in war.

He had no illusions about the hard realities facing the existence of a nation as an independent state; he realized the weakness which lay in separatism and the emptiness of all the talk of the great powers about nationalist ideals. He had after all witnessed the drastic parade of events for himself and lived through all the catastrophes which had brought about the ruin of the dream castles built by Masaryk and Beneš. In his self-chosen exile in America the bold ideas he had once served as a young Hungarian deputy in the intellectual retinue of Archduke Franz Ferdinand, with his reform plans for a new state, came alive for him again.

Wise in his experience, Hodža finally expounded his views in the book which he wrote shortly before his death, *Federation of Central Europe*, published by Garrick in London in 1941. In it he tells with warmth of his role in the "Belvedere Group" and the personal contacts he formed there. Developing the ideas which he had already held at that time, his book contains the ground plan of a federal state, extending from Central Europe down over the Balkans, a federation of states joined together to form a common currency and trade area and sharing common defense.

In this federation four Slav political units: Poland, Czechoslovakia, Jugoslavia and Bulgaria, were to join with five other states, some of them smaller: Austria, Hungary, Romania, Greece and Albania. The various nationality states would be represented in the federal administration in proportion to their population, and would participate in the common federal congress with certain stipulations which would prevent a domination of the smaller nations by the great. He expanded the old Austrian plan further by aiming for the federal organization of the conglomeration of small nationality states within the Danube region. In writing this book he was clearly not so much concerned with the development of an actual program as with laying down his belief in a great and timeless concept as expanded to the full.

A fourth member from Hungary kept the group informed and advised on matters concerning Magyar politics. Georg Linder, the former Hungarian deputy and a Transylvanian-Swabian, was addicted to politics with a passion to be found only in France or in Hungary. He was really happy only when he had all kinds of political threads running through his fingers, and on these threads he would cautiously pull—unseen, of course, by the outside world. He was a man of independent means whose son, Bela Linder, was a captain in the Honvéd.[3]

As a result of a tragic chain of circumstances Bela Linder was destined to play a most unfortunate role as Minister of War in Michael Karolyi's revolutionary government at the end of World War I. A keen soldier, he had the misfortune to be caught up on the Russian front in all the military miscalculations and catastrophes. He was seriously wounded and finally sent for convalescence to Baden,[4] only to volunteer in 1917, still on crutches, for service in the field as commanding officer of the small Italian fort of Palmanova. When I met him in August, 1918, his face already bore the visible marks of a man broken both in body and in spirit. Some months later he took over the office of Minister of War, an office for which he was to pay dearly in the errors he committed and in his bitter personal destiny; as a refugee he finally took up work as

[3] The Hungarian word *Honvéd* means "defender of the fatherland" and was originally the designation for the volunteer corps organized in 1848/49. In 1868 it was adopted for the defense force formed in that year and in due course became the recognized name for the Hungarian army.

a bookseller in Belgrade. Once more a refugee when the Communists took over in Jugoslavia, he fled to Paris in 1950, after which time I lost trace of him.

His father, Georg Linder, was in every way a genuinely loyal supporter of the house of Habsburg; he detested the Kossuthians and stood firmly for the old Liberal party. He was in close touch with many of the leading figures active in Hungarian political life. I cannot possibly tell how many memoranda and informative reports Georg Linder must have written for the Belvedere: they certainly went into thousands. Not all of these were good—at least such as I myself saw. He was nevertheless a most valuable member of the group, ably serving the common goal, not only by his extensive personal contacts but in his own selfless dedication.

From the German-National camp "old Steinacker" came to the Belvedere, a Transylvanian German-Hungarian by origin. A white-haired old warrior, wholly absorbed in the Hungarian question, he was a high-minded man with nationalist ideas who was entirely devoted to the Heir Apparent.

The leading figure in the "Civil Service" government formed by Fejérváry and also for the "Belvedere Group" was the Hungarian Minister of the Interior, Jôsef von Kristóffy. He came as a high official from the Komitat administration, a pure-bred Hungarian combining both the positive and the negative characteristics of this amiable and chivalrous people gifted with their innate inclination to politics. Kristóffy had grown to power outside the circles of the landed gentry and the high society of the nobility and was fired with the constructive concept of a universal equal suffrage which would finally break the antiquated rule of the upper class and free Hungary from the ever recurring and painful conflicts resulting from controversy on the constitutional issue.

Political literature has given far too little credit to Kristóffy for his service in so courageously pursuing this ideal in the face of strident protests from the privileged classes and the mockery he received as "the servant of the satellite government." For it was this predominating idea of Kristóffy's that forged the weapons which

---

[4] Baden is a celebrated spa fifteen miles south of Vienna.

finally defeated the nationalist dictatorship of Kossuth and indirect-
ly contributed toward the establishment of universal equal suffrage
in Austria. When at a political meeting in September, 1905, he first
developed the basic concept of his reform plan in public, he recognized from the enthusiastic response even to this first mild proposal
the tremendous import of the idea. The plan which he then completed and which was published as a government draft bill on December 19, 1905, already granted universal equal suffrage to all Hungarian citizens over the age of twenty-four. In the accompanying
report explaining his motives in drawing up this plan, Kristóffy reveals the fact that an average of only one in twenty of the Hungarian population had hitherto been entitled to vote. In some electoral
districts 139 voters sufficed to send a representative to Parliament,
while in others the electorate comprised as many as 12,000. There
was no parallel in the whole of Europe to this monstrous system, a
travesty of electoral rights. Kristóffy published a fat book[5] of memoirs covering his reform plan and the development of its historic
role, a book of which contemporary literature has curiously enough
made little use.

An excellent relationship existed between the men of this small
group in the Belvedere, representatives of divergent camps and
various forces. The strength of this bond lay in their common political convictions. If the expression "workshop" has sometimes been
used in reference to this intellectual community—and Milan Hodža
also employs this term in his book published during his emigré
period—this has been to emphasize the planned, systematic work of
the group so admirably headed and co-ordinated by Major Brosch,
the master in the workshop.

The Croats from Agram who came to Brosch and sometimes
were received in audience by Franz Ferdinand made up a special
group. They were the leading figures of the "Reinen Rechtspartei"
(Pure-Right-Wing-party) founded by the lawyer Dr. Frank which,
in contrast to the Serbo-Croatian coalition of the Agram Provincial
Diet, had begun a campaign against Budapest for the recognition of

---

[5] Kristóffy, Jôsef: Magyarország Kálváriája. Az összeomlás útja, Politikai
Emlékek 1890-1926; Wodianer F. és Kiuai Grafikai Intézet és Kiadóvállalat
R.-T. 1927.

Croatia as a national entity and envisaged a future Croatia, loyal to the Habsburg dynasty, safeguarded within a strong Habsburg Empire. I made the acquaintance of a high official in the administration, the Sektionschef Kršnjavi, an able, level-headed man, young Dr. Frank and the lawyer Dr. Horvath who remained faithful to this loyal Croatian national concept right up to the end.

I met old friends here too: Dr. Josop Sunarić and Dr. Mandić from Bosnia, the Agram university professor Dr. Milobar, the mayor of Trau Madarasz, and many others. All these men took part in some way in the great game which the little major of the General Staff directed with such skill for the Heir Apparent. Different again were the relationships established with the Austrian parliamentarians for whom Brosch once more acted as intermediary with the Heir Apparent. These men included Lueger, Gessmann, Schraffl, Dr. Ebenhoch and Baron Viktor von Fuchs from the Christian-Socials, Dr. Ivan Šusteršić and Dr. Korošec from the Slovenians.

Brosch worked sedulously to assemble the components of a forceful political group which shared the views held by Franz Ferdinand and which would co-operate in the realization of these concepts; he threw himself whole-heartedly into the work of compiling and distributing information, of ceaselessly encouraging, directing and urging forward. There were many at court, among the higher officials of the state administration, and indeed, some members of the imperial family itself, who sought to isolate this troublesome Franz Ferdinand, this innovator and ruthless critic. It was due to the active work of the military bureau which screened the Heir Apparent that these attempts at an isolation policy were unsuccessful from the middle of the first decade of the century onward.

The influence of Franz Ferdinand in state politics could be felt. He became the hope of countless thousands who were driven to despair by the endless contention, by the parliaments which were in fact no longer real parliaments, by the perpetually recurring exlex condition in Hungary which robbed the state administration of its revenue from direct taxation, and by all the talk of constitutional rights by the chauvinists who were driving the Empire to destruction and were blind and deaf to every remonstrance from other quarters.

Although the Civil Service ministry of Fejérváry was dismissed at the beginning of April, 1906, it had nevertheless fulfilled its function, in its announcement of electoral reforms, of forcing the fanatical rowdies of the frenzied opposition to come to an agreement: it exacted their promise first of all to introduce electoral reform by the establishment of universal equal suffrage, and then—in the new parliament—to raise the national demands in the army issue with the Crown. The specter of this electoral reform hung over the political stage and marred the electoral victories of the coalition. The *Reichspost* contributed daily to its further discomfort.

Six months had passed since the pledge given for electoral reform before Franz Kossuth referred for the first time to the matter in his New Year speech—he had followed here the practice of great statesmen. He gave the assurance that preparations were being made for the introduction of universal suffrage; this legislation, so he said, would be the crowning achievement of his party. It took a long time for this crowning achievement to materialize. It was the middle of October, 1907, before the subject was raised again in new promises from the Minister of the Interior Andrássy. More than a year later, on November 11, 1908, he eventually dared to produce the draft of an electoral law, a bastard creation remarkable for the cramped and desperate efforts to get out of the prescribed task. In the precarious situation confronting the Fatherland, so it declared, "the intellectually mature section of the population" should be entrusted with a share in determining the fate of the country; for this reason from the poor Romanian mountain peasants, 40 per cent of whom were still illiterate thanks to the old and well-calculated educational policy of Budapest, only one in ten had the right of a single vote, whereas every citizen with an elementary school education who paid 10 kronen in annual tax was entitled to two votes, and those with a secondary school education paying 100 kronen had the right to three votes. There was no question, however, of a secret ballot: voting had to take place publicly—so that a "control" could be kept. It was a shameful piece of work, a travesty of the concept of universal franchise. This monstrous creation soon disappeared from the scene in the face of the stormy demonstrations of the indignant workers. The *Reichspost* followed the issue alertly with appropriate commentary. It now followed that it was able to take a share in the "cleaning-up" process which had begun in Hungary. Many prominent figures in Hungarian public life, men whose nationalist attitude was unquestionable, lent their services to the newspaper in this action.

At the beginning of December, 1908, I received a bundle of manuscripts through a Hungarian friend of the old publicist Eötvos, a man who was highly esteemed in Hungarian public affairs for his personal integrity and his unswerving pursuit of truth. The contents were directed against the leader of the Independence party, Franz Kossuth, the Minister of Commerce, and contained annihilating revelations concerning this national hero. These included falsification of the balance sheets of a company formed by him for the manufacture of fire-fighting equipment, fraud against the state committed with the writings of his late father, intrigue in the sale of shares in the insurance company he had founded, the Allgemeine heimische Versicherungs—A.G., and similar shifty maneuvers in the founding of the organ of the Independence party *Független Magyaroszag*. A whole list of similar delicts followed with full details of the various swindles and large-scale corruptions in which many of the most prominent members of the Kossuth party were named as accomplices. All this was supported exactly by the necessary evidence.

The significance of the publication of this information was obvious, for it was the Hungarian Minister of Commerce who was indicted, the leader of the strongest party of the Hungarian parliament.

After having satisfied myself as to the authenticity of the manuscripts, I began in December, 1908, the publication in the *Reichspost* of a series of articles under the title "The Real Franz Kossuth," a series which was continued up to the end of January, 1909.

The first reaction was dead silence. Franz Kossuth, Minister of Commerce, raised no protest. The Hungarian press was clearly disconcerted and some newspapers personally involved in the affair betrayed genuine alarm. That was all to begin with.

When the third article appeared revealing still more incriminating facts and the awaited protest was still not forthcoming, I began to grow worried. What could lie behind Franz Kossuth's attitude?

On January 16, 1909, the answer came. That evening a man came into the office of the *Reichspost* and asked the employee on duty, E. Hör, for copies of the articles in the series which had appeared to date. He began a long conversation with Hör, and then he came to the point. He was interested, so he said, to discover who had written these highly interesting articles and if Hör could find this out for him it would not be to his disadvantage. His future would be taken care of if he knew how to hold his tongue and procure even a fragment of the manuscript itself. It would be worth his while to think the matter over, said the man, and promised to come back again shortly.

Hör immediately informed me of his strange visit. I had the premises watched by reliable men from the neighborhood, and on the next Monday the unknown man appeared again and asked whether Hör had been able to obtain the manuscript or even part of this for him and what his price would be. Hör, who had received precise instructions as to how he should act, pretended to agree to the proposition and declared his price. The visitor told him he would collect the manuscript and hand over the sum demanded within the next few days. Steps had been taken to establish the identity of the visitor so interested in our manuscript. He was an official of the Austrian Danube Steam Ship Company, a Dr. A.S. who lived in Vienna in the Valeriestrasse. He was soon to discover that nothing was to come of the business transaction which he had started.

A second conspiracy was to follow. An employee taken over by the *Reichspost* in the handover of the *Deutsche Zeitung* tried to break into the manuscript files during the night. The attempt was unsuccessful. The man was discovered immediately and it was established that he had been won over to commit the theft by the promise of a high reward. The connections were obvious. In an open letter addressed to the Magyar press the *Reichspost* declared that two imperial officials of the highest rank were prepared to testify that Franz Kossuth had himself known of the attempted briberies and had even agreed to the amount of money to be offered. The press men and politicians met in the Café Balaton in Budapest upon receipt of this open letter and agreed that the only thing in the circumstances was to hush up the affair, for "unless Franz Kossuth himself protests, the Hungarian public cannot be informed of the letter."

The *Reichspost* thereupon published a brochure containing the series of articles on "The Real Franz Kossuth" which had previously appeared in the newspaper, together with the accompanying story. The first edition sold like hot cakes and a second had to be printed immediately. The brochure became a sensation on both sides of the Leitha.[6] There had certainly been a lot of talk of late about the private affairs of the Herr Minister, but the supporting evidence had been lacking. This had now been provided and the facts revealed were staggering. So this was the revolutionary leader, the hero, the liberator, who had traded on his name to trick the people of Hungary.

Already in November, 1909, the same year as the *Reichspost* publications, the Kossuth party, the hitherto all-powerful party which had taken the lead in all the strident demands for independence, divided into two factions: from its 220 deputies 136 broke way to join the new party formed by Deputy Justh. The subsequent parliamentary elections of 1910 shattered forever their former glories. All that remained of the Kossuth party were three tiny factions, hostile to one another. They were triumphantly confronted by Stephan Tisza, the opponent of all those intent upon the suppression of rights and the disintegration of the Empire. This was the same Stephan Tisza those adversaries had thought to have put out of the way for good in their electoral victory five years before, but who had made a triumphal comeback to political life with the 201 seats gained by the *Nationale Arbeitspartei* which he himself had formed.

By the introduction of a reform of the rules for the conduct of parliamentary business, a reform which he had pursued resolutely from the very commencement of his political leadership despite all the scorn of the opposition, Tisza secured the absolute defeat of the Independents by removing for good their old weapon of ob-

[6] The Leitha was the river which constituted the border between the Austrian and Hungarian halves of the Empire.

struction in Parliament. He could, however, still not undo the work of the Kossuth regime. Not all the efforts of this old warrior, so fiercely loyal to his King and the Constitution, could repair the damage to the unity of the Empire and their curtailment of the defense forces of the monarchy, the consequences of which could be felt right up to World War I.

Even before Stephan Tisza had settled his accounts with the mystics and gamblers of the Kossuth regime, however, public opinion in Hungary and professional politicians alike had been faced by a sobering political reality. One of the foremost causes of this disenchantment was the vision of a future determined by universal equal suffrage, the establishment of which was inevitable. How was this new future to be faced, a future in which the old class privileges would disintegrate?

Even before 1908 tentative overtures had been made from within the coalition toward an understanding with the Heir Apparent. One such endeavor ended in my own private apartment. It was, as far as I can remember, one Sunday in June, 1908, when Count Theodor Batthyani, a deputy, accompanied by two other Hungarian gentlemen, came to pay me a visit. Our conversation was frank and unreserved and lasted for more than two hours. The count, who as a parliamentarian flirted with nationalistic ideas, confided to me with typical Hungarian humor his opinion of the battle being fought by the coalition. Nothing could result from the military demands. Sooner or later the electoral reform would have to go through, but in such a way that the vital nerves of the Hungarian nation would not be impaired. He and his friends were willing to consider the wishes of the future monarch; all sensible people realized that it was a short-sighted policy to pin their sentiments and destiny to a couple of bits of colored silk or heraldic devices.

I made it quite clear in our conversation that in my personal opinion only such an extension of electoral rights could be considered as allowed the non-Magyar nationalities full participation in state affairs and which provided an organic tie with the life of the monarchy. I reported the interview to the Belvedere. The contents of this report was a further contribution to the growing conviction that in the event of a change of monarchs drastic solutions were not the only means of achieving the necessary internal reorganization of the monarchy. For the moment the wholesome fear of the strong man was a serviceable notion.

In 1909 I was to become involved myself in the internal history of Hungary through a personal acquaintanceship the beginning of which was as strange as its outcome was to be significant for contemporary history.

During the second week in June I received an invitation from Georg Linder to visit the former Hungarian Prime Minister, Baron Desider Bánffy, at the Hotel Sacher at ten o'clock. The invitation was surprising. The *Reichspost* had certainly never accorded friendly treatment to this Hungarian statesman who during the years 1895 to 1899 had instigated the *Kulturkampf* legislation directed by the powerful Hungarian lodge, and who had held the notorious parliamentary elections which had ended in bloodshed. He received me with Hungarian joviality. Somewhat corpulent, with an easy manner, his eyes revealed humor and shrewd intelligence. He could have been taken at first sight for a good-natured Hungarian provincial lawyer. This impression soon changed, however, as he explained the reason for his invitation. He told me he wanted to talk to the editor of the Vienna daily paper with whose independent opinion in Hungarian affairs he was acquainted. It was his intention to place at my disposal at the right moment a political exposé the publication of which would help to unravel the dangerous tangle in Hungary, this Hungary which had become involved in conflict with its dynasty. In that inimitable Hungarian-German which the Viennese so love to hear, Baron Bánffy proceeded to describe the events of the past. Never had an important public man spoken to me like this before.

"I know only too well" he began "how you all criticized my elections, but nobody thought of what was involved. I had to secure the governmental majority which was threatened by all kinds of opponents whose sole aim was to secure the political field for themselves alone: magnates, greedy for even more than they unfortunately already possess, and clericals who were dissatisfied with the existing clerical-political legislation. The same clique were threatening to get the upper hand who are now in power—a pack of ambitious opportunists, profiteers and rogues who will end by bring-

ing about the ruin of our poor country. That was why I was forced
to fight. It was clear that soldiers had to be called in when force
was threatened and the mob seemed to be getting out of hand. Yes,
I know there was some shooting and even bloodshed. But do you
really think it is fair to hold me responsible for this? By and large
I chose less radical methods—as others have done before me.

"For example I would send for the district notary and pat him
on the shoulder. 'My good friend,' I would say, 'how would you
like to be made a royal *Hofrat?*[7] Just do this and that. If you don't
like the idea, it's a pity, for you'll probably not only not be made
a *Hofrat* but end up by being something very much less exalted!'
He preferred to be made a *Hofrat,* but was I to blame? At that time
when people came to see me about election matters I used to have
a bag of money beside me. I would ask the visitor how much he
needed to ensure that the next election would go through smoothly
without any unnecessary complications. On no occasion did my
visitor show the slightest trace of embarrassment when I drew so
and so much out of my money bag. Remember, we Hungarians are
a fighting, self-confident people, but a simple people and used to
simple tactics."

This had all been said in a tone in which primitive hilarity, cyn-
icism and contempt for human nature were curiously mingled.
Bánffy reverted to the current political situation. The Crown had
done well, so he thought, to set the question of electoral reform in
the forefront of political obligations; there was no hope for its realization as long as the supremacy of the present ruling classes over
the people continued. "But Tisza who is all set for a comeback is
himself one of the ruling class and will certainly only introduce the
semblance of an electoral reform," Bánffy pointed out. "He is the
cleverest man in Hungary—cleverer than all of us put together. This
brilliant, obstinate and proud man represents a great risk for our
country. Remember that, my dear fellow, Tisza is as dangerous as
a cutthroat razor."

Bánffy bade me good-bye. "I'm going to send you a memorandum in which I want to set down what I personally consider the

___

[7] *Hofrat* is the official title combined with certain higher offices in the
administration.

right thing for the future of Hungary and for the dynasty, in the light of my own experience. I shall bear in mind perhaps that much of what I have to say can, in view of its significance, be made public only after my death."

This man who still looked so well had certainly never remotely considered that he was soon to die as he spoke these words. During the next few years he kept me informed through Georg Linder of his opinion of the political situation. On Wednesday, February 22, 1911, Linder appeared in my office to tell me that Bánffy was seriously ill and to hand over to me on his instructions an exposé which was entrusted to me for publication after his death, as had been agreed upon in our conversation of some two years ago.

Desider Bánffy had a stroke some days later and died on March 24, 1911. Not without some emotion, I published the document entrusted to me on the leader page of the *Reichspost* on May 27 under the title "The Testament of Desider Bánffy." The text of this historical document is reproduced here:

"When I look back over the past forty years and consider who has most benefited by the Compromise, the Hungarian nation or the dynasty, there can today be only one true answer: never was the nation further from those aspirations which it had cherished up to 1867 than it is today, and never have these aspirations aroused less enthusiasm. Victory in Hungary lies in the hands of the dynasty.

"What has happened in Hungary? What has caused this change? Fünfkirchen is still Fünfkirchen and Pressburg remains Pressburg! The magnate class have brought about the ruin of the country. They have exploited the nationalist ideal for their own ends, incessantly provoking conflict with the dynasty in order to enforce their own political domination. The gentry has deceived the dynasty and at the same time the people. If a 'Hordar' gives his word or his promise, this promise is kept, but the gentry who are masters in Hungary have never kept their word. They have only been concerned with utilizing their power won out of the conflict with the dynasty. For this reason an electoral reform is imperative, a reform which would break the power of the gentry and introduce new blood into the country.

"If ten unbiased men were to sit down together to discuss

Hungary they would be bound to come to this conclusion: there is but one nation in Hungary—the Magyars (let's imagine the magnates out of the way!)—which has no possessions outside the Habsburg monarchy and whose future and destiny is conceivable nowhere else but inside the monarchy and in the development of the power of the dynasty. No other nation is so dependent upon the monarchy, for the Magyar nation has no blood brothers outside Hungary, possesses no concrete self-contained national territory and is even lacking in a real social structure. *This people cannot exist in perpetual contention with the dynasty if it is not to bring about its own ruin.* No other nation is so destined by nature and circumstances as a medium for a sound monarchist policy as the Magyar people.

"Look at the Romanians! It is small wonder that their yearnings for racial unification have been roused, for they have a nation beyond our frontiers—which the Magyars have not. I am not talking about today, I am thinking of the future, for the man who cannot look ahead into the future is no statesman and would be better off digging potatoes. *Why should the soundest element of a monarchist policy in Hungary be sacrificed for the future?* For this reason in my opinion the policy to be followed cannot be based exclusively on the nationalities. But I also maintain that *apart from the electoral reform* a sure development for Hungary is possible only if the nationalities are satisfied—but in such a way that their secret aspirations do not grow still further.

"But how can these nationalities be appeased? By good administration and by the taking over of the Komitat administration by the state. The power of the gentry must be broken!

"The district judge from the gentry today is a fine hand at drinking, cards, charming the ladies and everything else besides, but as for being able to understand a peasant's point of view or even hearing him out in patience ... Complicated methods are by no means necessary. If every district judge had to visit every parish or community in his area just once a year, listen to the people who came to see him and straighten out their difficulties, that would already be a step in the right direction.

"The Romanian or Slovak must at least be made to feel that

the state is not just a tax-collector, but that it also offers him the guarantee of an ordered legal system and a fair administration. What does it matter if forty or fifty Romanians are elected to Parliament as a result of the new reform? Our primary concern must be that in this Parliament elected by universal suffrage all obstruction is a thing of the past and that proceedings are conducted in the recognition that complications for Hungary constitute complications for the dynasty, and that it lies in the interests of the dynasty that the Hungarians should live together peaceably with the nationalities and work together for the greatness of the dynasty. Any Hungarian who thinks otherwise is an enemy of the dynastic ideal.

"Much as I support the necessity of an electoral reform, I nevertheless fear that it will not be possible to put this through by Parliament in Hungary. This view is also shared by Khuen,[8] and in his position I too would have followed the same course and concentrated first of all on settling the army reform question. This question must be solved once and for all; it has poisoned public opinion in Hungary long enough. Only Graf Khuen's Parliament can hope to put through the army reform, for a more battered and lame old hack than this Parliament we have never had in Hungary. It goes without saying that the government which introduces the electoral reform signs its own death warrant. Count Tisza is already getting ready today to step into Count Khuen's shoes, and, although this will mean the restoration of the lamentable rule of the gentry, the Crown will not be able to prevent this.

"There can, therefore, be only one goal: the electoral reform must be established, even without the Hungarian Parliament, for only this reform can assure the whole Hungarian nation of its rights and appeal to the people as a whole. Furthermore, this electoral reform would seal the peace with the dynasty so vital for Hungary. Austria need have no fear of this peace, for it is the pledge for the existence of the monarchy as a great power."

In the Budapest press the publication of the document was understandably met with the greatest surprise. Since doubts were voiced as to the authenticity of the document and Eugen Bakosi,

[8] Count Karl Khuen-Hederváry, Prime Minister for the second time, January 18, 1910, to April 16, 1912.

the president of Othon, the Hungarian journalists' association, evaded my challenge to have the document held by me examined by two delegates of the Hungarian press, I appealed to the special tribunal of the Vienna Foreign Press Association.

On July 6, 1911, this association sent a letter to all its members signed by the members of the special tribunal; the chairman, Wickham Steed (*Times*), and that associate members, Dr. Hugo Ganz (*Frankfurter Zeitung*) and Julius Seress (*Pesti Naplo*), to the effect that the tribunal had examined the original document submitted by me, considered my conduct in the matter to have been "beyond reproach," and established that the facts of the case fully justified "the publication of the material placed at his disposal as the political testament of Baron Desider Bánffy."

The events of the last years before the World War I only confirmed the good counsel and warnings which Desider Bánffy, the old realist, had laid down in his testament. When Stephan Tisza took up office as President of the House on May 25, 1912, he showed himself to be as rigid and uncompromising as ever in his tactics and soon gave the opposition fresh cause to transform the parliamentary building on the banks of the Danube into the scene of the wildest obstructionist demonstrations. He nevertheless succeeded simultaneously, by a bold decision, to put the matter to the vote in putting through the various readings of the new bill for the army reforms. He was, however, none the less "a cutthroat razor," for, despite his indubitable gifts and outstanding personal traits of character, he was lacking in moderation and infinitely preferred active combat to consistent striving to achieve peace.

He assumed office for the second time as Prime Minister on June 10, 1913, surrounded by a ring of personal enemies, and, worse still, he had lost the confidence of his confederates who had been waiting hopefully for the introduction of universal equal suffrage as the prelude to a new era. Tisza, however, obsessed by fear of revolutionary change that might be brought about by the appearance of some 150 newly-elected deputies, had prepared an electoral reform program even more hopelessly restricted than that produced by Andrássy. The electoral bill presented by the Lukacs cabinet on January 1, 1913, was a stilted and ineffectual creation which extended the right to vote to only 1,800,000 citizens—not even half the adult population—and limited the suffrage in the majority of cases to citizens over the age of thirty. The bill which was accepted by the House of Deputies on March 6 was such a disillusionment that a member of the government, the Minister of Justice, Dr. Szekely, resigned from office in protest.

A tragic political end awaited Stephan Tisza, that obstinate and proud old warrior who had stood so unrelentingly like a rock in the whirlpool of party political emotions. It was true that he had himself shared in the guilt and so contributed toward his own bitter fate, but he was nevertheless a man *integer vitae, scelerisque purus* and deserved a better exit from the tragedy in which he had become involved.

The true Magyar nation repudiated all the ideologists who thought they could ignore the natural conditions vital to the life of their nation in their high-sounding political concepts for the state.

Chapter 8
UNIVERSAL SUFFRAGE IN AUSTRIA

The movement for universal suffrage in Hungary was by no means an innovation for the Austrian Empire, for the initiative for electoral reform had originated from Austria itself where an extended franchise had already been introduced in 1897. Nevertheless the Hungarian plan undoubtedly brought about a new stimulus in Austria.

Powerful elements in Austria were active in the struggle for equal parliamentary rights. Universal suffrage had featured from the very beginning in the program of the Social Democrats, whose demands were voiced in the name of the proletariat, as yet denied any say in political affairs. The Christian-Socials too, as a people's party, had good reason to demand universal suffrage, for they also represented broad masses of the population who had so far no right to vote. A further argument influenced the Christian-Socials in their campaign. For years the legislation had been paralyzed as a result of the obstruction caused by the various nationalist party conflicts: the people felt that such a state of affairs could arise only because of the indifferent and irresponsible attitude of those in power in Parliament, "those lawyers and high-sounding journalists," who could well afford to carry the costs of the national conflicts since they were not concerned with the real needs of the people. Thus the Christian-Socials viewed universal suffrage, in the sense of an appeal to the people, as the summoning of the most powerful existing means of safeguarding the state.

The determination with which the Christian-Socials exerted all their energies in their demands for electoral reform (and the *Reichspost* did its best to support them) produced a remarkable change in Parliament. The Christian-Social party, formerly so small, suddenly developed and rose to take over the acknowledged leadership in the House as the only non-Marxist German party with clearly defined aims in the electoral reform issue. It even resulted that from its ranks Dr. Gessmann was appointed within the Electoral Reform Committee as speaker. The new political parties of the future began clearly to differentiate from the obsolete political "party unions" of the old days. On the German side only the Christian-Socials and the Social Democrats seemed really to count.

There was nevertheless tremendous opposition to the demands for electoral reform. An extremely tenacious and vigorous group of opponents contested the reform from among the members of the powerful upper classes. The interests of the aristocracy and liberal middle class were widely represented by the existing *curia* system, essentially based on economic considerations. Nor were these interests simply the political expression of a mutual egoism on the part of these classes. This aristocracy was deeply rooted in the very history of the nation: the very designation of the aristocracy as Bohemian, Styrian, Tyrolese, Hungarian, etc., revealed their intrinsic ties with the old provincial federalism and with the dynasty. Whether on the field of battle, in diplomacy, in public administration, in the arts, science, research and as patrons of the arts and of literature, there was no field of human activity in which the aristocracy had not achieved honor and distinction. The high achievements of the men of the nobility were complemented no less admirably by the practical social and welfare work of the women. Representatives of an age-old tradition and way of life, this aristocracy had helped to form the culture of Austria.

As a class, however, they had all too complacently accepted the fate of all human institutions which gradually grow obsolete, a fate which cannot be warded off merely by the enforcement of law, but rather by the moral strength inherent in the class itself. Where this strength lives on, a true aristocracy will endure in the future, unconcerned with considerations of ostentatious title. This restriction of the power of the aristocracy and the lessening of the political influence of the urban upper middle classes appeared to many to constitute a capitulation to the revolutionary elements and the handing over of public affairs to the lower classes.

The electoral reform announced by the Prime Minister, Baron Gautsch, was already regarded in wide circles as a threat. He had submitted his plan for electoral reform at the beginning of February, 1906, and within three months his defeat had been decided. His successor, Prince Conrad Hohenlohe, fared no better and also resigned within a few weeks.

Was the outcome of the battle already to be decided merely by the rapid downfall of two successive governments? Everyone was aware of the seriousness of the demonstrations for the new electoral reform, as the Christian-Socials and Social Democrats marched through the streets. On the other hand, there had been similar protests before on other issues by these unruly political crowds. No decisive action had been taken as a result of their demonstrations and all the same the world had not come to an end.

Those who took comfort in such thoughts this time, however, were unwilling to recognize the unprecedented fact that behind this electoral reform campaign stood no less a figure than Emperor Franz Josef himself, this Habsburg monarch who had hitherto always been a conservative, the guardian of old recognized forms and privileges. This same old monarch, regarded by so many as emperor-bureaucrat, had now decided to appeal to the people. He had been influenced in this decision by the events in Hungary during the past years, the renewed outbreak of the subversive Kossuth movement, and the deserting of leading Hungarian politicians who had been destined to represent the interests of the Empire; he was furthermore strongly influenced in this course by the events in Russia which were demanding the establishment of a constitutional state.

Baron Max Wladimir von Beck replaced Conrad Hohenlohe as Prime Minister. From the very beginning the way in which he took up the reform project of his predecessor left no doubt as to the firmness of his intentions. In his speech introducing his program before the House of Deputies on July 7, 1906, his declarations were far more emphatic than those of Hohenlohe and Gautsch. He spoke of a sacred task, the fulfillment of which should be the expression of the common will of all the peoples of Austria.

The Electoral Reform Committee hastened to consider the government proposals which skillfully made provision for the jealous demands of the various nations in its plan for the distribution of seats in Parliament by reducing these to a common denominator. To compensate for this the number of seats in the future House of Deputies was to be increased to 516, as against Gautsch's 455 and Hohenlohe's 495. In Gautsch's plan the ratio between the German-Italian-Romanian bloc and the Slavs was 225 to 230; Hohenlohe reduced the difference by three seats; in Beck's plan for the distribution of seats the gap was virtually closed with 257 to 259. Despite various objections, the German-Nationals and Liberals finally agreed to the plan.

Various critical episodes followed in connection with demands for the plural vote, but by the end of December the great work was finally concluded. These seven months, during which Beck had weathered many a storm, saw the final end of the *curia* parliament which, even in its last stages, had used all the devices of parliamentary combat. A great and memorable work had been accomplished, a task in which the Crown, as the pre-eminent power of the state, had worked together with the mass parties to achieve the victory of the democratic ideal. Among the non-Socialist Vienna newspapers the *Reichspost* had stood in the vanguard of the press campaign for the reform.

In the subsequent elections the Christian-Socials and Social Democrats emerged decisively from among the German parties as the two significant political parties of the future. The German Liberal press was totally disconcerted by the disintegration of the Liberal parties, and vented its shock and helpless vexation in angry cries of "Red is better than black!"[1] a catchword which was taken up throughout Austria in campaigns for the second polls.

In general the results of the elections were highly satisfactory for the Christian-Socials, who received 57 per cent of the non-Socialist German vote. Already on the first victorious day of the election the Catholic Conservatives of Upper Austria declared their decision to amalgamate with Lueger's party. Prince Alois Litchten-

---

[1] Up to the present day political experience has shown that approximately two-thirds of the middle classes, predominantly Liberal or pan-German in political outlook, tend to vote "red" when faced with the alternative "red or black." The color "red" here stands for Socialist, while "black" signifies the Christian party.

stein had been working quietly behind the scenes, preparing for this unification.

The Christian-Socials were justified in their jubilations over the electoral victories, for, in addition to the 66 seats which they had gained, they could furthermore count on an increase of 30 as a result of the merger with the Catholic Conservative People's party. The Social Democrats had also good grounds to be proud of their achievement, however, for with a parliamentary union of 87 seats— 50 German, 23 Czech, 7 Polish, 5 Romanian and 2 Ruthenian—they entered the House as the second largest party. Unfortunately, however, their multi-national union was short-lived, a loss as viewed from the standpoint of the interests of the state as a whole. The grave significance of the whole Socialist movement in Austria had, however, become apparent. Most unfortunately all too little effective use was subsequently made of this realization in practical social politics.

Beside the 96 Christian-Socials in Parliament stood representatives of five independent German parties: 47 German-Nationals, 21 Liberals, 18 German Agrarians, 14 German Radicals of the Karl Herman Wolf school and 3 Schönerer pan-Germans, the latter two parties being remnants of a parliamentary group which ten years previously had given good cause for fear and trembling during the conflict resulting from the language ordinances.

For the first time in the new Parliament there now appeared political groupings of different nationalities sharing common concepts, replicas, as it were, of the Austrian multi-national state itself. Such parliamentary unions were furthermore voluntarily formed by the representatives of the people themselves, representatives freely elected by the common will of the working Austrian population. Unlike the Social Democrats, the Christian-Socials representing the German, Slovenian and Italian nationalities were not organized in a single party, but were closely associated in the recognition of common principles and pledged to work together; here too their varying national dissimilarities were bridged by a great common ideal. Thus the vital principle of the monarchy—the solidarity of the various nations within the Empire through their historical, cultural and economic interdependence—was embodied in the two leading party groups in Parliament. It seemed really as though this were an auspicious sign heralding the rebirth of the whole inner political life of the nation. It looked as though this were the realization of the hopes cherished by so many in the campaign for universal equal suffrage. Great possibilities were opening up. It remained to be seen whether these would be turned to good account.

The new Parliament in fact gave good grounds at first for optimism. The new era began hopefully with a government composed of four Civil Service ministers beside seven parliamentarians and in which Young Czechs and German-Nationals worked peaceably together. In the first parliamentary cabinet Dr. Weiskirchner, the Christian-Social, was President of the House and there were two Christian-Social members in the new government, Dr. Ebenhoch and Dr. Gessmann.

The first negotiations of the new regime went well. Beck entered into the *Ausgleich*, or Compromise, talks with Hungary with energy and great political skill. He succeeded in substituting a true compromise, an ordered and stabilized relationship between Austria and Hungary, in place of the permanent element of insecurity which had hitherto existed between the two halves of the Empire, a state of affairs which none of his predecessors had been able to achieve. It now remained to be seen whether he would be equally successful in dealing with the language contention in Bohemia and restore peace at last by a similar German-Czech *Ausgleich*.

On January 18, 1908, Dr. Ludwig Wahrmund, professor of canon law, delivered a public lecture at the faculty of law at Innsbruck University on "The Catholic Concept and Free Science." Soon afterward the lecture appeared in pamphlet form, published by Lehmann, a firm of publishers in Munich. Not content with disregarding completely the first rules for logical discussion, Wahrmund further indulged in downright blasphemy. This professor of canon law declared the religion proclaimed by the Catholic Church to be "merely in theory still a monotheistic religion, in popular practice, however, it indulges in polytheism in a manner scarcely surpassed by the much-combated practices of the heathen religions." According to Wahrmund, Catholicism was "an antiquated philosophy, a mockery of all the scientific achievements of modern times, a superstitious pagan polytheistic cult." All this called itself the Catholic concept, said Warhmund, according to which one was required to believe in "Gods which come down in person from heaven or in beings who ascend in person into heaven."

Professor Wahrmund added further coals to the fire, calling the Catholic students "parasites" against whom "war to the knife must be declared." The affair grew more critical from week to week. Beck, the Prime Minister, was so disconcerted by the turn of events that he would have preferred to ignore the whole affair, had this been possible. Nevertheless he and his Minister of Education, Dr. Marchet, felt compelled, in the face of Christian-Social demands that Wahrmund be removed from his professorship at Innsbruck University, at least to promise to suspend Wahrmund's lectures for the coming summer term.

The righteous indignation of the Christian-Social electorate for whom the *Reichspost* acted as guide and interpreter led to the resignation of the Christian-Social cabinet members. The exit of the two representatives of the largest German party sounded the death knell for Beck's ministry. The government further contributed toward its own downfall in the sharp public criticism which it aroused by its weak attitude in the Magyar army demands. The Beck regime came to an end on November 14, 1908, and with it the leadership of a remarkable statesman who, despite all his gifts, was nevertheless unable to cope with the over-heavy burden of the cultural and political affairs of state.

Chapter 9
BOSNIA HERZEGOVINA

I was on vacation with my family in July, 1908, when reports suddenly appeared in the newspapers of the outbreak of the Young Turkish revolution, and of the burning down of farms belonging to Mohammedan small landowners in northern Bosnia by Serbian *Tscheten*. The news was ominous. For many years now since the Austro-Hungarian occupation (1878) there had been peace in Bosnia-Herzegovina; the robber bands which had ravaged the countryside during the long Turkish domination had been finally wiped out by the highly-organized special military police, the famous *Štrafuni*. These new outbreaks of violence were clearly alarm signals. I myself knew these countries only too well and was greatly perturbed by the newspaper reports.

We hastened back to Vienna and a few days later I was on my way to the Bosnian capital, Sarajevo. The political situation had in the meantime become quite clear. Turkey had suddenly reverted to her old 1876 constitution: the Young Turkish League was proclaiming the indivisibility of the Ottoman Empire. New parliamentary elections were to be held as soon as possible in all provinces, including of course Bosnia-Herzegovina which, though still constitutionally part of Turkey, was occupied by Austria-Hungary as officially sanctioned by the Concert of Powers in Berlin in 1878. The Young Turks were demanding the restitution of both provinces in which elections for the new Turkish central parliament were shortly to take place.

In practice, however, the situation was by no means that simple, for the majority of the population, for the most part Serbs and Croats, protested violently against such a course. It was an acknowledged fact that the monarchy had introduced law and order in

129

these wild half-barbarous regions overrun by the bands of brigands which the Turkish regime had never succeeded in stamping out. An excellent road and railway network had opened up a country formerly unknown, and extended and encouraged trade and commerce. Not only had substantial sums been invested in this country, but law and order had been established, often in the face of armed resistance and at the cost of the lives of Austro-Hungarian troops. The attempt to reincorporate these[1] provinces into the Ottoman Empire could only end in a civil war which would reduce the land once more to its former chaos.

The situation was grave. On my arrival in Sarajevo I expected to encounter swarms of journalists from home and abroad, summoned by the ominous turn of events. To my surprise I found no one there. For weeks I was the only journalist in Sarajevo. The Bosnian capital might just as well have been a city on the moon for all the interest the outside world showed in events there. I found Sarajevo like a seething witch's cauldron about to boil over. The emotions of all three national elements which made up the population of Bosnia-Herzegovina had reached white heat. The Mohammedans, a third of the population of 1,800,000, were demanding unification with the Sublime Porte, to which they constitutionally but not in effect belonged; they insisted upon their rights to vote for the Turkish central Parliament. In opposition to these Mahommedans, the approximate 800,000 Serbs were loud in their demands for a union with the Serbian kingdom. Wedged between these strongly divergent masses were the 400,000 Catholic Croat minority who differed from their Serb relatives, not only in their religion but in a strong sense of patriotism which bound them to their racial and religious compatriots within the Habsburg monarchy. The Croats were confronted by Western civilization and thought on the one side and a Byzantine, Oriental way of life on the other.

The Habsburg Empire found itself in a complicated and un-

---

[1] The population was 1,359,000 in 1878 before the occupation, but had increased since then by some 400,000, the majority of whom were Christians (*Notizen über militärische und politische Verhältnisse in Bosnien und in der Herzegowina Ende Juni 1878*, Vienna, Verlag der Hof- und Staatsdruckerei, 1878).

enviable position. It had to protect the Catholic minority which in any case, whether the provinces concerned were to become Turkish or Serbian, were faced with an extremely uncertain future. It was the Empire which would have to face the music if it permitted the wrong solution in this old volcanic territory. Yet on the other hand both the apparent alternatives could only end in catastrophe. Were the Empire to agree to the Young Turks' claims for the restitution of the provinces to the Ottoman Empire—a decision which *de jure* appeared to be the most feasible—it would certainly have to reckon with an insurrection, doubtlessly backed by Russia, of immeasurable consequences and with repercussions in Serbia and Dalmatia. If, however, it were to yield to the demands of the Serbian population and the heated propaganda which originated from the kingdom of Serbia, it would have to face the complications of the Turkish reaction. There was very little time in which to weigh the decision.

I was able to form a general picture of the situation and the various opinions and intentions through numerous conversations with members of the divergent camps in the capital. Even when the difficulties were acknowledged there seemed no way out of them. The atmosphere was moreover so electric that a calm and dispassionate discussion with Serbs and Mohammedans was virtually out of the question. The leader of the Serbian (Orthodox) Orientals of Mostar, Athanas Šola, spoke frankly with me in a heated discussion about the use of armed force and of active rebellion should the Empire dare to prevent the integration of the two provinces in a Serbian national state.

Completely different in temperament and outlook was the lawyer, Dr. Dimović, a highly-educated Serb; it was rare to find men sharing his more moderate views among his countrymen of the same race and religion. Dimović supported an autonomic program which aimed to give the Serbs of Bosnia-Herzegovina the leadership within the framework of the Empire, and he became the leader of the moderate Serb faction in the Provincial Diet.

One of the first men I saw was the Archbishop, Dr. Stadler, a great Croat held in the highest esteem by the Catholics of the country for his untiring efforts in building up his new archdiocese and for his own good works, his selflessness and the warm and close contact he had established with the people. On my visits to Bosnia in former years this loyal Croat subject of the Austrian Emperor had given me proofs of his good will and of his confidence on repeated occasions. This time too he spoke quite openly with me. In his opinion there was only one way out of the apparent impasse, and that was for Austria-Hungary to unite both provinces within the Empire. Only thus could the Gordian knot be severed. The Habsburg Empire, so said Dr. Stadler, was indeed committed to this step by virtue of its position as the bastion of Western Christian civilization on the frontier of the Balkans. The Croat population was unanimous in this view. Even in the cultured home of one of the Croat political leaders, the lawyer Dr. Nikola Mandić, the atmosphere was charged with the tension of the political unrest in the country.

The same opinion was shared by the wise Franciscan Provinvincial Fr. Alois Misić,[2] a true son of Saint Francis. From the early Middle Ages his order had kept alight the wavering flame of Christianity in this land. Its members had lived as peasants in solitary mountain huts, Catholic priests disguised in Turkish national dress. One generation had followed another, fearless, self-sacrificing and resolute, the furthest outposts of Christian culture. They were now looking toward the dawn of a new era. The Provincial spoke glowingly of the age-old dream of the Catholic Christians of the Bosnian mountains, the realization of which now seemed so near. How could it be otherwise?

There could be no further doubt. Only strong action by a firm hand could put out the smoldering fire. Compliance with the demands of the Young Turks would certainly result in the outbreak of bitter civil war. Adjacent Serbia was already quite openly preparing to support an insurrection. If Europe were to be spared a Balkan conflagration of incalculable dimensions, the monarchy must intervene and put an end to the perilous state of indecision by creating a new and tolerable situation.

Upon my return to Vienna I was already able to observe the

---

[2] Fr. Misić died shortly after World War I as Bishop of Mostar, Herzegovina.

effect of my first reports from Sarajevo. I am still convinced today that in principle no other solution was possible than that indicated in these reports. In view of the political discord in Europe as a whole, a conference of the signatory powers such as England had desired later would only have been a waste of time; the problem would have been discussed to no purpose and further confusion in the Balkans would have been provoked. The diplomatic procedure adopted by the Ballhausplatz[3] in not previously informing the great powers of its intentions was no concern of mine.

In mid-August I was asked to come and see Count Aehrenthal, the Foreign Minister. I received a warm welcome from the minister who was full of thanks for what he called my reconnaissance work in the occupied provinces, my enlightening reports on the situation there and for having pointed out the inevitability of the solution about to be taken. As Aehrenthal said, it was unfortunate that so many people were voicing their opinions on the subject without any real knowledge of the true facts and circumstances.

"We are facing a momentous decision of historical significance," declared Aehrenthal. "Rest assured, I shall do everything within my power to prevent war. No, I have not the least desire for war, and for this very reason I am concerned to avoid prolonged and dangerous discussions. The decision has in fact been taken and you will soon have the satisfaction of seeing the result for yourself. Go on, in the meantime, along the same lines." He paused significantly. "On October 5"—he gave the date a particular emphasis— "we intend to incorporate Bosnia-Herzegovina into the Empire with all due solemnity and with the utmost consideration for Turkey."

This was certainly a disclosure of the greatest significance. I realized the honor and distinction which Aehrenthal had shown me. By confiding this state secret to me, a secret of international importance, the Foreign Minister had expressed in his own way his gratitude for my services to him in a difficult situation. His confidence may well have been further prompted by the fact that, al-

---

[3] The Ballhausplatz was the seat of the Austrian Foreign Ministry and the name thus became synonymous with the ministry. The present-day office of the Federal Chancellor and of the Minister of Foreign Affairs is still situated in the same building on the Ballhausplatz in the center of Vienna.

though the Heir Apparent (with whom Aehrenthal was not on a good footing) did not share his views on the Bosnia-Herzegovina question, the *Reichspost* had not allowed itself to be influenced by this fact.

The annexation took place on the date appointed, a date which was not disclosed until the very last moment. This very reticence on the part of the Ballhausplatz to reveal its intentions beforehand might certainly account to some extent for the surprise which the annexation aroused in diplomatic circles in Europe. It was, however, a somewhat inadequate explanation for the universal astonishment professed, for surely no one could seriously have believed that Austria-Hungary would have abandoned the fine cultural work she had successfully built up with so much sacrifice in the Balkan provinces committed to her charge.

International tension, caused rather by the strained relations between England under Edward VII and Germany under Kaiser Wilhelm than by the actual Balkan episode as such, but further aggravated by the new turn of events, largely accounted for the unfavorable reception of the act of annexation. Repeated emphatic assurances from the Ballhausplatz to London and Saint Petersburg that Austria-Hungary had not the slightest intention of violating Serbia's position in no way helped to ease the situation. London took offense at the fact that Emperor Franz Josef had given not the slightest intimation of the plan when King Edward VII had visited him that year in Ischl after his usual annual visit to the spa at Marienbad. Although the historical facts have in the meantime been clarified, the well-known writer André Maurois has unfortunately revived the old accusations in his book *Edward VII and his Time* (1951): "At the same time [the royal visit in Ischl] Aehrenthal, the Archduke Franz Ferdinand and the Chief of the Austrian General Staff, Conrad von Hötzendorf were preparing not only to annex Bosnia but possibly also to seize the whole of Serbia" (p. 301).

Anyone who still doubted the advisability of the annexation move had only to look at the results. Serbia immediately began buying war material and started to arm at all speed; the Serbian press was full of bitter invective and bands of partisans began to gather along the Drina frontier. There were *Tscheten* attempts to break through into eastern Bosnia. Events took such a serious turn that the Empire was forced to take military precautionary measures and reserves of the Sarajevo Corps were the first to be mobilized. Montenegro also joined in the turbulent demonstrations for Serbian national claims. Everything pointed to war. More than once during the annexation crisis the situation looked perilous.

The annexation secured peace for both the provinces themselves. There were no signs whatever of internal unrest. Delegations of Mohammedan notables and official Serb civic bodies, such as the municipal council of Srbrenica, expressed gratitude for the annexation. The whole country felt a sense of relief after the tension and apprehension of the preceding months. A deputation of Mohammedans arrived in Vienna to pay homage to the Emperor. Plans were even seriously considered for the erection of a mosque in Vienna as an expression of good will toward the new citizens of the Empire.

In 1908 Russia resummoned her bellicose Serb friends, for she had no desire for war and had enough to do as it was with her own affairs. The Balkans could wait. In Belgrade, however, nationalist feelings were still running high. Unrest flared up across the Hungarian and Bosnian frontiers. On March 31, 1909, Serbia solemnly declared her recognition of the situation created by the annexation and pledged herself to friendly relations with the Austrian Empire. At the same time, however, a new underground movement against Austria-Hungary, first started by the newly-formed militia *Narodna Odbrana,* was joined by the already existing rifle and *sokol* organizations. Syrmia, Bosnia-Herzegovina and southern Dalmatia were swarming with political agents. The Serbian press made no secret of the fact that the nationalist leaders had no intention of conforming with the notes of the diplomats and were prepared to take matters into their own hands.

In October and November, 1908, shortly after the annexation, I published in the *Reichspost* five documents with the aim of throwing some light on these proceedings. I had received these documents, which were German translations of the Serbian original text, from the military bureau of Archduke Franz Ferdinand. I gave no information as to the origin of the documents, but everyone in Vienna could easily guess the source.

The documents charged various members of the Serbo-Croat coalition of the Provincial Diet in Agram with having seditious relations with Belgrade. Shortly afterward the historian Dr. Heinrich Friedjung published a whole series of similar documents in the *Neue Freie Presse*. It was known that the Foreign Ministry was behind the publication of the papers by Friedjung. The reaction was inevitable: the deputies of the Serbo-Croat coalition against whom the grave accusation had been made brought an action for libel against the *Reichspost* and against Dr. Friedjung. The outcome of the proceedings in the Vienna court is well known: the trial ended with a settlement which was introduced by the declaration of Dr. Friedjung withdrawing the documents and the relevant accusations, and which constituted a victory for the plaintiff.

In a two-hour exposé I gave the court a general picture of the scheming activities and intrigues of Serbian chauvinists against the Empire at the time and of the dangerous political relationships in the southern regions of the Empire. There could be no doubt that the facts recounted gave ample proof of a conspiracy on the southern frontiers, a conspiracy which would stop at nothing to attain its ends. The paper *Srbobran*, brought out by a group of Serbian refugees in the United States, defined most virulently the aims of this movement with the words: "We shall not rest until the last Archduchess puts on mourning!"

But the documents, allegedly pan-Serbian, the supposed proof of the pan-Serbian subversive activities, were false. On this point the great impressive political trial which would have justified the introduction of strict measures on the part of Austria-Hungary for the maintenance of order in her southern territories collapsed. The Imperial Ambassador in Belgrade, Count Forgach, had been the victim of a fraud, and not only the ambassador but the Foreign Ministry in Vienna as well. The most calamitous aspect of the whole affair, however, was that it was not the facts themselves as shown in the falsifications nor the general situation evident from them which were false, but rather that the supposed documents had been constructed on the basis of real facts, interspersed with fictitious details, documents which had never existed. The sorry outcome of the trial could have furnished the conspirators against the Empire with no better cover and their friends such as Masaryk, Wickham Steed and associates with no more welcome justification for their attitude. From now on in the eyes of public opinion Vienna was held responsible for everything in its allegedly underhand and ill-disposed political policy in the Balkans—until the day came when the shots of the assassination in the Bosnian capital shattered the illusion and revealed the terrible truth.

Seton-Watson was one of the many who were shattered by the outcome of the trial. I had held this British journalist, who had now gone over to the ranks of the enemy, in the highest esteem. He had been a good friend to the Empire and had constantly warned in the past against the errors committed, particularly by the Magyars, in the treatment of the Slovaks and the South Slavs. In his great work on the South Slav question he devoted a long chapter to the Vienna trial. In this he says of me that, in making use of the supposed documents which had been received from a source which was felt to be sufficiently high to guarantee their authenticity, I had acted "as any journalist would have acted in his place."

The shadow of this regrettable affair fell over the Empire right up to the tragedy of Sarajevo. The Austrian Empire would most certainly have received a better international press after the Sarajevo assasination had it not been for the damning attacks leveled against its diplomacy and policy in the allegedly unjust treatment of the Serbs.

The damaging falsification affair was not the only unfortunate appendix of the annexation.

On the other hand, the visit of Emperor Franz Josef to Sarajevo (1910) was a happy occasion which helped to dispel to some extent the growing feeling of pessimism. He met with an enthusiastic reception. I was in Sarajevo myself during those lovely days in May when hope and happiness seemed to have been regained once more and saw for myself the moving reception which the vast crowds, not least of all the Mahommedans, accorded to their old Emperor. There was not a single incident to mar those cloudless days. It was touching to see the genuine devotion of the Turkish Begs with their retinue in gold-embroidered national dress.

The visitors from Vienna were, however, unaware of one fact: care had been taken to keep the Serbs away from the festive demonstrations in the streets. Later I heard about this from Dr. Josip Sunarić, at this time already President of the Bosnian Provincial Diet. "We had taken all precautions," he told me, "we representatives of the Croats and Mussulmans formed a deputation and approached General Appel, the general commanding the provincial forces. We informed him that we would undertake to guarantee the safety of His Majesty. We told him that there was not the slightest danger of an incident so long as we had the authority for one thing: all Serbian houses must be closed on this day and no window opened while the Emperor drove through the city and during the demonstrations of loyalty by the people. There was no need for a military cordon—we Catholics and Mahommedans would see to that! Appel agreed and everything went according to plan."

One year later the Heir Apparent expressed the wish to visit the newly-acquired imperial provinces. Here again Sunarić gave me a personal account. In 1911 the Archduke had sent Fr. Augustinus Galen from the Benedictine Abbey of Saint Emaus in Prague, a man in whom he had the utmost confidence, on a special mission to Sarajevo. As a nonpolitical observer, it was Galen's task to sound the reaction in Bosnia to a visit by the Heir Apparent. It was Franz Ferdinand's earnest wish to put an end once and for all by such a visit to the foolish stories which were current concerning his allegedly hostile attitude toward the South Slavs, stories against him, the very man who had so vigorously opposed the use of armed force in the annexation crisis and checked the ardor of General Conrad. To the day of his death he was preoccupied with the old idea of a triple alliance between the three emperors.

Galen received a positive and enthusiastic answer from Archbishop Stadler, and likewise from General Potiorek, then the commanding officer of the province. He had then been to see Dr. Sunarić, only to receive an equally emphatic condemnation of the project of a visit by the Heir Apparent to Bosnia.

"I knew the Serbs only too well," he told me afterward. "I

knew that there would be assassins lying in wait for him. I was so sure of this and put forward my objections with such vigor that Galen was quite astonished and asked me how I could account for the fact that he had received exactly the opposite answer from both the Archbishop and the General. I was summoned next day by the Archbishop himself who caught me by the ear, half-playfully, half-serious. 'Well Josip,' he asked me, somewhat unwillingly. 'What have you been up to this time? With all your talk you've done us out of the Archduke's visit. Whatever came over you?' I persisted in my warning, however, and so at that time the visit did not take place." Sunarić recounted this story again to me after the tragic events of June 28, 1914, when Archduke Franz Ferdinand and his wife were assassinated in Sarajevo.

Chapter 10
WAR IN THE BALKANS AND SARAJEVO

Storm clouds were gathering on the horizon. We watched with growing apprehension from our office in the *Reichspost* the unfavorable developments in the international situation. Now and then there would be a warning flash of lightning, distant as yet but a signal of the approaching storm. When at the end of February, 1910, the Bulgarian royal couple paid their state visit to Zarskoje Selo, General Paprikow who accompanied them openly declared that the situation in Bosnia looked dangerous. The Christian population had been roused by the Turkish attitude in the Macedonian Vilajets so that there was every reason to fear the outbreak of hostilities. A few weeks later King Peter of Serbia arrived on an official visit to the Russian court, greeted with a loud pan-Slav fanfare from the Saint Petersburg press. A Serbo-Bulgarian pact had just been signed, closely followed by another even more spectacular agreement with the non-Slav state of Greece, a country with which relations had hitherto been anything but friendly. In November news leaked out of a secret alliance between Serbia and Montenegro, and from then on one military agreement followed another between the various Balkan states. The Balkan League was formed and the significance of this highly explosive phenomenon, never before fully realized, was suddenly all too evident. The question was now whether the great powers were sufficiently united in a common desire to prevent an explosion.

In Russia two opposing forces stood in open conflict. On the one side was the pan-Slav movement which was rapidly thrusting its way to the fore with every means at its disposal, a movement in which Russian national pride sought a European compensation for losses sustained in eastern Asia. On the other side was the official political policy directed by Isvolski, a policy which viewed the moment as inopportune for a Russian trial of strength and was prepared at least for the moment to bid for time. Thus on March 20, 1910, the Three-Point Agreement was signed. In this agreement, which was highly favorable for Austria-Hungary, both powers were committed to the following: maintenance of the status quo in the Balkans; recognition of the new regime in Turkey which had adopted the principle of equal rights for all nationalities within her territory, and finally the independence, consolidation and peaceful development of the small Balkan states. In the meanwhile, however, unconcerned with official state negotiations, the Balkan states were feverishly going ahead with underground preparations for war.

A strange episode which affected me personally was interwoven into the events of this time. On our way home from a trip to Montenegro at the beginning of August, 1910, we found my brother-in-law Anton Mangold, a harbor official, waiting for us at Trieste. He brought us the astonishing news that I had been awarded the Komtur Cross of the Bulgarian Civil Order of Merit. I was highly skeptical at first, for I had never rendered any special service to the Bulgarian state, nor indeed had I any special connection with Bulgarian affairs. All the same when I arrived in Vienna I duly found the official parchment scroll and the decoration itself, complete with casket, reposing on my desk.

Somewhat embarrassed, I went to pay my official call to the Bulgarian Ambassador. He received me most cordially and remarked with great shrewdness and amiability that his sovereign had expressed great interest in the *Reichspost* and was well acquainted with the point of view of the newspaper, for which he had the greatest admiration. It slowly dawned upon me what lay behind the mysterious decoration. The King was in need of a newspaper in Vienna upon whose support he believed he could count as the Balkan political situation developed, a newspaper of standing whose political point of view coincided approximately with his own.

The bellicose intentions of the Balkan states had been evident for months. There were open military preparations, especially in Serbia and Montenegro, and hostile feeling was directed against Austria-Hungary with even more vehemence than against Turkey.

Indeed, one had the impression at times that even the Belgrade journalists were in some doubt as to whether the war should be waged against Turkey or against Austria. The municipal council of Belgrade passed a furious resolution calling for the demolition of the former residence of Prince Eugene of Savoy as a penalty, as it were, for his having liberated Belgrade from the Turks at the head of the victorious imperial troops. For Belgrade Austria represented the arch-enemy who threatened the freedom of the South Slavs and the future of their state.

Trouble started in earnest in the Balkans in September, 1912, with skirmishes on the frontier of Montenegro and mobilization in Siberia. A recent and invaluable member of my staff was Hermenegild Wagner, the former editor of the *Bosnische Post*. Half-Croat by birth, Wagner was fully conversant with the Serbo-Croat language. He was an officer of the reserve, a man of great courage with a free and easy manner, always on the lookout for adventure. He was, moreover, a first-rate journalist and a born war correspondent. I sent Wagner to Sofia. When war finally broke out he attached himself to the Bulgarian army.

In the first phase of the fighting he succeeded in bringing off a journalistic *coup* which earned his reports world-wide recognition. It was he who discovered the Bulgarian rochade towards Jambol and published the news in a dispatch in the *Reichspost*, thus arousing the attention of the whole of Europe. This sudden change of front was the prelude to the battles of Lüleburgaz and Kirk-Kilisse, the outcome of which was so victorious for the Bulgarians. While the Turks were expecting the main attack from Adrianople, the Bulgarian troops surprised the enemy positions from the flank. So began the three-day battle of Lüleburgaz. A whole crowd of war correspondents from all the well-known European newspapers had witnessed the early operations, but, unacquainted with the language of the country, none of them had realized what was happening. Hermenegild Wagner, with his flair for military reconnaissance, was out scouting one night when he discovered a troop train back from the front. It was clear to him at once from the chalk-scribbled Cyrillic inscriptions on the cars that those same troops which he had seen at dawn that morning departing for Adrianople had then been diverted in the opposite direction. He realized immediately what the maneuver meant. A chat with a group of hard-drinking Bulgarian officers confirmed his conjecture and provided him with further valuable information. The Jambol maneuver was successful and the unprepared Turkish troops were surprised and routed at Lüleburgaz.

Wagner's comprehensive report, which appeared in the *Reichspost* on November 12 concerning the operations of the Bulgarian army, gave an exact tactical picture of the strategical development and for the first time provided the world with a clear insight into the sensational events in the Balkans which from the very beginning had given a decisive turn to the war. From then on the entire world press quoted Wagner's dispatches. In order to ensure the simultaneous publication of these reports the London *Times* had a special contract with the *Reichspost* which enabled its Vienna correspondent to work in our offices during the night after the arrival of our dispatches and so to forward his report to London without loss of time.

In its political articles too (which echoed the intentions of the Ballhausplatz) the *Reichspost* took the side of Bulgaria. In the main the relations of the newspaper with Sofia were free of opportunism; they encouraged and supported a closer contact between the two states, a contact which was to prove especially valuable in World War I. Wassil Radoslawow, the Prime Minister who had taken over the leadership of the government from the Russophile Bulgarian Democrats, sent me a special photograph of himself, accompanied by a cordial letter.

The Serbian victories had only served to intensify still further the self-assurance of the Serbian nation, and the political arrogance of Belgrade knew no bounds. It was clear to the objective observer that south of the Sava River a power had developed which had to be reckoned with. A state had now grown up across the southern frontiers of the Empire whose armies under their fine leaders had achieved outstanding victories. This state had emerged from the war not only with substantial territorial gains but, even more important, with increased international prestige, and it was understandable that its enthusiastic younger generation was seized by ambitions for the future; they were no longer content with mere daydreams. The series of attempted assassinations in Croatia-Slavonia which followed from October, 1912, on showed only too plainly how this nationalist high feeling had also taken root across the frontier.

The chaotic state of affairs was further aggravated by the pan-Slav agitations which, by the end of 1912, had reached such a degree of intensity that the Russian publicist Prince Meschtscherski warned in his paper *Graschdanin* in mid-January, 1913, against elements "whose criminal intentions it was to force Russia to intervene in the Balkan crisis." He feared that Russia was facing "the most significant and jeopardous situation in her history"; the *Nowoje Wremja*, the conservative organ of the state, was already talking about war as a patriotic necessity. Although the actual moment had not yet come, Russia nevertheless introduced partial mobilization. When, however, in May and June the dispute flared up between Serbia and Bulgaria over the war gains question, she sought to settle this by the Czar's intervention. Russia continued to stand by, all ready and armed, for Belgrade refused to recognize this arbitration and war broke out between the two former allies. It was clear now, however, that Saint Petersburg had changed its positions in the Balkans, and it was the new and rising state of Serbia which was now given preference over its former Bulgarian protégé.

The annexation of Bosnia-Herzegovina had well been accomplished, but the necessary adjustment, the political reorganization within the Empire necessitated by this move in the South Slav region had not been made. *There was no sign of any revision of the old domestic political policy in regard to the South Slavs within the Austro-Hungarian Empire.*

A people so fundamentally loyal to the Habsburgs as the Slovenes in Austria at that time deserved a better educational and public administration system than was in fact provided. On grounds of its importance to the Empire as a sea power alone (no matter how little contribution it made on paper to the state's revenues), the wide coastal area of Dalmatia would long since have warranted a broad general scheme of economic development. That nothing had in fact been undertaken in this field could hardly be explained away by the hostile attitude displayed by certain Dalmation deputies, representatives only of a thin nationalist upper stratum.

How the people themselves felt about things was demonstrated by the enthusiastic welcome the crowds gave to Dr. Karl Lueger when he landed at Split on May 9, 1909, on his official visit to Dalmatia. A Croat poem, circulated in leaflet form, praised Lueger as the man who had everywhere roused the spirit of Christianity and secured better living conditions for the working people of Vienna. The verses went on to stress the loyalty of the Christian-Social party among the working people of Dalmatia to their Habsburg Emperor and expressed the hope that their sovereign would further Lueger's aims, consider the just petitions of the Dalmatians and so improve the lot of the workers of Split.

The situation was perhaps most serious in Croatia where the Magyar overlords in Budapest had succeeded in cultivating the spirit of pessimism which had resulted in the Fiume resolution of 1905. This was the first open disavowal of the traditional loyalty of the South Slavs to the Habsburg Empire. This was all part of an unfortunate past. It was now, however, high time to work out a constructive solution of the South Slav problem, a solution long overdue and urgently recommended by the Emperor's most loyal subjects. In fact, however, nothing whatever was done; the matter was comfortably left over "for the next monarch" to deal with.

This passive attitude is perhaps somewhat easier to understand in the light of assurances by a realiable observer, Ambassador Friedrich Wiesner, that, incredible though it might seem, there was in effect no central office either in Vienna, Budapest or Agram capable of providing planned authorative information and commentary based on documentary evidence on the South Slav movement as such and its various activities. Decisions and negotiations such as they were were therefore robbed from the start of any real stability and precision as to aims and objectives.

On November 12, 1912, I received a letter full of dark forebodings from a man with an intimate knowledge of the South Slav situation. Anton Puntigam, S.J., had formerly been a professor at the Jesuit *Gymnasium* in Travnik, a school through which almost all the rising generation of the Croatian intellectuals in Bosnia-Herzegovina had passed.

"My devotion to the Church in Austria prompts me to send you these lines," he wrote. "We all consider it highly improbable that the formation of a great South Slav bloc can be prevented. There is every danger that this new empire will incorporate the Austrian South Slavs—the Croats and Slovenes. Two years ago the Croats had a strong antipathy toward the Serbs, but today much has changed: the suicidal political policy in Croatia, the neglect of Dalmatia, the constant degradation of the Catholic population in Bosnia in favor of the Serbs and Turks—not to mention the effect of the Balkan victories in particular—all these facts have now borne fruit, even for calmly thinking people.

"The great majority of the Croats (and it is said almost all the Dalmatians) have in effect left the side of Austria. They are only waiting perhaps for the right moment outwardly to demonstrate this change of course. Some Croats, particularly the clergy, are still somewhat reluctant to join the Serbs out of their loyalty to the Catholic faith. While on the one hand, however, there is much indifference among the educated Croats, on the other hand it is hoped that religious freedom could be achieved from the Serbs. 'If we can attain religious freedom,' said a Bosnian priest recently, 'then we would gladly throw in our lot with the Serbs.' It would be only foolish to indulge in false hopes in Austria: a great and real danger exists for Austria and for the Church with this loss of the South Slavs. This can only be prevented by an immediate and far-reaching change of the present policy for Croatia and the introduction of special emergency provisions before it is too late. Since the *Reichspost* is the leading newspaper in Catholic Austria, I would ask you to do everything possible to draw the attention of leading public figures to this very real danger."

In a memorable speech on May 30, 1913, Dr. Korošec, one of the leading parliamentarians of the Slovene People's party in the House of Deputies, strongly emphasized that the future of the Empire lay in the Balkans and the Adriatic. Though the Austrian South Slavs had no real leanings outside the Empire, he said, they nevertheless desired the same rights as the other nationalities; they pinned their hopes on the dynasty, a dynasty which, supported by a loyal army, was strong enough to abolish the dualistic system which at present failed to guarantee the proper fulfillment of the just national demands of the South Slavs within the framework of the Empire.

In response to a general inquiry organized by the *Reichspost* as to how events in the Balkans were expected to have a bearing on the constitutional organization of the Monarchy, Josef Schraffl, deputy of the Tyrol, sent the following reply, which accorded with the opinion the *Reichspost* had held for several years:

> Unless a completely new political course is adopted by Austria in the South Slav issue, a policy first and foremost directed by these events, it can only be feared that in these southeastern territories of the Empire the same thing will happen as has happened in Piedmont and Tuscany. If means are not found to placate the Austrian nationalities within the Empire, it is only logical that with the development of uninational states across the frontiers of the Empire, the influence and attraction of these states on their fellow nationals within our Empire is all the greater, the more powerful these states are.

The Slovene deputy and university professor Dr. Janez Krek, undoubtedly the most significant intellectual figure of his nation, declared:

"The attitude of the South Slavs, particularly of the Slovenes, to events in the Balkan peninsula is based primarily on sympathy for the Balkan peoples. For all that no representative of the South Slavs seriously supports a pan-Serb concept which aims to create a Serb empire extending to the Adriatic and up to Trieste. The political aims of the Croats and Slovenes are still strictly centered within the framework of the Habsburg Empire.... It must, however, be clearly stated that the present dissection of the Slovene and Croat nation within the Monarchy into nine provinces (apart from the Slovenes in Hungary and on the Italian border outside the Empire) *cannot possibly be maintained as a permanent solution*. Political tendencies might in due course otherwise develop which are as yet foreign to the present-day generation."

In the May issue of the *Süddeutsche Monatshefte* in 1917 Dr. Krek once again voiced his appeal for a positive solution of the problem within the Empire:

The solution of the South Slav question is more vital than ever at this moment, but a solution can never be achieved by the existing simple, not to say over-simple, formula of the status quo, seemingly useful though this is. *The Habsburg Empire is able to provide this solution,* for within her dominions are now concentrated almost all the South Slavs, with the exception of the Bulgarians, among them all the Catholic Croats and Slovenes. She must provide the solution—in her own interests. Bosnia and Herzegovina, whose peoples, though in fact citizens of the Empire, still do not belong to either of the Dual States and are denied a voice in the conduct of Empire affairs, cannot possibly be held in the present circumstances....

These statements in no way veiled the truth when they proclaimed the loyalty of the Austrian South Slavs to the Habsburg Empire, they were indeed positive in their approach to the problem, but at the same time they frankly and courageously expressed what everyone acquainted with the intellectual movements in the South Slav area already realized as the unavoidable truth. The problem was now how to persuade the aged Emperor to face the risk of the conflict which was virtually inevitable as a result of the ensuing controversy with Hungary over the question of these constitutional reforms so long overdue.

The situation in Bosnia grew critical: thirteen Serb deputies, representatives of the supposedly moderate faction, walked out of the Provincial Diet. They demanded the abolition of the "denominational" *curiae* divided, according to the old distinction, into Mahommedan, Croat (Catholic) and Serbian (Orthodox); they further demanded the right to elect the President of the Provincial Diet (hitherto appointed personally by the Emperor), and desired the resignation of Archbishop Stadler. In *Srbobran,* the Agram counterpart of the paper of the same name appearing in Chicago, Svetozar Pribicević, the power behind all the disturbances and agitations, declared that "Belgrade was the determining factor" for his political policy. The Belgrade *Mali Journal* (September 29, 1913) also declared quite openly that Serbia need have no fear of Austria-Hungary "for she is weaker than the smallest nation."

This dangerous theory was seized upon by the small nation of Serbia, herself only too ready for war, and won such popular recognition that the deputy Voja Marinković even came out in the Belgrade Skupschtina with reproaches against the Serbian government for having given in to Austria-Hungary at the end of the Balkan war, a speech greeted with great applause. It was, so he said, an established fact that Austria-Hungary was incapable of conducting a war. The speech finally came to an end with the words: "The policy adopted by Austria-Hungary brought about unification in Germany and likewise in Italy; it now only remains for her to complete the mission of the unification of the Serb nationalities. After that Austria-Hungary can then be laid aside as an exhibit in the museum of history."

Within the freedom of the United States the language used was even more radical and outspoken and the trumpet call resounded in an open appeal for prospective murderers for Sarajevo. On December 3, 1913, for instance, the following words appeared in *Srbobran*, the paper published in Chicago and circulated among the *Narodna Odbrana*, the seditious nationalist society sponsored by Belgrade:

> The Austrian heir to the throne has announced his state visit to Sarajevo for the spring. Let every Serb take note of this fact. If the Archduke comes to Bosnia, we will defray the costs... Serbs, lay your hands on every weapon you can find: knives, guns, bombs and dynamite! Now is the moment for sacred revenge! Death to the Habsburgs and everlasting glory and honor to the heroes who raise their hands against them!

This sort of language was hardly surprising, for it received encouragement enough from other quarters. Shortly after the end of the first hostilities in the Balkans an article had already appeared in his Sofia newspaper by Dr. Dantschev, the Bulgarian writer and former instructor at the Sofia military academy. He reported on an interview which took place in a hotel in Vienna in which Hartwig, the Russian ambassador at the Serbian court, had declared to him: "You must understand one thing, we have need of a strong Serbia; after Turkey the Austrian question has to be dealt with, and this is where Serbia will be our best tool. You Bulgarians will then get Macedonia and Serbia will get back her Bosnia and Herzegovina!" This crude and brutal declaration from the lips of a man schooled as a diplomat may well sound almost unbelievable, but was confirmed by Hartwig's attitude both before and after the assassination in Sarajevo.

The Serbian wildcat was crouching on its tree, all set to spring.

Spring of 1914 began comparatively peacefully. Though the tension within the Empire and in international relations had not been eased, there was a general feeling of marking time for the moment, as though in preparation for some new development. Emperor Franz Josef, now over eighty, continued to deal meticulously and punctually with the daily affairs of state with a conscienciousness deserving of the highest admiration. His strong sense of duty outweighed the physical frailities of old age and he continued to perform his duties as monarch with the same precision as ever. It was nevertheless understandable, however, that on both sides of the Leitha people looked more and more toward the Heir Apparent as the man of the future.

It was well known that Archduke Franz Ferdinand had had several draft schemes drawn up in the event of a change of monarchs, schemes prepared by various competent authorities, which largely fitted into his own personal concept of the constitutional reorganization of the Empire. There was much discussion and speculation on this subject and fabulous myths gave rise to both hopes and fears. The situation began to look clearer, particularly in Hungary where years of perpetual struggle for a just and proper electoral system had opened the eyes of the Hungarian people to democratic measures and a constructive constitutional solution of the complex problems confronting the Empire.

In this world full of expectations, of high hopes and uneasy apprehensions the news of the assassination of the Heir Apparent in Sarajevo on June 28, 1914, broke like a clap of thunder. People were paralyzed with shock and genuine grief. The dark prophecy of the American *Srbobran* had been fulfilled: the time had indeed come for the last Archduchess to put on mourning!

Much has been written about the assassination and the circumstances surrounding it. I am only concerned here with a few details, for the most part unknown.

I received the following account from Dr. Sunarić, President of the Provincial Diet:

"Once again I had warned emphatically against this visit by the Heir Apparent and sent a special dispatch to the Imperial Minister of Finance, Bilinski, who was responsible for the Bosnian arrangements, urging him to use his influence to prevent the visit. I knew exactly what to expect of the pan-Serb irredentists; I knew that they would stop at nothing and would certainly resort to murder itself should the opportunity present itself. No one could have had a better knowledge of these people than we Croats, for we had witnessed at first hand the lawlessness of the pan-Serb chauvinism in the history of our country and had ourselves fought against it.

"It was our fate that no one really believed us and attributed our warnings to the traditional strong contrast between the Catholic Croats and a nationalist Serb Orthodoxy. Whether as a result of my own repeated warnings of the current situation there, or perhaps of some sinister foreboding of his own, I know that the Heir Apparent undertook this journey against his better judgment. I know that on the very last day he had still hoped, unlike him though it was, for a counter-command from the Emperor relieving him from the duty of attending the maneuvers in Bosnia. Both the Heir Apparent and his wife came to Bosnia fully aware of the danger. Everything apparently went off well, the maneuvers were conducted to everyone's satisfaction and the journey was completed according to plan.

"The evening before the procession into Sarajevo a gala dinner was given in Bad Illidze, just outside the city, in honor of the royal visitors. I was myself among those invited. After dinner the Archduke had the tables cleared and moved informally among the guests, obviously in the best of spirits. A small group of the male guests, including myself, had gathered at the left hand of the banquet table. On the other side of the room the Duchess had drawn several of the ladies into animated conversation. She suddenly noticed me in the distance and came laughingly toward me, wagging her finger in mock reproach. 'Well, Dr. Sunarić,' she said warmly, her face radiant with pleasure. 'It seems that you were mistaken after all, for it is by no means as you are always telling us. We have been received everywhere in the country—and the Serb population is here no exception—with such genuine warmth and friendliness that we are both quite overjoyed.' Whereupon I replied: 'Your Highness, I only pray to God that when I have the honor to see you tomorrow evening you will be able to repeat these words to me. It would be a weight off my mind, a great weight.' The next day I was to see the lifeless bodies of the Duchess and her husband."

Chapter 11
FRANZ FERDINAND

Much has been written about Franz Ferdinand. Willfully or unwittingly, through prejudice, malice or sheer ignorance, the character of probably the most remarkable Habsburg since Josef II has been largely misrepresented. A clear unbiased picture of the true character of the heir to the Habsburg throne is, however, provided by two men with perhaps the most intimate knowledge of both the Archduke's role in public affairs and of his private family life.

Alexander von Brosch was the Archduke's aide-de-camp and the first chief of his Military Bureau from 1905 to 1911; he was his most intimate confidant during this significant period of political activity. In a strictly confidential letter written to General Woinowich, one of the greatest soldiers of the old imperial army, Brosch analyzed, clearly and objectively, the character of Franz Ferdinand with all its virtues and defects. This letter (used by Leopold von Chlumecky as an appendix to his documentary work *Erzherzog Franz Ferdinands Wirken und Wollen*, 1929) was written two years after Brosch resigned from the Archduke's service to take over the command of the famous Second Regiment of the Tiroler Kaiserjäger and one year before he himself was killed in action. No prince and no statesman could wish for a more fitting testimonial.

Colonel Karl Bardolff succeeded Brosch in the Archduke's service and remained his close friend and adviser up until the murder at Sarajevo. In his autobiography Bardolff is largely concerned with Franz Ferdinand and succeeds in giving an authentic impression of the personality, life and political aims of this controversial figure. The book was written during the Hitler regime when it would have been infinitely easier to show the heir to the Habsburg throne in an unfavorable light, the more so since the author was himself for a time not without National-Socialist leanings. Franz Ferdinand emerges, however, as an outstanding figure, and Bardolff's opinion, for all its objectivity, is charged with a very real warmth.

It is not my place to add to these exhaustive descriptions. I would, however, just like to mention some of my personal experiences and one or two pieces of firsthand knowledge, if only to supplement the information available about this historical figure whose own tragic destiny was so closely bound up with that of the people of Austria-Hungary, of Europe and indeed of the whole world.

As a young man Franz Ferdinand was threatened with consumption, his younger brother was in fact regarded as the actual heir to the throne, and he was relegated, as a sick man, to that second-rate treatment at the court which he never forgot or forgave all his life. He took no pains to conceal his bitter contempt of the superficial court life, with its ceremony and rigorous Spanish court etiquette, and he was impatient of red-tape bureaucracy in any form. He made many enemies in consequence, especially among the powerful court hierarchy, and was accordingly subjected, together with his wife, to almost unbelievable indignities and humiliations. He loved above all to dress informally and live at home in the country as a simple man, enjoying nothing more than to smoke a leisurely pipe with his good old friend and neighbor the parish priest at Maria Taferl. Had he been born an ordinary mortal and not an Archduke of Austria and heir to a great dynasty, he would certainly have encountered much friendly appreciation and respect. At times, however, his temperament and disregard for outward form ran away with him, though he would do his best to make amends afterward.

Critics of Franz Ferdinand were quite incapable of understanding that the heir to the throne felt a very real need to escape from the formalities of the superficial court life. Furthermore it seems that there were few chivalrous people among the high-ranking society who could genuinely respect the motives of this man who, in order to win the woman he loved, was prepared to do battle, if not with the dragon, at least with the recognized traditions of the House of Habsburg and the monstrous Spanish court etiquette. His marriage was a model of Christian family happiness, but he was forced to renounce the right of succession for his descendants.[1]

I myself was among the few hundred Austrians who, with a few thousand wild Communists from Germany, were herded together in the concentration camp in Dachau. So were the two sons of Archduke Franz Ferdinand. They shared our fate with us and were a constant example of courage and faith. In the highly dangerous commando "Kiesgrube" run by a tormentor by the name of Sterzer[2] they still remained unbroken, cheerful and undaunted, noblemen of the aristocracy in the true sense, despite their torn and filthy clothing. They would squat together with us in the dust of the roadside during our brief recreation period and share the few lumps of sugar which we had somehow managed to get hold of. There was no one in the whole camp who did not speak of "the Hohenbergs" with the greatest respect. They were pointed out with affection and pride to every newcomer.

Only the best stock can produce such offspring. Those who had once been so opposed to this marriage were proved wrong once and for all, just like those others who had been only too willing to criticize the character and actions of the Heir Apparent. They saw Franz Ferdinand as an intolerant fanatic, a man of coarse habits, a brutal despot with dark moods; yet this morose tyrant, this reactionary clerical delighted in cultivating flowers, was an enthusiastic patron of the arts and an authority on folklore. As his understanding of art and of its preservation increased, he graduated from the status of a private collector to become the guardian of valuable public art treasures, fine old buildings and paintings of the Austrian countryside and towns.

Much in Franz Ferdinand's own way of life had been adopted from his parents: the moral and religious standards, the sound active spirit and the strong sense of duty.

---

[1] Children of a "morganatic" marriage, according to the Habsburg family statutes, were excluded from dynastic succession. Franz Ferdinand's wife was a Countess Chotek by birth. After her marriage she was given the title of Duchess of Hohenberg.

[2] Sterzer was himself a prisoner, not a "political" but an ordinary criminal. It was part of the concentration camp system to appoint criminal inmates with the requisite streak of bestiality as "bosses" over their unfortunate fellow prisoners.

Only in the light of these circumstances and connections, scarcely known or heeded by the world in general, is it really possible fully to understand the personality of Franz Ferdinand. The family life in the Belvedere with its balanced routine and natural informality was also based on these same values. Franz Ferdinand was an early riser; when not prevented by important affairs of state, his first visit was inevitably to the nursery. A hilarious hour would then follow, in which the children would also be encouraged, half-jokingly, half-seriously, to discuss the duties and work which lay before them for the day. Both parents would then often have breakfast together with the children. The family would be reunited, even when guests were present, at the luncheon table. In contrast to the custom in other court households, it was evident in the Belvedere that here Franz Ferdinand's wife was mistress of her own house, a real housewife who devoted herself wholeheartedly to her various tasks, cared for the welfare of her servants and kept her own housekeeping accounts.

Franz Ferdinand adhered to a strict working program each day. He heartily disliked inactivity in any form and never idled his time. Even when he was out in his gardens marking trees which were to be transplanted or felled, he would have his Hungarian teacher accompany him so as to take advantage of the time for his daily hour of conversation. He had no talent for languages and these practice conversations in Hungarian were a very real burden to him, but he set his teeth and grimly pursued these studies with determination almost to the day of his death. Only something quite unexpected could make him put off these daily conversations, which he viewed as a special duty just as important as the study of constitutional law. His orderly method of dealing with the many thick files and dispatches and with his correspondence was indicative of his character and working habits. He always insisted upon dealing with these absolutely promptly within forty-eight hours.

A fanatic and a clerical reactionary? He was a Catholic, true to his creed who took his faith seriously, a man who in his Christian family life and his personal moral integrity certainly represented a strange phenomenon in the worm-eaten society of his time. His sense of responsibility and the high ideal he cherished of the monarchy as an institution were determined by this same faith. Nothing angered the Archduke more than to encounter too little sense of their official responsibility in public figures or to hear tales of bribery, corruption or the misuse of state funds.

Franz Josef had celebrated his Diamond Jubilee as emperor and statesmen and politicians were reminded that a change of monarchs could be only a matter of time.

One day Dr. Gessmann entrusted me with a delicate mission. It was my task diplomatically to sound, through Brosch in the Belvedere, the attitude of the Archduke toward a formal authoritative revocation of the oath of renunciation with which before his marriage he had given up the right to the Habsburg crown for his descendants; the matter thus involved the revocation of an act of the utmost constitutional significance. Although Hungary had not recognized this renunciation, it was unequivocally valid in Austria. Dr. Gessmann empowered me to inform the Belvedere that the Christian-Social party was prepared in every way to sponsor the revocation of this pledge, whose moral foundation appeared to them doubtful anyway. It would not have been difficult at the right moment to put through an act of legislation to cover this issue.

In the course of my difficult mission I spoke with Brosch and asked him to lay the matter before the Heir Apparent at what he considered to be the appropriate moment. I soon received the Archduke's answer which ran as follows:

"The Habsburg crown is a crown of thorns and no one who is not born to this crown should seek to wear it. An annulment of the act of renunciation can never be considered."

I had only the highest esteem for these classic words. The question was never raised again.

The Obrenovićs were still ruling in Belgrade and there was as yet no sign of the irredentist specter in Croatia when Franz Ferdinand first discerned what every other responsible authority declined to recognize: he realized the urgent necessity in the near future of revising the policy of the state as a whole in regard to the bloc formed by the South Slav nationalities. The Magyar oligarchy across the Leitha may well have wielded the power and commanded the police force, but it had not the Magyar nation behind it (these did not even constitute the majority of the Hungarian population). The Magyar overlords could continue to challenge the state as a whole and its legislation grew more and more out of control, but there was no one there who recognized the vital need of reforming the 1867 *Ausgleich* and who was prepared to fight for the same rights for the non-Magyar national elements in Hungary. Franz Ferdinand stepped into the breach. Was force to be used, and bayonets drawn to scare off the latter-day Ludwig Kossuths? He has been credited with such plans: an impetuous phrase perhaps indicated such a course, but it was certainly never considered in earnest.

There had been a whole series of tentative plans drawn up through the years at his request, with suggestions as to Franz Ferdinand's attitude on assuming his high office. Old Baron Johann von Chlumetzky speaks of conversations held with the Archduke many years before in which the latter had discussed the possibility, in the event of a change of monarchs, of the abolition of the existing dualistic system within the six-months period accorded by the Hungarian constitution for the taking of the coronation oath, and the establishment of an empire united as one single state. Probably because old Chlumetzky, shrewd as he was, advised against such a scheme, it is not to be found so strongly advocated in the text of later drafts. One of the authorities invited to contribute such a draft plan was the Vienna professor of constitutional law Dr. Turba. Polzer-Hoditz, a high official under Emperor Karl, also mentions such a plan. From literature dealing with Franz Ferdinand, a reform program is known published by Theodor von Sosnosky (*Erzherzog Franz Ferdinand*, Oldenburg-Verlag, 1926). In his notes Heinrich Lammasch mentions that the Archduke, who greatly respected this eminent lawyer, gave him a series of manuscripts to look at from Ottokar Czernin, Conrad von Hötzendorf, Sektionschef Spitzmüller and Professor Harold Steinacker. The manuscripts dealt with constitutional and other pertinent questions.

These plans were doubtlessly subjected to some amendments in the course of years. The plan which to my mind most closely corresponded to the Archduke's own last intentions was that drafted by Baron Johann Andreas von Eichhoff and published in the *Reichs-*

post on March 28, 1926. For Eichhoff's proposals were conceived as the result of a discussion held only two months before Sarajevo while he was staying at Miramar as a guest of the Archduke. Eichhoff comments on the contents of this state program:

"According to Franz Ferdinand's draft, the boundaries of the territories in which each of the racial elements in Austria-Hungary comprise the compact, indigenous, settled population should now be carefully defined. Where these boundaries were doubtful, they should be examined by means of a plebiscite carried out according to a simple and just system. The inhabitants of these regions would then be given complete autonomy; according to the constitution their national liberties should only suffer such restrictions as would enable everyone freely to deposit the fruits of his labors all over the Empire and correspondingly obtain all raw materials from Empire sources. No borders for trade and commerce between the various united states of Greater Austria. Tariff union, unity in the railroad system, unity in the eyes of other foreign nations, and—to this very purpose—military unity!"

In connection with this program Eichhoff published the manifesto which the new Emperor and King would have issued at the beginning of his reign. In an introductory commentary on this manifesto, which is obviously the product of co-operation between the Heir Apparent and Eichhoff, he says: "The spirit and wording of this proclamation redound to the honor of its author." The proclamation (in which the heir to the throne is referred to as "Franz II") in fact constitutes a document combining tenacity and fixity of purpose with wise moderation. The most significant passage runs as follows:

"We desire to observe and firmly to defend the old-established constitutional institutions and the state system of justice in which, according to the law, every citizen has the right of participation. In the interests of the welfare and prosperity of all peoples throughout the Empire we feel it to be our most urgent task and duty to secure their unification in one state and to establish their harmonious collaboration according to just principles on a clear and stable basis which, unclouded by separatist tendencies, stand above doubt and opposition. In the Imperial Constitution the ambiguities must therefore first be removed which at present exist between the laws of Austria and of Hungary valid for the common affairs of the Empire and which, in view of their inconsistency, render the taking of the prescribed oath on the Constitution impossible.

"As pledge of our sacred duty as sovereign it is therefore our purpose to ratify with the solemn coronation oath the unequivocal points of the Imperial Constitution simultaneously with the basic rights and liberties of all members of the Empire.

"In order to render this possible our respective governments will introduce the necessary measures without delay.

"We shall protect and defend with all our strength the unity of the Empire in the eyes of the world, upon which depends its position as a great power, and the provinces united under our scepter, vouchsafed as indivisible and inseparable by virtue of the Pragmatic Sanction.

"We shall ensure at all costs that the firm structure of the armed forces shall remain intact from one-sided political influences. We view our loyal army as protector and trusted weapon, not only for the maintenance of domestic security and order, but especially for the fulfillment of our most ardent wish—the continuation of the peace-loving policy of our late revered uncle.

"Since all nations belonging to our Empire should have equal rights of participation in the common affairs of the state, this very equality of rights demands that every race should be guaranteed its right of national development within the framework of the common interests of the Empire; all nationalities, all classes, trades and professions should be entitled to protect their own interests by means of just and proper electoral systems, where these have not already been introduced."

In his comprehensive work *Magyarország Kálváriája* on the part played by Franz Ferdinand in the Hungarian crisis and the battle for universal equal suffrage in Hungary, Josef Kristóffy, a witness worth listening to, remarks in his account of the relations of the Archduke with Hungary (p. 414):

It really was his intention to introduce changes in the dualistic constitutional institutions... he wanted to put everything through by constitutional means, as far as possible through the parliament, even perhaps by plebiscite. Franz Ferdinand sought this revision because he realized that, in view of the changing circumstances, the existing dualistic constitution could no longer guarantee the position of the Empire as a great power.

To my way of thinking, Kristóffy had with these words revealed the real truth. The Archduke had certainly entertained no thoughts of revolutionary plans of action against Hungary during the last years of his life. The passive, forbearing methods adopted by Franz Josef during the past five years had slowly worn down the resistance of the Magyar chauvinists; the uneasy evasion of all the Hungarian party leaders, even Tisza, of an honest electoral reform plan; the various covert and open overtures even from the ranks of the extremists, the bartering attempts at reconciliation, all these factors had suggested that more could be achieved by the accepted means of patience, perseverance and absolute firmness of purpose in the pursuance of the essential reform aims.

These aims were:

1. To secure a permanent unity for the Empire, the natural basis of which should be an inviolable economic unity.

2. Real universal equal suffrage, also in Hungary.

3. The grouping of the respective nationalities in federal national autonomies within an Austrian and a Hungarian state with the continued maintenance of national cross-connections.

This was a Greater-Austrian program which would have left Hungarian experts in constitutional law with a fitting say in affairs. After the foundations had been laid it would have been for state decrees of the greatest solemnity and constitutional significance to introduce the new order. Kardinal Piffl, who was held in the greatest esteem by both Franz Ferdinand and his wife, told me about this in a confidential talk in the summer of 1913.

The Archduke planned to proclaim the new reform by means of an act of state of the highest ecclesiastical significance and solemnity: *an Imperial coronation in St. Stephan's Cathedral*, to be followed by the royal coronation in Budapest and another in Prague. The pomp and splendor of these ceremonies would be a fitting setting for the important constitutional change.

Franz Ferdinand's attitude in all critical affairs of foreign policy was characteristic. Much as he valued General Conrad (the Chief of Staff) as a soldier, he opposed his plans of preventive war against Italy, the suspect ally, during the annexation crisis and the Scutari conflict. His aim was the establishment of a League of the Three Emperors which he not only viewed as the best safeguard of future peace in Europe, but as offering the requisite security ensuring each participant great power the freedom necessary for domestic reform, the best weapon against revolutionary elements from within.

A testimony is at this point due, a testimony doubly important in the light of contemporary history. It comes from the Russian General von Bünting, one of the several German Balts who by virtue of their personal qualities had risen to high and honorable office in imperial Russia. This officer was sent by Czar Nicholas II with a mission to Vienna, as newly-appointed colonel of the Twenty-sixth Bugsch Dragoons, a regiment of which Archduke Franz Ferdinand was colonel-in-chief. What is given below is an extract from the notes which I was given by General von Bünting for publication in the *Reichspost;* I would like to preserve the most interesting and important passages from the fate of most newspaper articles which are just forgotten with time, for they are of lasting value.[3] Bünting reported:

When at the beginning of May, 1907, I was received in audience by the Czar as newly-appointed regimental commander, he said: "I am especially glad that it is you who have received this appointment. I know you speak German. I am particularly anxious" (in Russian "it is very important to me") "that at this moment the somewhat too formal relations between the Colonel-in-Chief, the Archduke, and the regiment should be improved. For this reason I want you to go to Vienna, present yourself to the Archduke and do everything in your power to foster these relations. I hope you will be met in this by the Archduke himself, and wish you every success in this mission."

My visit was officially announced in Vienna and I received an invitation to stay for ten days as the guest of His Apostolic

[3] *Reichspost* March 31, 1929, No. 90, Vol. XXXVI; April 7, 1929, No. 96, Vol. XXXVI.

Majesty. I rather feel that certain preliminary diplomatic moves had led to this honor.

The General made the following comments in explanation of further statement:

"I have read many commentaries upon this era, but in none of them did I find any reference to an episode to the truth of which I hereby testify.

"A document even exists, can at least exist, but is, however, in Bolshevist hands. This document is a report submitted by me to the chief of the Grand Imperial Headquarters Count Fredericks dated at the beginning of June, 1907. The report was prepared at the personal request of Emperor Franz Josef and was laid before the Czar by Count Fredericks. Nicholas II read the report attentively and locked it up in his desk with the following words to Count Fredericks: 'Extremely interesting and important, this report—but my Foreign Minister (Isvolski) is not going to hear anything about it, that's certain. This is—*my* policy.' Count Fredericks repeated these words to me in the fall of 1907."

I would especially remind the reader of one truth: in 1907 there were genuine efforts not only on the part of both rulers but also on the part of Archduke Franz Ferdinand, to establish and foster the best possible friendly relations between both countries.

So much has been written about the differences and friction between both courts and the conflict between diplomatic representatives of both empires which finally led to the catastrophe of World War I that it is a real duty to prove that there was a time during which another spirit prevailed at both courts and that the tragic destiny of both countries could have been otherwise.

The reception accorded to the Russian general in Vienna was markedly friendly and attentive. The audience was of long duration. The conversation centered at first on military affairs, the Russo-Japanese campaign and various technical experiences. The Archduke then lapsed into silence for a few moments, as though to give added emphasis to his next words. Then came the great political idea which lay closest to Franz Ferdinand's heart:

"I must tell you the following so that you should know my

attitude toward your country and toward your Czar. Tell everyone in Russia with whom you may have a chance to speak of me
that I am a friend of Russia and her Czar. No Austrian soldier
has ever yet borne arms against Russia in combat and I should consider myself no man of honor should it ever be otherwise so long
as I have anything to say in the matter...."

Bünting had further opportunities for discussions with the
Archduke during the days he spent as his guest, and as a result he
says: "The relationship between the Archduke and myself grew
ever warmer and more intimate. The Archduke could not have
been a more charming and considerate host." At the end of May
Bünting was received in audience by the Emperor himself at the
latter's request. From the conversation, which lasted almost half
an hour, the Russian visitor comments especially upon the following pointedly political declaration by Franz Josef:

"We are Russia's neighbors and must be good neighbors.
Friends—despite many!" He laid particular stress on the last two
words. "Convey these words of mine to your Czar; tell him when
you return everything I and the Archduke, the Heir Apparent, have
said to you here. I earnestly desire that your Czar should be informed of this, not in the paper-and-ink way of the diplomats, but
in this confidential way."

Franz Ferdinand asked Bünting for exact details of the audience; he then spoke of the uneasy situation in the Balkans and
said: "Russia can look at things from a distance, but for us the fire
is burning at our own doorstep. We are engaged all the time in
trying to put out the flames—and it's a hard and thankless task. It is
dangerous to play with fire! God help us if it gets really out of
hand—the whole of Europe would be in danger! So now, General,
you must tell the Czar everything, everything His Majesty and I
have said to you, particularly my first words to you on making
your acquaintance. I repeat these words to you now: I am a
friend of Russia. Your Czar must hear this, in this way, not in the
'paper-and-ink way of the diplomats,' as His Majesty so aptly expressed it. Yes, we must be good neighbors. What a brilliant concept had been the League of the Three Emperors—Russia, ourselves
and Germany! What power!"

"These prophetic words of the Archduke still resound in my ears. I assure the reader," emphasized the General in his statement, "that I am in the position to quote these words of Archduke Franz Ferdinand, as well as all our later talks and everything Emperor Franz Josef said to me with absolute accuracy, for I made notes of the exact words used every day and thus was able to transcribe them into my report submitted in mid-June, some fifteen days later."

Eighteen months later General Bünting returned to Vienna on a diplomatic mission and was received once again by Archduke Franz Ferdinand, who in due course reverted to the former conversations. This time too the Archduke arranged an audience with Franz Josef who duly received the Russian visitor in Schönbrunn. The old monarch spoke with a gravity, urgency and warmth which if anything exceeded that of his earlier message to Czar Nicholas. Franz Josef asked Bünting to convey to his "Imperial brother" that the peace of Europe, the welfare of all peoples, demanded that they should find the way to a mutual direct understanding. This time, however, Vienna waited in vain for an answer. It has never really been ascertained just what events at the Russian court played a part here. Even the personal letter written by Franz Josef to the Czar in 1910 was to no purpose. Nicholas II, well-intentioned though he was, was too weak a personality to withstand the increasing pressure of the various movements in Russia which ever since the Balkan states had begun arming, had been agitating more and more stridently for war. All the efforts of the Emperor and Franz Ferdinand to avert the catastrophe over the head of Foreign Minister Aehrenthal were of no avail.

I remained in personal correspondence with Bünting right up to his death at the beginning of the 'thirties, and the photograph he sent me in token of his friendship is among my most treasured possessions. He was a fine man with a charming personality, a gentleman of the old school to his fingertips.

One day in 1913 Colonel Bardolff, that loyal friend and servant of the Archduke, told me of a recent interview he had had with Franz Ferdinand. He was still visibly deeply impressed by what had taken place. Some days before, in the course of his duties, he had presented a military-political report on the European situation to the Archduke. During the discussion of this report, which lasted over an hour and a half and which led up to the inevitable consequences of the general situation, the Archduke had grown more and more restless, and when Bardolff finally declared quite openly that in the light of the facts a war against Russia could not be avoided he had sprung up, his face scarlet: "Never! Never! Are we to push each other off the throne? Never!" Bardolff himself was deeply moved as he told me this. These words of Archduke Franz Ferdinand made a lasting impression upon me. The incident is mentioned in Bardolff's memoirs.

The very day Franz Ferdinand was murdered in Sarajevo I found on my desk an article by a scholar whose opinion was greatly valued by the Archduke, the director of the Imperial Court and State Archives, Sektionschef Schlitter. He had compiled an article based on comprehensive documentary material showing the close ties which had bound Russia and Austria-Hungary all through the changes of history.

Much as Franz Ferdinand desired a new League of the Three Emperors and friendly though his relations were with the German Emperor Wilhelm, he thoroughly distrusted the Italian partner in the Triple Alliance who made no attempt whatever to curb the patently irredentist activities in Dalmatia, Trieste and Trento. The political horizon was darkening ominously and it became increasingly clear that in the event of open hostilities the loyalty of Italy would be put to a dangerous test. In political circles centered around Dr. Gessmann there was much discussion as to how the critical relations between the two states could be improved.

It was obvious that the last moment had come for any such move. Italian espionage activities in the Adriatic littoral had assumed grotesque forms and Italy's aspirations in Albania were evident. Conrad von Hötzendorf had grounds enough for his plan for a preventive war against Italy. Yet realistic thinkers such as Gessmann and his parliamentary friends were opposed to such a scheme. So Gessmann asked me to intimate to the Archduke how valuable it would be if he could break the ice between Austria and Italy.

In the Vatican decree *Non expedit* Pope Pius IX permitted Catholic sovereigns to visit the Quirinal[4] only after a formal state visit to the Vatican. The House of Habsburg had hitherto felt itself bound by this ruling. The Vatican ruling (a reminder of the violation of Papal sovereignty by force by the Italian state and its dynasty in 1870) amounted in fact to non-recognition of the new state of Italy as successor of the Papal States. For this reason state visits in Rome by the Habsburgs had ceased since 1870. Nor had the alliance itself served to bring about a personal contact between the two ruling houses. Needless to say this gave great offense in official and political quarters in Italy. Gessmann now conceived the following plan in an attempt to heal this dangerous breach in the Triple Alliance. If the Archduke were prepared to lend his support, the Christian-Social party, as the political representative of Catholic Austria, would in its turn be prepared to do its best at the Vatican toward the establishment of a modus vivendi. I cautiously passed this proposal on, well aware that this was a matter of the greatest delicacy which would involve the subtlest political maneuvers. The answer which I received a few days later from Colonel Bardolff in the name of Archduke Franz Ferdinand was an emphatic "No." The House of Habsburg was a Catholic dynasty and it was not for it to take the initiative in an attempt to change the basic legal attitude adopted by the Vatican.

This was like Franz Ferdinand. He was capable of combating destructive forces directed against the state with a vehement determination, tenacity and grim inaccessibility, but he was not open by nature to surprise moves, breaks with tradition or vigorous initiative. His strong, often temperamental personality was tempered by his balanced Habsburg character which moderated all his thoughts and actions.

In the sunset glow of the old Austrian Empire the figure of Franz Ferdinand stands out as the personification of the Greater-Austrian idea. He died for this idea. It meant, beyond political

4 The Palazzo del Quirinale (called after the Mons Quirinalis, one of the original seven hills of Rome) was built in 1574 and until 1870 served as the Papal residence. Until 1946 it was used as the palace of the Italian royal family and since then has been the seat of the President of the Republic.

reality and constitutional organization, the promise of peace and freedom for the small nations living in the Danubian region of Central Europe.

Chapter 12
FOR THE FATHERLAND

The assassins of Sarajevo had not acted on the spur of the moment. They had planned their murder in cold deliberation and knew exactly what they were doing—and so did many others along with them. The crime they committed was only the culmination of years of conspiracy and seditious intrigue in Belgrade. They had done away with the heir to the throne of the Habsburg Empire across the frontier, they had killed the very man on whom were pinned the high hopes of the small nationalities within Austria-Hungary and whose aim it had been to create a new structure for Central Europe. In killing Franz Ferdinand they had aimed at the heart of the Habsburg Empire.

The assassination roused the shocked horror of the whole civilized world. The source of the crime was well known. An immediate reprisal, a punitive expedition undertaken without delay, would have been understood and accepted abroad. But despite all her experiences over the past turbulent decade in this volcanic area, the great Empire of Austria-Hungary was not prepared for an immediate military action. It was felt that it would be unwise to embark upon a punitive action only insufficiently prepared, for a military debacle would only provide the enemy with fresh laurels. And so nothing was done, nothing happened for a whole month.

This interval should have been utilized for diplomatic negotiations to establish the exact facts in justification of Austria's position. This omission was to be paid for dearly. The interval gave the enemy a heaven-sent opportunity to concentrate its forces. The first universal recognition that a crime which threatened the peace of the whole of Europe cried for redress in the name of moral justice, a justice applicable to all nations, slowly receded into the background in the light of political considerations.

On July 28, following the unsatisfactory reply received from Belgrade to the ultimatum, war was declared against Serbia; on July 30 Russia started to mobilize and so took the decisive step. Austria-Hungary began conscription the next day and twenty-four hours later Germany declared war on Russia.

It is not my intention to write a history of World War I. I am merely concerned with my own personal experiences during that terrible epoch, my personal impressions of those years viewed in the light of my devotion to my country and in the consciousness of my own responsibility.

Criminal force had been used. Throughout the past ten years the Habsburg Monarchy had had to contend with the activities of the trouble-makers in the small adjoining state of Serbia. The whole of Europe had borne witness to the provocations which Austria-Hungary had countered with warnings and with a long-suffering forbearance in the interests of preserving peace. This situation had been viewed with grave concern by friends of the Monarchy. Her rivals and opponents interpreted her attitude as proof of her weakness, and her active enemies were only encouraged to continue with their terrorist activities. The climax had now been reached in Sarajevo.

The state is after all also a human organism and as such cannot exist without its honor and due respect of its fundamental rights. The Habsburg Empire was more than just a family concern of a dynasty or a ruling caste. It formed the vital structure of a living community of nations and it was its task to protect the national existence and liberties of the small nations within its framework. What was more, it was the Habsburg Empire which guarded the balance of power in Europe. It was our moral obligation to defend this common house—no matter what defects the old building might have—and when others came in in support of those guilty of the crime of Sarajevo we ourselves had to take up arms in the name of God in defense of the precious heritage committed to our charge.

This was the line of reasoning which seemed to me clear and convincing at that moment and which guided us in our journalistic work on the *Reichspost*. And millions of Austrians thought just the same way. It was heart-warming to see the outburst of real Austrian loyalty in all classes and all nations within the Empire.

I myself had always believed implicitly in the strength and virility of the Monarchy, but I was nevertheless overcome by this manifestation of genuine devotion to the Fatherland which was to be found in every province as the call resounded to rally to the Empire's cause. I can still hear and see the vast crowds in the very core of a Social Democratic district of Vienna on the day war was declared against Serbia. There were throngs of working-class men and youths in the streets. They had already composed their own war song set to a popular tune and the rough singing could be heard far into the night. Many of these people living on the outskirts of the city were Czechs, and the Czech newspapers were loud in their enthusiastic assertion of the loyalty of their nation to their sovereign and their Empire.

This was the true Austria which had revealed itself during those summer days, the Austria which was to stand firm against many ordeals to come.

In the midst of the tension and anxiety of those troubled days and my strenuous work on the *Reichspost* I was faced with a terrible personal tragedy. My wife suddenly fell ill and died. She was indeed too good for me, and so God took her to Himself. Her death was an almost unbearable loss.

For a long time I made a little pilgrimage every day to Hietzing, where a bed of flowers had come to mean the dearest plot of earth to me.

Life seemed to have lost all meaning and I volunteered for service at the front. My wish was not to be granted, for by intervention of the Prime Minister it was declared that, at the express wish of the government, the editor of the *Reichspost* could not be released for military service.

Colonel Bardolff did, however, at least arrange for me to visit the eastern front, a visit which was instructive in many ways.

Berlin was in the meantime greatly concerned to strengthen Italy in her neutrality and to prevent her at all costs from coming into the war on the side of the Entente Powers. These admirable intentions were pursued with undue nervous energy and precipitation. It was intended that Austria should pay for this neutrality with territorial cessions in South Tyrol. Feeling ran high in Austria over the methods of negotiation, especially since the concessions in question were very considerable: the cession of the Italian-speaking region of South Tyrol known to the Italians as Alto Adige, the internationalization of Trieste and the dividing of the spheres of interest in Albania where Italy was to receive the southern half which included the harbor of Valona.

One evening a leading deputy of the Imperial Diet whom I held in the highest esteem came to pay me a visit.[1] He was an Austrian-Italian, and I had known him well since his student days. He had founded the Italian students' association Unione Cattolica Italiana at the University of Vienna and I had often had dealings with him as a deputy during the course of my work. His relations with the *Reichspost* were most friendly. He lost no time in coming to the point of his visit.

"Tell me quite frankly," he asked me, "what does the Austrian government really want? What are they going to do in the Ballhausplatz? Are they going to give up South Tyrol or are they determined to defend it? This is how things stand: 95 per cent of the Italian population in South Tyrol naturally gravitate in their own interests toward Austria to whom they have belonged for cen-

---

[1] The visitor was Dr. Alcide de Gasperi, at that time a deputy of the Imperial Diet. After World War I he became a deputy in the parliament in Rome, a member of the Partito Popolare Italiano (Italian People's party) founded in 1919 by Luigi Sturzo. He later succeeded Sturzo as party secretary. After the downfall of fascism in Italy, de Gasperi was one of those who founded the new People's party, the Democrazia Cristiana, of which he became the leader in 1944. In this position he headed the government coalition led by the Christian Democrats from 1945 to 1953. As Italian Prime Minister it was he who, on September 5, 1946, signed the "Paris Agreement" with the Austrian Foreign Minister at that time, Dr. Karl Gruber. This agreement envisaged autonomy for South Tyrol as compensation for Austria's renunciation of her territorial claims. This treaty went into effect on January 28, 1948, but up to the present day certain essential points have still remained unfulfilled, so that there is increasing justification for Austrian (and South Tyrolese) complaints that the sacrifice of territorial claims has not been fully compensated.

turies. Take our schoolteachers, for example, who have after all
a great influence among the people. Coming from Austrian schools,
they know very well that they will not remain in their posts if
South Tyrol is ceded to Italy; they know that they will be replaced
by Italian teachers. Nor have our mayors the slightest desire to
exchange the municipal independence accorded them in Austria for
the role of mayor in Italy. And as for our parish priests, how can
they possibly turn round and declare that they have always been
irredentists striving for unity with Italy—Italy which even today is
still in conflict with the Vatican! And what about the broad mass
of the population, the wine-growers and fruit farmers for whom
Italy offers only a poor market and whose economic interests are
closely bound up with Austria? What is going to happen to all
these people? Tell me that! You ought to know what they're going
to do!"

Whereupon I told him the view of the Emperor himself, a
view which had never changed. I could, however, not deny his
charge that the diplomats, driven by Germany, were pursuing a
different course. "Then you can hardly expect us South Tyrolese
to risk our lives for you," he said. "Just consider the responsibility
we deputies have toward our people in South Tyrol!" We shook
hands as good friends as he left me, but I knew that honest men
and women in South Tyrol had said farewell to us through him.
The reasons were only too clear.

On May 23, 1915, the Duke of Avarna conveyed the declaration of the Italian government to the Emperor that from then on
Italy was at war with Austria. This must have been a painful duty
for the Duke who was a convinced adherent of the Triple Alliance.

The opening stages of this war will go down in history as one
of the strangest introductions to a military conflict. As I learned
later from Field Marshal Boroević, the only defense that Austria
had prepared against the expected attack on what was presumably
to be the main front (the gateway to Trieste along the ridge of the
mountainous plateau of the Doberdo) consisted of a system of
trenches constructed by inexperienced troops of the reserve, and
in twenty-four antiquated artillery posts at intervals along the rocky
slope and manned by these same troops. The Italians could easily

have made short work of this "defense." But no attack came. The enemy advanced slowly in cautious preparation. At this juncture Boroević arrived on the scene with his army which had been withdrawn from the Serbian theater of operations.

"We had no idea as we came up where the enemy was located," he told me afterward. "At every station the further west we came we expected to be given the signal to get out of the train and to receive details of the enemy positions. But nothing happened! To our great astonishment the train went on as far as Görz. Cadorna had apparently such a fundamental respect for the Austrians that he failed to strike at the right moment. And then it was too late—he could no longer get through!"

The Italian declaration of war had been preceded by the great victory at Gorlice on May 5, 1915, which had driven the Russians on a broad front out of Galicia. Although this victory brought about the long-awaited change in the situation in the east, it could no longer be effectual in reversing the predetermined decision of Italy to enter the war.

A week after this great battle the Slovene deputy Dr. Anton Korošec appeared in my office. He was the militant leader of the Catholic Slovenes, far more robust than his intellectual compatriot and fellow deputy Professor Krek. He came to the point at once: after this great victory of the Central Powers on the eastern front which was probably decisive for the whole course of the war it seemed as though the time had now come for the politicians and party leaders to pave the way for peace. I pricked up my ears as he went on. The Slovenes—and he was speaking here in the name of their greatest and most authoritative party—had a proposition to make. As he continued to speak Dr. Korošec now emphasized every syllable:

"If the government and the German parties are prepared to guarantee a Slovene national school autonomy within their own language region, then my party is prepared to concede to the use of the German language as the official language of state."

This was an extraordinary proposal indeed. The demand for the use of German as the language of state was the most far-reaching national demand that had been raised from the German side in the German-Czech language controversies. This was a demand which had been retained only in the programs of the German Radicals of the Karl Hermann Wolf brand and by the followers of Schönerer, whereas the great German parties, the German Nations and German Liberals, had been content with a milder version in their claims for the use of German as a "language of convenience." And now here came Korošec with the surprising offer which, for what was surely a small price in comparison, would seem to constitute the guarantee of permanent national peace in the western sector of the Austrian South Slav area, a matter of the utmost political significance for the frontier regions in view of the imminent military conflict with Italy.

I passed on this sensational political proposition. It would have been easier to make bread out of stones than to influence the German National potentates in South Styria and Carinthia toward such a pact.

The summer of 1915 was fine and warm. The days were long and sunny in Vienna, and in the vineyards on the Nussberg the vines stood in their golden splendor. But all the same it seemed to me as though a sort of dark veil of foreboding hung over the landscape.

With the death of King Carol of Romania and of old Bratianu Austria had lost two of her strongest pillars. Romania, once the friend of Austria, had fallen into the hands of cynics, greedy despots and corrupt rabble. The hostile attitude was for a time modified by the colossal bribes which, according to a fixed tariff, had to be paid to the mistresses of the ministers before the wagons with ammunition needed by the Turks for their campaign in the Dardanelles were allowed to pass through. Romanian nationalism, fostered by the propaganda of the Western powers, was already troublesome and voicing its claims to the Romanian region of Hungary. Austria had to face a new enemy.

Matthias Erzberger returned to Vienna full of concern. He was aware of my connections with the Hungarian-Romanian leaders and rightly argued that the aim to be followed at this juncture was now to reward the tested loyalty of the Hungarian-Romanians, thus protecting these people in Hungary from the irredentist influences of their neighbors across the frontier. Prime Minister Tisza had already sent a letter to Dr. Vajda formally withdrawing his censure of the Hungarian-Romanian political leader, appealing to the unity of the two nations on Hungarian soil, but this reconciliation now demanded concrete and visible expression. It was time to grant the important and undoubtedly just demands of the Transylvanian Romanian Peasant party leaders. As long as the Romanian-Hungarians remained a firmly established entity, the danger of war from Romania would be considerably lessened.

In a discussion between Erzberger, Gessmann, the latter's trusted adviser and friend, Sektionschef Josef Khoss, and myself a plan of campaign was evolved. Dr. Alexander Vajda, who was in Vienna at the time working as a military doctor in the Allgemeine Krankenhaus, was asked through my intervention to invite the leaders of the Hungarian-Romanians to Vienna for talks. The conference took place on the Feast of the Annunciation, 1916, in the *palais* of Prince Alois Liechtenstein in the Valeriestrasse. Prince Liechtenstein took the chair and in addition to Gessmann, Erzberger and myself, the others present were Dr. Vajda, Dr. Maniu, Dr. Aurel Popovici, the deputy Pop and another Transylvanian Romanian deputy whose name escapes me. The outcome of the conference, which lasted several hours, was the setting up of a concrete program of political demands for the area populated by Romanians. The demands were purposely kept moderate. Erzberger had merely been present as an observer, taking no active part in the discussion. In order to secure the presence of Popovici, against whom certain old political charges were still in process in Hungary, it had been necessary to obtain a special *laissez-passer* from the Hungarian government. This government had, therefore, been informed in advance of the conference.

The program agreed upon was confined to two points: 1. The extension of the same language ordinance which already existed in two *comitates,* ensuring the equality of both the Romanian and Magyar languages in law and administration, to the remaining *comitates* with a Romanian majority. 2. The re-establishment of the Romanian secondary schools which had already existed before Apponyi's school legislation. Signed by Prince Alois Liechtenstein and myself, this program was telegraphed to the Hungarian government that same day. I sent off the telegram myself, full of good spirits on that wonderful spring day, confident that an important step had been taken toward national appeasement in Hungary, and perhaps also toward the averting of a very real military danger.

The effect of the telegram was, however, quite different. A few days later the Foreign Minister, Baron Burian, asked me to come to the Ballhausplatz. He told me that the Hungarian government was indignant at this Viennese interference—German-assisted at that —in Hungarian domestic affairs. The Foreign Minister warned me against a repetition of similar enterprises in the future, with a stern reminder of martial law and its consequences. A protest from the Hungarian government was also sent to the Austrian Prime Minister. Tisza gave public vent to his anger at this episode in the Hungarian press.

Dr. Maniu was to pay dearly for his part in the affair. Shortly after our conference he was removed from his post as Syndic of the Greek Uniate Bishopric of Blasendorf and called up for immediate military service at the front. This was no mere chance. By a strange coincidence he was himself to discover the reason for this sudden call-up. He described this to me after the war.

In the chaos which followed the collapse in 1918, some 56,000 Romanian soldiers who had passed through Hungary on their way home (having first relinquished their arms), found themselves in transit in Vienna and Lower Austria. These troops were in good condition and they were well-disciplined. Among them was Dr. Maniu, a captain in an artillery regiment. Vienna was at this time at the mercy of bands of armed plunderers and soldiers streaming back from the broken front lines, not to mention the terrorist activities of the so-called *Volkswehr,* a motley and undisciplined Communist *soldateska.* Julius Deutsch, the Secretary of State for the Army, held office in the Ministry in the heart of the capital without any reliable instrument for the restoration of law and order. When Dr. Maniu came to him with the proposition that, so long as the Romanian troops were held on Austrian soil, they were prepared to assist in the maintenance of order, Deutsch had the good sense to accept his offer and gave Maniu command of the city. He was provided with administrative offices in the Ministry of War and Romanian soldiers of the defeated imperial army took over sentry duty in Vienna. This was the last act of Transylvanian-Romanian loyalty to the Empire which now lay in ruins.

At the invitation of the chief of the Military Press Department, I had frequent opportunity from 1917 onward of visiting the Italian front and witnessing several important military actions. I was present during nearly all the battles of the Isonzo campaign in 1917.

A longer trip took me up to the Romanian and Russian front. I encountered almost exclusively Hungarian troops here. As I learned later on, those responsible now viewed the time as ripe to comply with the demands of the Magyar politicians in regard to the Hungarian contingents of the common imperial army: the army would thus cease to feature as a bone of contention in party political conflict. I was to be won over for this move, but I must admit that what I saw for myself at the front could hardly be said to accord with the plan as such.

In the fall of 1917 I married again. My second wife was Marianne Nothaft, the favorite cousin of my late wife, also from Styria. I had spent three lonely and troubled years and now there was once more to be a woman in my neglected household. Things promised to be different in the future.

The offensive against Italy was now imminent and my place was once again at the front. In Krainburg, the base of the commander of the Bavarian Alpine Corps, Krafft von Delmensingen, I was given the chance to choose for myself which unit I would accompany. I picked the Edelweiss Corps, a unit confronted with a particularly difficult task on the northern flank in Alpine country. Glorious weeks now began for me, weeks in which the Empire once again gave open proof of her strength and the unity of her people. When the twelfth Isonzo battle was launched, extending from the district of Görz in a broad front across the Italian mountain range to South Tyrol, the Italian defense wall was shattered. Soldiers from the Italian ranks fled, panic-stricken, as far back as Bologna and Florence, spreading the news that the war was over.

The Edelweiss Division, one of the best in the whole army, was commanded by Major General von Wieden, a first-class soldier and highly popular with his troops. This crack division was made up of regiments from Salzburg, Upper Austria and Carinthia.

I accompanied this division in its offensive against the northern flank. I had made my way through to the corps commander, General Krauss, over the romantic mountain road named after Archduke Eugene which ran from Kronau in Krain to Flitsch, and so took part in this historic campaign from the very first day. Below Flitsch I reached the headquarters of the Edelweiss Division and on the same evening I made my way on foot up toward the Nivea Ridge over which the attack down to the Resia Valley was to be launched with the purpose of opening up the enemy's north flank which was firmly concentrated in the vicinity of Raibl.

The practical geographical difficulties involved were enormous. With the utmost difficulty the Alpine light artillery had crossed the steep ridge. Heavy showers of rain prevented our advance in this wild, almost impassable country, with its seething mountain torrents, swollen by the rainfall. General von Wieden went ahead as quickly as possible with his staff, leaving the officer commanding the artillery with his men and myself behind just below the ridge. In the miserable little village where we stopped I sat for hours operating the field telephone. Down in the valley the attackers had been met by the resistance of the permanent Italian fortifications; our ammunition was insufficient, even for the light artillery, for many of the pack mules had fallen over the precipice on the way up the steep and narrow mountain path.

But the hour of victory finally came, the reward for those almost superhuman exertions pitted against the forces of nature and the resources of the enemy. We entered the friendly little town of Resiutta. The march down the Tagliamento now followed, a glorious march with the rough riflemen firing across the river from their hiding-places, and then we stopped to rest in Tarcento, an unforgettably peaceful idyll. There were still blue figs in the garden of the house which took me in, and the asters glowed, crimson, purple and mauve in the warm Italian sunshine. At midday officers and men sat down to the sort of meal we had only dreamed of.

The truth could no longer be concealed. The encircling of the Central Powers, the systematic hunger blockade directed against them, was proving more destructive than the enemy mortars.

The sight of the troops as they passed by in rapid advance was revealing. The men marched past, wan and exhausted, in miserable, faded uniforms; these were front-line troops that had endured hunger and privation for months on end. Overjoyed at the sight of a land literally flowing with milk and honey, they fabricated victory wreaths for their pack mules out of the corn cobs which they had not seen for so long. They streamed as though driven by hunger into this Promised Land. From what I witnessed during those days I knew instinctively that, great though this victory was, it was the last that we could hope to achieve with this army. I also took part in the offensive of June, 1918, from the Assa gorge of the Sette Communi, those fateful battles which only served to confirm what we had seen coming six months before.

In the battle of the Piave, however, this army once more gave great proof of its substance as the army of a league of nations in the true sense of the term. In this powerful offensive, launched by the Italians and their allies, German-Austrians, Slavs, Italians and Magyars fought side by side in the mountains along the frontier, and, in a heroic common attack, won back the vital strategic position of the Sisemol and then struggled tenaciously right up to October 27 to regain the adjoining positions at Pertica, although everything had disintegrated on the other fronts. Truly a great and tragic drama.

Now, however, there was no longer any strength left. The end drew near. The army had been the cement which had held together the motley conglomeration of the Habsburg nations, unsurpassed in strength by any other organizing body.

It was true that there had been cases of felony and treachery among the Czechs in the field, but a wholesale judgment would bear no relation to the facts. Loyalty and devotion to duty were also to be encountered among them, right up to the end. I shall never forget a special incident during the tenth Isonzo battle. The Italians had penetrated into the Brestovizza Valley; only three more kilometers and the road to Trieste would have been free and the Austrian front broken through at the most strategic point. The Italian artillery directed a murderous hailstorm of fire against the slopes of the Hermada, the most vital position, the batteries on the heights of which had been put out of action. Poison gas spread death across the mountain side.

I followed the action from a bunker high up on the Hermada. The earth trembled beneath us, the enemy fire flung sand and stones against the shaking walls of our shelter. Beneath our bunker was a great natural cave in which we had laid our wounded and into which we ourselves would retreat every now and then to regain our breath and escape for a few minutes from the infernal noise around us. At our feet lay Point 136, the other gatepost of the doorway to Trieste. The point changed hands from one minute to the next. The sky above this terrible scene was as blue as steel.

The Italian breakthrough was suddenly stopped by the action of our 30 cm. mortar! The shells sent towering fountains of smoke and stones into the air. Only by the intermittent flash of the Italian officers' sword blades was it possible to distinguish friend from foe in the inferno of fire and smoke. The landscape had been transformed into a fiery volcano. Death was all around us on the heights of the Hermada. I was suddenly flung against the wall by the repercussion of a shell and left the bunker for a moment to snatch a breath of air. Death and destruction were so near that it seemed pointless to seek shelter any more.

To my astonishment as I came out of the bunker I saw long rows of soldiers feverishly hacking a trench out of the rock with their pickaxes in a last desperate attempt to stave off the danger of the Italian breakthrough by the construction of a last line of resistance. I recognized from the scarlet lapels of the soldiers at work on the entrenchments that they were from the same Czech regiment which I had seen the night before marching back from the front line for a brief respite and regrouping. Hardly had the regiment reached its resting place than it was recalled to the threatened front, the same front which it had just left, worn out and cut to pieces after days of ceaseless combat. Once again they were called upon to throw their last pitiful remnants into the defense of this vital stretch of front. This was a Czech regiment, made up of all classes—peasants as well as workers. Unfaltering in their devotion to duty, these men gave an example of admirable heroism which I feel bound to record here.

One of the most significant figures among the many great soldiers of World War I was Field Marshal Svetozar Boroević, Baron von Bojna, the victorious commander of Komarov, the liberator of Przemysl and west Galicia and the army commander in twelve Isonzo battles. I am, however, not concerned here with the celebrated soldier whose name will go down in history, but rather with the personal character of this great man.

I often visited Boroević at his headquarters in Adelsberg whence he directed the complicated mechanism of his broad front which extended for miles across the mountains and valleys. He was the personification of all those splendid characteristics which for centuries had made the Croat people the bulwark of Western Christian civilization and of the Habsburg Empire against the advance from the East. The personality of the Field Marshal dominated the headquarters. His strong sense of duty, the simplicity of his way of life, his absolute personal integrity, exercised a tremendous influence on all around him.

The same hard, selfless discipline to which he subjected himself was also applied to his fellow officers and men. He despised weakness and softness in any form and was hot on its trail. Certainly he was not an easy chief. Had Boroević not set this hard personal example to his officers and men, however, he would probably not have succeeded in such difficult circumstances in resisting the enemy army, superior as it was both in numbers and in war material. As it was, they could only hope to some extent to follow the example of this extraordinary man who seemed to be made of steel and for whom no hardship seemed too great.

His ability to regulate his need for sleep was reminiscent of Napoleon. All through the great defensive battles, which would sometimes go on for days and nights at a time, he would go without sleep. Throughout the tenth battle of Isonzo, during which the Italians maintained a constant battering for ten days on the

Isonzo positions, Boroević remained fully dressed, never relinquishing his command for as much as an hour, only now and again snatching a few minutes of half-sleep in an armchair. Then, all of a sudden, when no one even dreamed that the enemy storm had come to an end, he surprised his staff with the announcement: "I'm off to bed. It's all over." He had sensed the decisive slackening of the enemy attack with an extraordinary alertness. The devotion of his officers and men was mingled with an awed admiration.

At the end of World War I Boroević could perhaps have been instrumental in changing the course of history for Austria. The events connected with this episode are not generally known and I give an account of them here with the authorization of the former Prince Bishop, Dr. Hefter, himself closely concerned with Boroević at the time. I quote below from the memorandum which he gave me:

"In November, 1918, Field Marshal Boroević conducted the withdrawal of the Isonzo army from his base in Klagenfurt.[2] He came to see me. On this first visit he told me that he hoped to have the Isonzo army back within twenty days. In effect, thanks to the fine autumn weather, he completed the withdrawal in twelve days, an example of devotion to duty. The troops marching back through Klagenfurt were well-disciplined and in excellent condition, as I could see for myself. Boroević often came to see me and now and again he would give me an insight into his own state of mind and the terrible spiritual conflicts which he had endured in decisive moments on the Isonzo front.

"All the time he was in Klagenfurt his last hopes were pinned on an expected mission from Emperor Karl. When this summons did not come his last hopes receded. He came to me, perhaps in the hope of easing his pain. 'Now it's all over,' he said in despair. 'Twice I telegraphed to His Majesty requesting him to receive me, and twice he had the same telegram sent back in reply: he would take the first opportunity at a more opportune moment to thank me for my services. But I did not send these telegrams because I wanted thanks. Now that everything is over and it's too late to do

[2] Klagenfurt is the capital of the south Austrian former crown province and present-day federal province of Carinthia.

anything I can tell you what I wanted. I wanted to occupy Vienna and so restore freedom of action for the Emperor. But I could do this only on the Emperor's direct orders and not on my own initiative. I am not an Austrian, I was born in Croatia, which today belongs to Yugoslavia. The Austrian Imperial Field Marshal with the power to act on his own responsibility no longer exists. Only the express command of the Emperor himself could have authorized me to take this step. I had everything in readiness. Troops who were not one hundred per cent reliable had been sent off by rail. I had posted reliable troops at the most important railway stations as far as Wiener Neustadt. In twenty-four hours after the receipt of the command Vienna could have been occupied—and now it's too late'!"

So much for the contents of a historically interesting memorandum.

It is interesting to consider how very different the history of Austria might have been had Boroević been able to present his plan to the Emperor. It must, however, be noted that the Emperor himself was very probably not unaware of the plan envisaged by his gallant field marshal. He knew of the loyalty and decisive courage of this great soldier and guessed his intentions. The Emperor undoubtedly was reluctant to undertake an action which by the use of force would almost inevitably have resulted in bloodshed. This was certainly the reason for his opposition to the plan. The Emperor was confronted with similar decisions on subsequent occasions and always took the peaceful way out, declining to use force even when the interests of the Crown itself were at stake.

The Field Marshal ended his days, together with his wife, in the most modest circumstances at his home near Klagenfurt. His sole income consisted of a tiny pension which, as holder of the Theresia Cross, he received from the Maria Theresia foundation and which was worth almost nothing in the inflation of the postwar years. His depth of character and moral integrity were revealed to the full in the manner in which he accepted his bitter personal destiny.

On May 23, 1920, Boroević died as the result of a stroke in a Klagenfurt hospital at the age of sixty-four. He had remained physically and mentally full of energy and vigor right up to the end.

Officers formed a guard of honor at his bier. The *Volkswehr*[3] had declined to give the coffin a military escort, but the French and English commission present in Carinthia[4] at the time for the purpose of conducting the plebiscite accorded their former adversary on the field of battle this last chivalrous honor. A Capuchin priest had come to officiate at the funeral, but Prince Bishop Hefter, who had by chance heard of the funeral at the last moment, stepped into his place and spoke a few moving words at the graveside. On October 21, 1920, the mortal remains of Field Marshal Boroević found their last resting place under the arcades of the Central Cemetery in Vienna where his emperor had endowed a special tomb of honor for him. This funeral ceremony was conducted with fitting dignity and pomp. Many thousands of old soldiers from all classes of the population followed the coffin.

The old imperial army was indeed a remarkable institution, this army of Prince Eugene, of Daun, Archduke Karl and Radetzky. It was like a ring composed of many precious stones in a fine setting: it united the many and varied nationalities which made up the great Habsburg Empire. For decades the army had been exposed to the chauvinistic passions which shattered political life in the Sudeten provinces and in Hungary, but its inner structure had always remained unshaken.

[3] The newly-formed so-called *Volkswehr*, or "People's army," supposedly the new army of the Republic, was a collection of soldiers of widely differing origin and reputation. It was an undisciplined body of men, many of whom were deserters from their units and few of whom had seen front-line action. It was in fact a veritable *soldateska*, whose members were only too ready to make use of their rifles to serve their own ends.

[4] At that time Jugoslavia was claiming part of the present-day federal province of Carinthia. In a plebiscite conducted by an Allied commission in 1920 the region elected to remain part of Carinthia and thus of Austria. In February, 1956, Austria remembered in gratitude the American authority on international law, the late Miss Sarah Wambough. Miss Wambough rendered an inestimable service to Carinthia at that time by her protest against the dissection of Carinthia, in her capacity as the American expert on the minorities question and on plebiscites. Her book *Plebiscites Since the World War*, published in 1933 by the Carnegie Foundation, contains one of the best and most objective accounts of the Carinthian plebiscite.

Chapter 13

FAREWELL

There was a great deal of talk against Emperor Karl, based on misinterpreted fact and ill-natured gossip, but the most serious criticism arose out of the regrettable "Sixtus affair." Much has been written about this matter, but most of the commentaries have been lacking in objectivity, so that the true picture has become totally blurred. The attempt of the peace-loving Emperor to initiate peace talks with France through the mediation of his brother-in-law, Prince Sixtus of Parma, was made at the beginning of 1917, at a moment particularly favorable for such an advance. In a letter from the Emperor the Prince was entrusted with the confidential mission of informing the President of the French Republic that the Emperor was prepared "by every means and using my personal influence to the full with my allies to support the justifiable French claims to Alsace and Lorraine."

Although Ottokar Czernin was not conversant with the exact text of this letter, he had been informed of the move for peace and had agreed to it. It was no longer a secret that the restitution of Alsace and Lorraine to France would be one of the absolute conditions for a peace treaty. When finally in the spring of 1918 a diplomatic indiscretion on the part of Czernin provoked an angry reply from Clemenceau bringing to light the mission confided to Prince Sixtus, the general situation had changed so much, and public opinion both in Austria and Germany was already so irritated and warped, that it was quite impossible dispassionately to judge this peace move which, had it succeeded, might have spared the Central Powers the bitter end of the war and thus saved Germany from far greater losses than would have been involved by the restitution of Alsace and Lorraine.

Count Czernin had certainly done himself no good and could

not have served the interests of his imperial master worse. No enemy could have done more harm to the Emperor's cause. That dreadful scene in my office in the *Reichspost* made such an impression upon me that I can still see the count standing by my bookcase and can still hear his words. I know of no more terrible admission from the lips of a former imperial minister.

Public opinion was now unjustly biased against the young Emperor. People were used to the time-honored concept of the Monarchy of Emperor Franz Josef's day: this was a new concept, and it brought confusion. It was true that the new ruler was no Hercules, but he was nevertheless full of honest good will, a conscientious and deeply religious man, light-hearted, fond of Viennese music, a devoted husband and a gallant soldier. His simple nature was ill-fitted for the post of a great ruler; he fulfilled the high office of emperor in the role of helper in distress, a man genuinely concerned for the welfare of his subjects. He earnestly desired peace and happiness for the people committed to his charge. But with all his noble endeavors he was no match for the demons which seemed to have taken possession of humanity.

Among the many letters of appreciation received by the *Reichspost* after his tragic death, one comment made a very deep impression upon me. Strange and paradoxical though it sounds, it seems to me even today the best characterization of this good man, burdened in a terrible moment of history with the onerous office of sovereign: "He was a lieutenant and a saint."

He bore his tragic fate with real fortitude. Instead of following the example of Emperor Wilhelm, who sought out a quiet and peaceful place in the sun to establish himself and his family, far away from all hatred and conflict, he felt it his duty to do battle for the heritage still allotted to him. For him this heritage signified a real mission in the fulfillment of which his own personal destiny was of no importance. So convinced, he ventured to take a plane to Hungary, supported by only a handful of loyal men, and so, with his head unbowed, accompanied by his wife and child, he accepted the banishment inflicted by the victorious powers with so little understanding and humanity, a banishment in which he was to die.

In another more peaceful era this warm-hearted young man would certainly have been an emperor who would have won the affection and loyal devotion of his people. As it was, he was confronted with a superhuman task, a bitter turn of fortune. Even a stronger man would have failed here. His tragic destiny was to mark the way that many millions of men, women and children were soon to follow—the way of suffering of persecuted and mourning humanity.

As was to be expected, the South Slav problem increasingly dominated political developments within the Empire in 1917-18. The fact that this problem had hitherto remained unsolved was now the root of all evil. The final and irrevocable decision lay in this sphere, and here Austria helped to dig her own grave. The question was approached with extraordinary lack of foresight.

The Austrian Slovenes were a small nation of some two million, but theirs was a zone of the greatest strategical importance. They formed a valuable security belt for Austria against Italy in time of war. Almost exclusively Catholic and united in their Catholic People's party, they had for decades existed in a state of nationalist feud with the Italians, who had robbed them of a substantial wedge of territory in the Italian Friaul in 1866.

When hostilities broke out in 1915, people were seized by a sort of war psychosis which spread confusion and caused great harm. Even some in the entourage of General Scotti, Chief of Staff of the Tenth Army, were caught up in this feeling. Nothing else could account for the fact that as soon as this staff arrived in Villach the names of all the stations in the Slovene region of the Gail Valley which had formerly been given in both languages were now changed exclusively into German on the instructions of the General Staff. This was a measure of not the slightest military significance which gave justifiable offense to the Slovene population. But worse was to follow. At the outbreak of the war twenty-seven Catholic Slovene priests from Carinthia and South Styria were arrested on the charge of having betrayed the Austrian mobilization movements to Italy. In several cases they were openly escorted to prison in chains, exposed to the rough treatment of the incensed

Austrian frontier population, though the accusations were without any real foundation.

In the Slav south the newspaper with the widest circulation was the Laibach daily paper *Slovenec*, the organ of the Slovene Catholic People's party. The paper became increasingly Jugoslavian in tone. Things looked black among the Slovenes. The Austrian Government saw the way things were turning and attempted to intervene.

One summer day in 1917 the Prime Minister, Baron Seidler, in an optimistic mood, disclosed to me his idea and policy in the South Slav issue. He told me he had succeeded in completing arrangements for the subdivision of the Slovene-speaking region into administrative districts and thus solved the highly controversial problem of the establishment of school autonomy for the Slovenes.

It was certainly high time to reinforce the broad mass of the Slovene Catholics who had remained loyal, above all since a rift was developing in their camp as a result of the Jugoslav policy adopted by Korošec in the *Slovenec*, and the very definite opposition to it displayed by various leading figures including many of the clergy. There was openly bitter protest on the part of the clergy who accused the *Slovenec* (published by the Catholic Press Association) of "turning away from its obligations as a Catholic newspaper" and held it mainly responsible for the dissention which now divided the nation into two camps. This was a case unique in the history of the Austrian Catholic press. Prime Minister Seidler, with his optimistic plans to fulfill the national obligations by the establishment of national administrative districts within the Austrian provinces, was sailing the "German course" supported by a group of active men of the German National *Verband*. It was saying a great deal for him to fit the Slovene school autonomy into this course. But Seidler was a kindly and well-intentioned optimist whose high hopes and confidence, refreshing though they were, were not infrequently without foundation.

I asked him doubtfully whether the Carinthian and South Styrian German deputies had already agreed, whether they had in fact been asked at all. The Prime Minister replied that they had not, but that this would present no difficulties whatever; he had already talked the matter over and reached complete understanding with the leading men in the German National *Verband*. I knew my countrymen too well and I knew that Seidler had not found the solution.

Every subsequent plan and pact aimed to conciliate the South Slavs likewise came to nothing. Nevertheless, the political feeling of the Slovene clergy could certainly have been influenced up to the early summer of 1918. The situation was recounted to me after the war by the bishop of Carinthia, a man with a broad knowledge of public affairs.

"As long as the war lasted," he said, "the leading national figures among the Slovene clergy in Carinthia still were looking for an Austrian solution. Domvikar Smodej, one of their leaders, came to me requesting me to inform the Emperor that the moment had now come for him to assert his authority in the South Slav issue. The matter should not be postponed, so he urged me, for in a fortnight's time it might be too late. Smodej was later to become a senator in Belgrade. I went to Baden to inform the Emperor. I was warmly received, but I had the feeling that the Emperor viewed the situation as already hopelessly beyond repair." Certainly the Emperor's trusted adviser, Prime Minister Seidler, held this opinion. He was not the man equal to the task of solving this intricate problem.

The situation in Croatia was infinitely more critical. On September 24, 1918, the Agram university professor, Dr. Milobar, a well-intentioned Croat of high integrity, wrote the following bitter words in the *Reichspost*: "Jugoslavism among the Croats is an expression of the despair of an improvement of the fate of the Croat nation within our Monarchy in general and under the hegemony of the Magyar gentry in Hungary in particular." Without the intervention of a higher authority, Croatia saw herself as a mere appendage to Hungary, with no measure of autonomy or equal rights; nor could the leaders of a people so proud of their own state as the Magyars understand that these ancient Croat people were not prepared to see their historic kingdom as a relic of the past, but were aiming toward its practical realization within the framework of the Monarchy, bringing about the unification of all Croat peoples.

For all that the Hungarian Prime Minister Wekerle remained

inflexible. Such promises as he made were merely to evade the issue, to play for time. When Hussarek (the Austrian Prime Minister) came to him demanding a positive decision, he replied that he would discuss the matter further in six weeks. He must surely have realized that the last hour for any discussion had already come—or had he lost his head? Wekerle was also responsible for the enemy propaganda and treachery which found its way into Croatia under the regime of the *Banus* Mihalovich, a figure from the Serbo-Croat coalition.

The minds of young people, still at school or university, were systematically poisoned. In the royal printing office in Agram a special brochure was published for the secondary schools to commemorate the centenary of the poet Peter Preradović, a brochure which misrepresented the character of this great Austrian and politically distorted his work. One of his poems was turned into a political lampoon, directed against all those who "ogle unconditionally with the double-headed eagle." On July 9, 1918, a secret congress of representatives of the pupils of all the secondary schools in Croatia took place in Agram which among other things drew up a "black list" of all teachers known to resist the Jugoslav aims. Hundreds of letters were received by the *Reichspost* from Croats who violently protested against the growing political devastation of their country.

In the middle of March the *Reichspost* correspondent in Sofia, Oskar Bam, arrived in Vienna. He had spent several weeks in Croatia on his way to the capital. A man well acquainted with world affairs and a first-rate journalist, Bam had taken good note of the state of affairs in Croatia. He had also seen the *Banus*. The description he gave of the conditions in Croatia, supplemented by various details, was a fitting backdrop for a tragedy. I felt it my duty to lay his report before the imperial Minister of Finance, Baron Alexander Spitzmüller, who had only recently assumed office. The Minister who, in connection with Bosnia-Herzegovina, was also responsible for South Slav questions, received me at once, together with Bam. He listened attentively to all Bam had to tell him. "The reports I have here read quite differently," was his first comment, half in astonishment at what he had just heard and half in official reserve. He thanked Bam warmly and made no attempt to conceal his concern at the general situation in the South Slav sphere.

At the beginning of October the *Banus* Mihalovich was removed from office and the former Hungarian Minister for Croatia, Unckelhäuser, was nominated as his successor. Any further investigation as to the justification for such a step was, however, no longer necessary for the National Assembly of Croats, Serbs and Slovenes convened in Agram on October 18 officially proclaimed the fully sovereign state of Jugoslavia and recalled Mihalovich to office.

In September the South Slav tragedy began to precipitate toward its sudden end, the final climax of decades of neglect, mistaken policy and lost opportunities.

The atmosphere in the House of Deputies in Vienna, which reassembled on January 22, 1918, was electric. Political events followed one another in rapid succession.

In mid-January a strike broke out in Wiener Neustadt which spread to Vienna and many industrial towns in the crown provinces. The Social Democratic leaders were scarcely able to keep matters under control. For the first time in this strike (which had a strongly political character) the increasing influence of a revolutionary faction among the Social Democrats made itself felt. At this same moment the Poles showed renewed signs of unrest. On January 23 there were noisy demonstrations against the Government in Crakow, and the Polish Social Democrats walked out of the Polish Club in Parliament.

This weakening of the government majority encouraged the Czechs to rebel against Seidler's ministry. With the utmost difficulty a majority of 155 to 105 votes could be achieved against the Czech deputy Stanek's motion not to take cognizance of the Prime Minister's declarations. When on January 29 the government presented its budget estimates to the House, the decision of the Polish Club to vote against these proposals as well as against a provisional budget caused Seidler to ask the Crown to accept his resignation on February 7. The Emperor declined to accept his resignation, but the signing of the Peace Treaty of Brest Litovsk with the Ukraine produced a new crisis, for in accordance with the so-called Cholm clause the district of Cholm was made over to the Ukraine, despite the fact that the majority of the population were Roman Catholics. The Poles in both chambers of Parliament formed a closed front in opposition. The German Social Democrats now came to the rescue and for the first time declared themselves prepared to vote for the provisional budget, although they still refused to support the war credits. With this somewhat uncertain assistance the motion was put to the vote and on March 7 Sec. 1 of the provisional budget was in fact carried by 240 votes to 121, and the war credits were secured by 202 votes to 165.

The division had, however, followed a new declaration on the part of the Prime Minister who had at long last decided to approach the problem of national autonomy, to further the policy of self-determination and to acknowledge the existence of the South Slav question. Only a fraction of the Poles and the South Slavs had voted against the government motion, the majority had abstained. All the same this was a light in the darkness. Unfortunately Seidler did not follow it. The tension had hardly been eased before Czernin produced the explosion over the Sixtus affair which brought about his own resignation on April 14.

A new government crisis developed out of the confusion which now broke loose, with instantaneous political consequences. To add to the alarm signals in the Czech, South Slav and Italian camps, now came the resignation of Dr. von Zolger, the Minister for the Slovenes, a loyal man who found his position untenable in the midst of the South Slav movement. Finally Seidler's plan for the subdivision of the provinces into administrative districts in an attempt to reach a solution to the national question only added coals to the fire when on May 19, by means of a general order, steps were taken to set up seven Czech and four German administrative districts in Bohemia. This order placated neither side, for it was only a half-measure and above all provided no scope for national autonomy. The Minister for the Interior was forced to pay for the order with his own resignation, but this in no way alleviated the general situation.

The provisional budget expired at the end of June, and as from July 1 no legislation was provided for the administration of state finances. On July 16 Prime Minister Seidler held his last Cabinet

meeting. His successor, Baron Max von Hussarek, made his first appearance as Prime Minister in the House of Deputies nine days
later with a short speech introducing his program in very general
terms. He spoke of a "reconciliation of nations" and of the necessity
of creating "the basis of mutually confident co-operation." His
speech before the reassembled House of Deputies was a masterly
piece of rhetoric, but it was a failure. His words concerning the
"home of the peoples of Austria, never to be lost" were met with
a sharp call of "Too late! Too late!" from the Slav section of the
House.

A whole series of lost opportunities now began. I heard details
of these five years later from the lawyer, Dr. Horvath, who at that
time had been a Croat deputy and leader of the Croat right-wing
party. He came to see me in mid-October, 1918, half in despair. If
urgent steps were not taken now, in the eleventh hour, the Empire
would surely collapse. He had to see the Emperor. A few days later
I met Horvath, who was just coming out of the Hungarian government *palais*. He told me that he had been received in audience on
October 21. The Emperor had listened attentively to Horvath's report and shown great insight; he had instructed Horvath to negotiate
with Tisza, "the most powerful man in Hungary." Horvath's eyes
were shining with new hope and confidence as he hurriedly told me
that he was just about to leave for Budapest and had just been to the
Hungarian administrative office to ask for an appointment with
Tisza. I wished him every success in his mission and refrained from
uttering my own grave doubts.

Political events now followed one another in a positive ava-
lanche. The connection with Agram was severed, and I heard nothing more from Dr. Horvath until to my surprise I received a letter
from him at the end of May, 1923, referring to our last meeting in
Vienna and explaining an article which had appeared under his
name in the Agram paper *Pravaš*. In his article Horvath reported on
his mission at that time and wrote that he had had a detailed conversation with Stephen Tisza in the Parliament building in Budapest,
in the presence of Prince Ludwig Windischgrätz and Dr. Ivo Frank.
Tisza had listened to Horvath and then declared slowly and solemnly, as though weighing each word carefully: "Hard though it is, I

am bound to confess that the policy I followed personally, and indeed the entire Hungarian attitude in regard to Croatia, was quite wrong. I can well see the legitimacy of your claim that Croatia must be given complete independence and that all Croatian territories, including Fiume, must form their own state."

Prince Windischgrätz requested Tisza to inform the King in Reichenau immediately that he was prepared to accept the proposals submitted by the Croats. On the same day a meeting of the leaders of the Hungarian opposition was held in the *palais* of Count Aladar Zichy which, after some preliminary difficulties, finally led to the acceptance of the Croat concept. In his report Horvath then made the following surprising declaration:

"That evening Prime Minister Wekerle informed me that his ministry supported Tisza and that all details would be arranged in two or three days after the King's return from the official inauguration of the University of Debreczin."

There can be no doubt as to the reliability of Horvath's statement. But it was too late. On October 29 Croatia formally joined Jugoslavia, and on October 31 Stephan Tisza was murdered.

The day after Hussarek had announced his program many members of the Christian-Social Union were present in the Club rooms in Parliament. I was talking with a group of friends when Prälat Hauser came in and motioned me to join him. He was visibly upset and his face muscles were twitching. He whispered in my ear: "The German front has collapsed, the Siegfried Line has been broken and the German armies are retreating in disorder toward the Rhine. We are facing a military catastrophe." The news was concealed for a few days from the general public and only those versed in the art of reading between the lines of the newspaper reports could guess the truth. The Austrian front in the south still remained intact.

It was President Wilson who now brought about the ruin of Austria-Hungary.

The President had gleaned his information about the Austrian Empire from unreliable books and propaganda pamphlets and had gained the impression as a result that the Monarchy was nothing more than a "prison of nations." He had little or no idea of the national problems in Central Europe, of the diverse economic and cultural interests of the various nations and their historic interdependence. Thus he presented his Fourteen Points to the world and they were avidly seized upon by a group of men only too anxious to set the fuse once and for all to the Central European structure. Wilson's Fourteen Points provided them with the dynamite they needed. Far too late, Wilson at last realized during the peace negotiations in Paris that he had got himself into perilous waters. On one side were the conspirators of the Beneš-Masaryk group, on the other the Jugoslavian intriguers, Clemenceau and his followers preached their doctrine of hate, and behind them all stood the sinister secret powers who pulled the strings and who, through Beneš, proclaimed the death sentence upon Austria: "*Détruisez!*"

From the confusion which followed the disintegration of the Central Powers on the western front and which increased daily as a result of the hectic political developments within the Empire itself, the concept of a *Mitteleuropa* might still have been salvaged by a constructive solution. Wilson, however, chose to ignore the peace offer made by Austria-Hungary on September 14 and those who had any say in the matter were not interested in a constructive solution: their attitude was to bring about terrible consequences for their own nations. The disappearance overnight of the state which despite all the changes of fortune had for centuries held together the conglomeration of small nations of the Danube-Moldau countries was the prelude to tragedy in Europe.

One of President Wilson's most widely-quoted phrases was that concerning "the self-determination of nations." The *Reichspost* commented on this slogan:

In reality there is no such things in this world as the absolute right of self-determination, neither for the individual state nor for the individual nationality; just as man as an individual being is limited in his personal freedom by his environment and the well-being of his fellowmen, the society in which he lives and with which his own needs, a common civilization and common tasks as human beings are bound up in a thousand ways, neither can the individual nation exist alone. This nation too is dependent upon its neighbors by the numerous ties of natural law and the necessary conditions imposed by life itself.

Since these words were written millions—indeed whole nations —have been sent into slavery and misery, and the despots and over-lords were in no way concerned with the observance of Wilson's fine precept of self-determination. In October and November, 1918, the phrase went a long way toward helping to bring about the dis-integration of the great Danube empire of nations.

Now came a veritable cloudburst of disaster for Austria. The military breakdown went hand in hand with the complete inner col-lapse of the Empire. Nor could the flimsy dam of the Emperor's October Manifesto appealing to the nations to co-operate in the es-tablishment of a new federal state based on national principles any longer stem the flood waters. The Hungarian Prime Minister Wekerle proclaimed the end of the 1867 *Ausgleich* agreement with Austria and the substitution of a "personal union" for the old "real union." Michael Karolyi was all set to take over the power in Hungary. In those terrible days when values and the old order changed overnight only sleep could bring a few hours of blessed forgetfulness, oblivious escape from hard reality.

Abandoned by the others, there was no other course open but to form a new state out of the remaining German territories of Aus-tria. It soon, however, became evident that not only the determina-tion of the frontiers but also the vexed question of the new constitu-tion was involved. Wilson's challenge addressed to the German Em-pire to relinquish her Emperor and dynasty in return for peace with-out capitulation (some months later in Versailles Germany was granted peace in exchange for her capitulation) had immediately roused republican propaganda in Germany. Underground elements added coals to this fire, which began to flare up also in Vienna.

When during the third week in October the question of the constitution was first raised in the Christian-Social Club the depu-ties in favor of a republic were only a small minority. In the debate which followed Professor Schoepfer and Wilhelm Miklas expounded the old principles of the party with great eloquence; even more moving was the speech by the Tyrol deputy, General Athanas von

Guggenberg, who since his election had only very rarely spoken in the club and was not noted for his gift of oratory.

The white-haired old soldier from Tyrol now rose to speak of true Austrian patriotism, the Emperor and the Monarchy. He spoke with the dignity and ardor of a man prepared to live and to die for his cause. In all my twenty years in the Christian-Social Club during the course of which I had heard many fine speakers, I never heard a speech which more profoundly impressed those present than that of the old general from Tyrol who seemed to regain the vigor of youth in his infectious enthusiasm. The Empire had endured through the centuries, supported by the firm loyalty and devotion of men like him.

At that meeting the club decided to continue to support the monarchist constitution. The motion was passed by a large majority, only a very few members abstained from voting. Since Prälat Hauser was sick with the flu and could not be present, the deputy chairman of the club, the Tyrol deputy Schraffl, was delegated to speak at the Provisional National Assembly convened for October 21 in Vienna. He was charged with a declaration in principle which stated: "The Christian-Social Union of German deputies is prepared to contribute toward furtherance of democracy in German Austria by encouraging measures for the active participation of the people in the legislation and in the administration, but on the strength of the fundamental adherence to the monarchist form of government. If, in the light of the geographical position and the historic and economic ties, the new nation states should of their own free will wish to amalgamate in a federal state, the Christian-Social Union would be prepared to support the formation of such a federation while continuing to protect to the full the national, political and economic interests of the German-Austrian people."

To the satisfaction of the Christian-Socials, the declaration delivered by Dr. Steinwender on behalf of the German National Verband contained the following words: "The force of circumstances has brought the old state to an end. We Germans now stand together, fully united and independent. We continue in our devotion to our country and remain convinced adherents of the constitutional monarchy as the form of the state."

In a speech remarkable for its rhetorical elegance and *noblesse*, Dr. Viktor Adler, leader of the Austrian Social-Democrats, pledged the loyalty of his party to a democratic republic.

While the solemn assembly was taking place in the historic building of the Provincial Diet of Lower Austria in Vienna, in an atmosphere which reflected traditional surroundings, a newly formed National Socialist party was actively demonstrating in front of the Landhaus for a republic and for *Anschluss* with Germany. For all that, the concept of a republic for Austria was by no means universally accepted at that moment. But there were trouble-makers enough. There were newspapers that took advantage of the moment to scorn the new small Austrian state, and advocate *Anschluss* with Germany. Reports of popular feeling in the various federal provinces were far from favorable. Tyrol was bitterly concerned about the fate of South Tyrol, but even from the conservative province of Upper Austria the reports were critical.

Back again in Parliament after his attack of influenza, Prälat Hauser went about with his head bowed gloomily, and Jodok Fink, chairman of the Christian-Social Deputies' club, lapsed into unhappy silence. I knew Fink well and realized that the laconic answers he gave when pressed for his opinion on the all-absorbing question of the moment inferred that he considered another solution than that which we all envisaged as almost inevitable. One day Hauser took me aside, his face full of concern. "I've serious news for you," he said. "Things look far from good in Upper Austria. I've never encountered such a rebellious spirit in the country before."

The people of Vienna gathered in a mass meeting to pray for peace, largely organized by the various Catholic bodies of the capital. This impressive religious assembly was followed by an address to the vast congregation by Cardinal Archbishop Piffl in which he indicated the attitude of Catholics toward the new state form for Austria. The Cardinal spoke to the masses assembled to hear him with the popular touch which he understood so well, emphasizing that the final decision as regards the state form must rest with the whole nation.

"In this turbulent era in which the after effects of the lost war tend to confuse and distort political thought," he said, "it is not for the politicians whose seats in Parliament are no longer valid and who are unduly influenced by confused public opinion to decide on the state form to be adopted. This ultimate state form must be decided by the nation as a whole, at the right time and after careful consideration. A national plebiscite must be held in which the people themselves can choose between the republic and the monarchy."

The Cardinal's words were greeted with unanimous enthusiasm by the Catholics of Vienna. In the name of the Christian workers of Austria the authoritative commission of the Christian Workers' Congress declared:

"The Christian workers demand a monarchy as the state form for German Austria, a monarchy based on broad, democratic principles. The people's rights must be guaranteed by the introduction of universal, equal, and direct suffrage for men and women alike. Questions affecting the basic principles of the constitution must be decided by a national plebiscite."

The various Viennese Catholic university associations also solemnly proclaimed their fundamental attitude on this question in a special declaration emphasizing their loyalty to the new Austrian state and supporting the monarchy as its state form.

A strange conversation took place during the tumult of those days. Dr. Rudolf Sieghart, member of the Upper House, invited me to come and see him in his charming small house near the Türkenschanzpark, for he wanted to talk to me privately about a matter of the utmost importance. I had not seen him for a long time. In the previous year he had been relieved of his post as governor of the Bodencreditanstalt at the express wish of Emperor Karl. His fall from such a high office had created quite a sensation. There had even been a rumor about a written recommendation found among the papers of the murdered Heir Apparent suggesting this step to his nephew.

Dr. Sieghard now sketched the current political situation for me with the skilled precision of a trained political strategist. All was not yet lost, he assured me. In such a situation the press was one of the most important instruments in the directing of popular feeling. Among the daily papers the *Neue Wiener Tagblatt* was indisputably the newspaper with the widest circulation among the middle classes in Austria. In view of its position and its enormous circulation—the largest of any Austrian paper—this newspaper was the most valuable weapon in forming public opinion. The paper had up to now maintained a reserved attitude on current political developments, but Sieghart was resolved at this point to use the newspaper against those forces in the country hostile to the state and the dynasty.

"Dr. Funder," he said, raising his voice impressively. "I own 90 per cent of the Steyermühl shares. I have complete freedom and the firm desire to use the paper in a campaign against the left-wing trend in public opinion. You are a newspaperman yourself and must see that this is a unique opportunity. I have, however, one stipulation to make. When I was forced to resign from my post as governor of the Bodencreditanstalt, a post to which I was appointed by Emperor Franz Josef, I was granted no audience of any kind in which I would have been afforded the opportunity to say one word in my own defense. What I now demand, as a condition for the use of the *Neue Wiener Tagblatt,* is an opportunity to justify my position before the Emperor."

At this moment the Crown was not widely supported by the press in Vienna. Many editors in chief were lying low in fear and trembling at the thought of the approaching revolution. Had the *Neue Wiener Tagblatt* indeed gone into battle, public opinion would probably have improved, at least in the capital. Such a press campaign was certainly not to be underestimated and could perhaps even have been decisive. The answer I received to my intervention from the chief of the Imperial Cabinet, Baron Seidler, was not an outright refusal, but a concrete decision was never made either. The *Neue Wiener Tagblatt* did not attack the old regime—but neither did it make any active contribution to its defense.

Rudolf Sieghart died in exile in Switzerland. He was one of the most brilliant men of the last era of the Habsburg Empire, an Austrian who always adhered firmly to the strict sense of duty which typified the officials of the old Austrian bureaucracy. He was a man whose many human failings were accompanied by exceptional qualities which should not have been lost in this time of need.

The imperial palace of Schönbrunn was not a good place to be in during those revolutionary days in Vienna. The number of palace guards was quite inadequate for the enormous building. The increasing general unrest in the capital made this situation too dangerous. Cadets from various military academies therefore took over guard duty from November 3 until November 12. The imperial family had left the palace the evening before and moved to Eckartsau.

Toward the end of October conditions in the capital became at times chaotic. Countless thousands of half-starved men, still armed, streamed back from the front. Undisciplined bands of marauders poured into the towns and roamed the countryside. Soldiers returning home were received at the various railway stations by revolutionary committees and subjected to "democratic" propaganda. "Red Guards," armed Communist bodies, were sounding the call everywhere for a social revolution. But there were still fortunately some signs of law and order. For example formation from Lower Austria, and especially the Saint Pölten Regiment,[1] arrived home in perfect discipline under the command of their officers.

The national confusion and disintegration had by now reached such a point that we were forced to print the following statement in the Reichspost on October 24:

"The mechanism of the Austrian central government can no longer function efficiently. Regulations issued by the various central administrative offices are ignored. Orders are no longer obeyed, not even by provincial governors." The article went on to demand "the setting up of an impartial body for the establishment of law and order with authority over all the various new factions. This authorative body, though not the legal successor of the Hussarek central government, would exercise its administrative functions in the government of the future national states until such time as these are formally constituted, able to take over the work for themselves. After these national states have been formed, it would then be for them to decide of their own free will to what extent and in which form they desire to co-operate within the necessary limits in the future."

The Reichspost proposed Heinrich Lammasch as the man most fitted to take over the leadership of such a provisional government.

[1] The officer commanding the Saint Pölten Regiment at that time was former Lieutenant Julius Raab, since 1951 chairman of the Christian Democrat Austrian People's party and since the spring of 1953 Chancellor of Austria.

Noted for his impartiality and strong sense of justice, Lammasch was the perfect man to maintain order between the divergent opposing political elements.

This proposition was more that a mere journalistic sensation. It was seized upon with approval by the various parties as a constructive plan, a practical solution in the chaos of the moment. Conversations with the leaders of the opposition gave grounds for hope. Immediate steps were taken in Parliament for the formation of a "Lammasch ministry for the maintenance of order." On October 27 the new government took over from the Hussarek cabinet which had resigned. Although the Lammasch administration lasted only two weeks, it functioned as an invaluable breakwater in those turbulent days. Moreover, as a result of his activities in this administrative body the public was made aware for the first time of a figure that was to play a leading part during the next few years in the new state of Austria. This man was Ignaz Seipel.

The provisional basic law passed by the German Austrian National Assembly on October 30 had made no mention of the form of the state foreseen for the commonwealth which the Assembly had created and furnished with legislative and executive powers. This Assembly, made up of party men whose seats in Parliament had already expired in 1915, considered themselves incompetent to effect any change in the existing form of the state; nor, however, had they the courage to follow the course indicated so clearly only a few days previously, on October 21, by Schraffl and Dr. Steinwender, spokesmen of the majority of the deputies, the Christian-Socials and the united German Nationals. The masses had been aroused by propaganda hostile to the state, and the pressure of popular feeling made itself felt.

The Catholics of Vienna fought tenaciously against such pressure. Their great organizations set up a working committee of seven members as a center to co-ordinate a counteraction. This committee was made up of Leopold Kunschak, Dr. Viktor Kienböck, Richard Schmitz, Dr. Franz Hemala, two ladies, Dr. Motzko and Dr. Hildegard Burjan, and myself. The committee set up its headquarters in the rooms of the *Volksbund* (People's League) in the Predigergasse. A meeting was called of the leaders of the *Volksbund* groups in the various districts of the capital, as well as the leaders of the Catholic Workmen's Association and the Catholic Students' Union. It was like the military headquarters of a divisional staff during some great battle.

Conferences were held throughout Vienna which in their resolutions affirmed the creation of the German-Austrian state, but firmly declared that this state should be built upon truly democratic principles. They demanded a federal union with the other national states and a constitution founded on the monarchistic principle. On this highly complex question we of the Catholic press consistently maintained the point of view that men who were elected seven years previously in quite different circumstances and whose term of office as deputy had expired must in all conscience leave the answer to the difficult and controversial question "Monarchy or Republic?" to the people themselves. The answer of the people—no matter what this might be—would be considered universally binding. This attitude was adopted daily, throughout those chaotic weeks leading up to the general election for the Constitutive National Assembly which was to draw up the new state form. Those days have long since been forgotten.

The provisional government created on October 30 was made up of fourteen state secretaries, augmented in the course of the next few days by eleven deputy secretaries. Few of those holding office were professionals in the sectors for which they were to be responsible, five of them were parliamentarians.

"It seems to us" we of the *Reichspost* complained, "that the error has crept in that democracy is merely a charitable institution for parliamentarians, a misconception against which an emphatic protest must be made. Whatever is the purpose of this enormous government? Whatever are we going to do in our poor little German-Austria, with all these secretaries of state and under-secretaries of state, enough to administer a state of a hundred millions? If we are already starting to throw out good money like this—and not even for first-rate men—where are we going to end up in our poverty by such a system of parliamentary nepotism?"

Four days previously, on the instructions of the German Imperial Chancellor, the Prussian Minister for the Interior had already urged his Hohenzollern Emperor voluntarily to relinquish his crown. One week later one German prince after another had abandoned his throne. The Duke of Braunschweig was the first of these to abdicate, hastily followed by Emperor Wilhelm II himself. Germany was turned into a conglomeration of motley republics almost overnight. Pan-German propaganda in Vienna increased in intensity in the face of these events, as though the pan-German agents were seized by the sudden panic that the new German-Austria might still remain loyal to the Habsburgs and reject an *Anschluss* with a republican Germany. The Vienna newspaper *Wiener Mittag* was loudest of all in its vehement anti-Habsburg propaganda.

In the capital itself public opinion was divided. But for all that the old imperial Vienna was still there. I shall never forget, for instance, a political meeting at which I spoke on All Souls' Day in a working-class district of Vienna. The place was packed. There were many ex-soldiers, home from the front, who followed my words with special attention and increasingly loud applause. I spoke uncompromisingly as an Austrian, as I had so often spoken all over the country in more peaceful times.

The Christian organizations in Vienna had announced a public meeting in the People's Hall of the *Rathaus* for November 3. As one of the speakers, it was my task to convince the vast audience of the grounds for the resolution to be framed as the climax of the meeting. I had prepared my speech beforehand, although this would hardly have been necessary for the crowd bore me along with them in their enthusiastic calls of approval which greeted every sentence. The demonstration was overwhelming as I declared:

"We want to retain our own accustomed monarchist form of state, a structure deeply rooted here in Austria for over a thousand years. We have no use for foreign building styles and tastes. We have no wish to impose our conviction upon anyone else, nor to turn this question into the object of an open conflict. We are firm in our own conviction, however, regarding this as something sacred. But above all we are here and now prepared to co-operate with all those of honest good will to restore social order and peaceful conditions for the people and so ensure that we are not overcome by something even worse than the terrible war just ended. Later, when order and public liberty has been secured, we can peaceably discuss plans for our future with our compatriots. The people as a whole shall freely decide this question."

This was the unanimous opinion of the Christian population of Vienna.

There was not much cause for optimism among the Christian-Socials and German Nationals in Parliament. News from the western provinces was far from good. Parcels containing leaflets summarizing the resolutions passed by the meeting of the Catholic organizations in Vienna were returned unopened from various country towns in Lower Austria. The Christian-Socials met on November 11 to discuss the situation and decide on the line they should adopt at the forthcoming Provisional National Assembly. Feeling was markedly pessimistic and a decided change was evident in the mental attitude of many of those present. It was already known in the parliamentary clubs that the Emperor was to issue a proclamation that same day renouncing any further participation in the affairs of state, and declaring that he "would recognize the decision which German Austria chose to make in regard to its future form of state." This proclamation was not an act of abdication, but merely a personal renunciation of the Emperor's participation in government affairs.

"On November 12, 1918, the National Assembly adopted the proposal of the Council of State (a body under Social Democratic leadership composed of the highest officers of the Executive vested with government functions) and agreed to a provisional constitution for German Austria, the first article of which envisaged the establishment of a democratic republic. The three Christian-Social state councilors, Athanas von Guggenberg, Wilhelm Miklas and Karl Prisching, published a declaration to the effect that their names had wrongly appeared in the communiqué issued by the Council of State, and that, true to their fundamental principles, they had spoken in favor of a democratic monarchy and against a republic in the debate on the future form of state. Since, however, another decision had in fact been reached, they declared themselves prepared to submit to the majority decision. In the National Assembly Deputy

Miklas, speaking on behalf of the Christian-Social party, reminded the House that, according to his party's belief, only a national plebiscite to be held as soon as possible could finally decide upon the form of state. Miklas further declared, however, that the Christian-Socials would refrain from introducing a motion to this effect "so as not to disturb the unity at this historic moment." The draft bill for the constitution was thus unanimously accepted by the Provisional National Assembly on all three readings.

That same day on which the National Assembly agreed to this provisional constitution in the midst of unprecedented tumult and commotion, the House of Deputies of old Austria met for the last time. A few Poles and Ukrainians and some Romanians and South Slavs appeared beside the German deputies. The Romanian deputy Simionvici took the chair in his old capacity as Vice-President of the House. It was an ironic twist of fate that the President was unable to announce the dissolution of this parliament on the grounds of a division; he could only propose that "this meeting should be adjourned and no date should be fixed for the next meeting."

On November 13 the *Reichspost* printed the following lines on its front page:

We are in conscience bound as German-Austrian Catholics, just as it is the duty of every citizen of our country, to devote all our energies with loyalty and devotion to the service of the new state of German Austria, even if the form of state adopted is not that of our own choice. The loyalty of Austrian Catholics to the Emperor and the old state of Austria has caused offense to many, for the most part to those for whom it is all too easy to trim their sails according to the wind. This very loyalty and their genuine sorrow at the change and at the passing of the institution so dear to their hearts is not only in no way hostile to the new state, but offers a far better guarantee for the trust and devotion with which the German-Austrian Catholics are resolved to serve their country than the importunate enthusiasm of those who first discovered their republican principles with the promise of material advantage.

The grim aftermath of the lost war was making itself felt throughout Austria. For weeks on end the country was without any system of law and order. Illegal patrols and commissions roamed through the towns and villages, pillaging private houses and apartments. People were robbed of food and clothing and anything else which might take the fancy of these undisciplined rebels. The imperial family had moved in time from Vienna to Eckartsau, a lonely hunting lodge not far from the capital. In the Hofburg and in Schönbrunn so-called guards set up their quarters in the palace, using the imperial apartments for their wild carousals. While the population of Vienna was almost starving, reduced to a diet of gruel three days a week, the hundreds of uniformed "guards" who had all of a sudden gathered at the palaces seized avidly everything they could lay their hands upon from the palace cellars, larders and storerooms.

Strange things can happen when law and order no longer protect private property. People suddenly viewed former imperial possessions as public property and great parcels of table linen, embroidered with the imperial crown, would disappear from the linen rooms at the palace to find their way into the linen cupboards of respectable middle-class Viennese families. Even officials were not slow to profit from this "clearance sale." On the strength of some flimsy authorization or other issued by the Ministry of Agriculture, piles of woolen blankets and valuable harnesses disappeared wholesale from the imperial stables; the horses formerly owned by the court were sold, often finding new homes in the stables of some dignitary or other. People who had hitherto affected good manners and considered themselves as belonging to the educated classes of society were suddenly infected by the revolutionary spirit and developed a taste for daring cultural-political enterprises.

Shortly after the declaration of the republic a meeting was held in the Konzerthaus in Vienna of a short-lived organization which called itself the Association of Intellectual Workers. According to reports in the press, a speech by a man called Rudolf Goldscheid to the effect that "the downfall of the crown must now be followed by the downfall of the church altars" was greeted with "thunderous applause" by the vast audience assembled.

Was this democracy which the radical Socialist press had promised the people? At times the country seemed on the verge of succumbing to lawless Bolshevism.

On the Feast of the Annunciation, March 25, 1920, Prince Alois Liechtenstein, leader of the Christian-Social party, died. For fifty years he had given of his best to the people at the side first of Vogel-sang and then of Lueger and Gessmann. He was a staunch upholder of the monarchist tradition and a deeply religious Catholic to the day of his death.

The early days of the Republic were anything but tranquil. Tension grew up between the provinces and Vienna, the capital being accused of centralist tendencies, and even the economy was threatened as a result. During those troubled weeks the relationship between Professor Ignaz Seipel, who had now succeeded Dr. Schindler as president of the *Herold*, and the *Reichspost* drew even closer. When his brief term of office at the side of Lammasch in the latter's provisional government came to an end, Seipel wrote a series of leading articles for the *Reichspost* which we published during the second half of November. These clearly defined the rights of the people in a democratic state, the essence of a democratic constitution, the urgent tasks which confronted the country at that moment and the prerequisites for the determination of the future form of state.

Elections were about to be held for the Constituent National Assembly. Despite all the noise, a great deal of foolish talk and deliberate disturbance, some good work was nevertheless done by some state departments. Administrative details in connection with the forthcoming elections were organized with speed and efficiency. In this election women were for the first time to have the right to vote on the grounds of the universal equal suffrage in the system of proportional representation now adopted.

On February 16 the people of the newborn republic of Austria went to the polls. The Social Democrats gained a majority of 1,211,-814 votes, as against the 1,068,382 polled by the Christian-Socials. The Social Democrats were unable to achieve an absolute majority, for the German Nationals accumulated a total of 617,984 votes for their various factions. The Social Democrats nevertheless succeeded in ousting the Communists from the political scene. Augmented by deputies from German South Tyrol and South Styria, the new National Assembly was made up of 72 Social Democrats, 69 Christian-Socials and 26 German Nationals.

Among the newly-elected Christian-Socials was the university professor Prälat Ignaz Seipel. The Christian-Social Union elected him as its chairman.

The Constituent National Assembly was confronted with problems of great difficulty. The peace treaty had to be negotiated, the question of an *Anschluss* with Germany had to be solved, order had to be restored within Austria itself and a basis created for a sound economy. No easy task faced the deputies in their new House.

Chapter 14
THE FIRST COALITION GOVERNMENTS

The New Year of 1919, the year which promised peace for the people of Austria, saw the country completely transformed. The great Empire lay in ruins, the small German Austria which remained had been wrenched out of the economic organism that had grown up through the centuries. Formerly an integral part of a great European power, this new Austria had become a small, landlocked country without safe frontiers; it was even doubtful whether it could exist at all.

In order to attempt to mold its future it had first of all to find its precarious way between internal discontent, chaos, the deliberate interference of the trouble-makers, fear, discouragement and despair. Many people viewed the union with Germany, the "return home" into the fold of the great German fatherland, as the most feasible solution. The national idealists, the poets and the harmless man in the street were carried away by this idea. Faced as they often were by almost insuperable difficulties of their own, people naturally tended to view the *Anschluss* with the "big German brother" as a simple political way out of their troubles. There were, however, other reasons for such a solution, realist, practical, party-political reasons.

Dr. Otto Bauer was the first of his party to advocate the idea of a union with Germany among the masses, thus out-trumping the National Socialists. His voice could be heard in the central organ of the Social Democratic party which commented on the resolution of the Provisional National Assembly to declare "German Austria a component part of the German Republic according to Article 2 of the Law of the Constitution:

"It is now a Red Germany, a proletarian and Socialist Germany, with which we desire to unite ourselves and shall indeed be united. German Austria is a poor Alpine country with an inadequate agricultural economy, backward industry and a conservative peasant population. Forced to rely upon its own resources it would not yet be ready for a Socialist order of society. *Anschluss* with Germany means *Anschluss* with Socialism. For this reason the proclamation of an *Anschluss* with German is the most important and far-reaching of all the achievements of this great day."

The resolution and the various developments which followed, carried out with all the persuasive eloquence of Dr. Bauer and Dr. Renner, more than justified the words "the most far-reaching of all achievements." The methods adopted in pursuit of the aim envisaged, not to mention the goal itself, gave good cause for doubts. Those who expressed these doubts, however, or openly opposed the propaganda for an *Anschluss*, denouncing the unrealistic political considerations as dictated by emotion, found themselves unpopular. This *Anschluss* campaign was, however, at least in the manner in which it was launched—in open defiance and with undue haste—coupled with such obvious dangers for our new state that we of the *Reichspost* felt it was our duty to voice our opinion.

In this we found ourselves alone in the journalistic world, aware that our attitude might well be interpreted as influenced by unworthy intentions. For all that, we went into battle, for too much was at stake. The attitude of the *Reichspost* was then subjected for a long time to such violent criticism for its opposition to the *Anschluss* campaign, and the political errors committed at that time in the name of national policy and necessity were in fact so far-reaching, that a brief review of this fateful episode seems to me appropriate here.

The severe conditions of the peace treaty, dictated by force and the urge for retribution, threatened to deprive the German nation of its political, military and economic power. Far from increasing its national territory, the German state was indeed facing degradation. There was no longer any doubt that the victorious powers were about to enforce these dictates. What then was to be the fate of Austria?

On December 25, 1918, Dr. Otto Bauer, in his capacity as Secretary of State for Foreign Affairs, delivered a note to the diplomatic representatives of the victorious powers which culminated with a sentence referring to *Anschluss* with Germany as the "only and right way" to handle the Austrian problem. Negotiations with Weimar, the capital of the new German Republic, were begun.

A fortnight later the Provisional National Assembly adopted, with the two-thirds majority necessary for the passing of a constitutional measure, a bill introduced by the Council of State which provided that all citizens of Germany registered as domiciled in Austria on the day the Austrian election was announced had equal rights with the citizens of Austria to cast their vote in the forthcoming election of the Constituent National Assembly. The implication that Austria wished to be regarded as a constituent part of the German Republic was obvious. These elections were held in February, 1919.

Before the newly-elected National Assembly had a chance to discuss the *Anschluss* issue, that most delicate of all problems, the Secretary of State, Dr. Otto Bauer, hurried off to Weimar on February 23. A semi-official communiqué from Berlin published on March 3 revealed that this five-day visit was devoted exclusively to negotiations covering "all the essential details of the form and substance of the *Anschluss*." Dr. Bauer was evidently in a great hurry.

The Secretary of State was able to report on March 12 that a whole row of specialist commissions for the preparation of the *Anschluss* was being set up and would shortly begin work. In his program speech delivered on March 15 before the Constituent Assembly Dr. Renner declared: "Our foreign policy will always be directed toward achieving the reunion of our state with the Motherland."

The Secretary of State paid scant attention to bureaucratic procedure, not to mention the provisions of the constitution, in securing the services of Dr. Franz Klein, a permanent official, to whom he formally confided the organization and general administration of the *Anschluss* action on March 28. He thus gained the ardent support of a recognized legal authority with outstanding organizing abilities, himself an enthusiastic adherent of the *Anschluss* idea.

A fortnight before the Austrian delegation left for the peace conference at St. Germain, the National Assembly adopted the motion proposed by the Chancellor, Dr. Renner (as the result of an invitation from the Berlin government), to send a five-member deputation to attend the meetings of the German Constitutional Committee in Berlin. This was a bold decision indeed for the leading statesman of an impotent, small, defeated state.

The provincial government of Tyrol shortly afterward raised a protest against this risky course. Already on February 25 the leading political representatives of the people of Tyrol had made it clear, as a matter of constitutional principle, that the Pragmatic Sanction, the bond which had hitherto bound Tyrol with the other Austrian provinces, was no longer valid after the collapse of the Empire. The Provincial Diet of Tyrol was, therefore, alone competent to decide upon the future destiny of the Province. On March 6 the Tyrol deputy, Dr. Michael Mayr, expressed this point of view in the Constituent National Assembly in a protest based on legal principles which stressed quite clearly the threat to German South Tyrol. Dr. Ignaz Seipel sharply emphasized the need for a considered and responsible state policy in contrast to this *Anschluss* plan, the fruit of political calculation and sentimentality. Diplomatic representatives of neutral states well-disposed toward Austria warned against such an *Anschluss* policy.

On April 16 the Secretary of State for the Army, Dr. Deutsch, received certain information through Lieutenant Colonel Seiller, the Austrian liaison officer charged with maintaining contact with the military missions of the Entente powers in Vienna. This information, described as "useful hints and advice," came from the chief of the British military mission in Austria, Colonel Cunninghame, and drew attention to the fact that Austria could expect favorable peace terms (she would be able to keep South Tyrol, would receive territory in western Hungary and certain German border territories in Bohemia and Moravia to which she laid claim, as well as economic concessions) if she refrained from her striving for an *Anschluss*. Though not the official diplomatic representative of the Entente, Colonel Cunninghame was nevertheless one of their most important officials. The Secretary of State for the Army was clearly not the appropriate authority to make use of the information which he had received. It was, however, evident that this information had been given him to pass on to the responsible member of the Austrian government. The "hints and advice" concerned should obviously have been examined more closely, for the information was clearly of vital importance to Austria if proved correct. This was no private matter, but something which concerned the very life of Austria.

It was a whole month later, on May 15, before the parliamentary deputies and the general public learned about these hints and general advice from a leading article in the *Reichspost*. We referred to the "alchemistic secret science" of Dr. Bauer who had "ignored" the information which he had received. The Foreign Secretary maintained the view that the information supplied was of a private nature only and not intended to be passed on.

The *Reichspost* replied with the publication of the text containing the "hints and advice" which Lieutenant Colonel Seiller had noted in a memorandum immediately after his conversation with the chief of the British military mission in Vienna:

Colonel Cunninghame gave Lieutenant Colonel Seiller certain official information on April 16 which was not of an official character, but was intended as friendly information. The conditions of the peace settlement with Germany were about to be announced. These would be exceedingly severe. The friendly attitude toward German Austria shared by England and the United States will also be adopted by France. German Austria is to receive South Tyrol, West Hungary, considerable regions of Bohemia and Moravia, and can count on certain economic advantages.

Austria must, however, undertake as a primary condition in return to give up every idea of an *Anschluss* with Germany. To the objection that England and the United States had never hitherto displayed any interest in this question, Colonel Cunninghame replied that their point of view on this issue had now changed. On being further asked whether the Entente powers were aiming toward a Danube confederation, Colonel Cunninghame declared that this was not their intention but that they desired to see Austria remain neutral. The peace treaty would never permit an *Anschluss* of German Austria with Germany. The Social Democrats would do well to make allowance for this fact in their policy, for politics should not be dictated by sentiment or by party political interests.

But it was too late. By the time the text was made public the Austrian delegation to the peace conference was already in St. Germain. The "hints and advice" proferred by a figure who at that time ranked as the most distinguished official of the Entente powers played no part in the preparation of their mission, and very probably the leader of the delegation, the Chancellor, Dr. Renner, was quite unaware of the existence of such confidential information. He would otherwise scarcely have referred in a speech on the *Anschluss* question to "the eternal rights which we shall obtain, if need be from the stars themselves."

In accordance with the invitation received, the Austrian delegation to the Peace Conference was due to arrive in St. Germain on the evening of May 13. The negotiations for a peace treaty for German Austria were scheduled to begin the next day. The composition of the delegation was of paramount importance. In the person of Professor Heinrich Lammasch Austria had the services of a man regarded with the highest esteem in international circles, for he had gained a name for himself before the world as a courageous advocate of peace during the war. A man with his authority should have been entrusted with the leadership of the delegation. But Lammasch was no adherent of the *Anschluss* policy and he had moreover been a friend and adviser of Emperor Karl. Chancellor Renner and Secretary of State Bauer decided upon the former minister Dr. Franz Klein, trusted adviser in the *Anschluss* issue, the man summoned by the Secretary of State himself for service in his own ministry.

Klein had the Vienna Liberal press behind him. The delegation was to be chosen on May 8. A few days before I received through a diplomat friend a piece of information originating from French Ambassador Allizé, which had been given me in confidence to be passed on to the Christian-Social Club in Parliament:

"The appointment of Dr. Klein, a recognized protagonist of the *Anschluss*, as leader and spokesman of the delegation to the Peace Conference, will be interpreted as an offensive demonstration in Paris. Such an attitude on the part of Austria can only considerably worsen her position at the Peace Conference. Any chance there still may be of saving German South Tyrol for Austria can only be nullified if this man is chosen to head the delegation."

Allizé, who knew Vienna before the war and was full of warm-hearted appreciation of the Austrian national character, had recently given another proof of his good will in arranging for the supply of food from France for an almost starving Austria to reach us before negotiations for the corresponding credit action had been concluded. He now urgently appealed to us not to jeopardize Austria's position still further.

Since I was not myself a deputy, I had seldom made use of my right to speak in the Christian-Social Club. This time, however, I claimed the right and rose to voice a protest. Prälat Hauser, one of the three former presidents of the provisional government, had returned after the election of the first coalition cabinet to take over once again the presidency of the club.

The information I had to give caused quite a stir. I gave good reasons for a change in the leadership of the delegation to the Peace Conference. Dr. Seipel rose to support me, confirming the information I had just laid before the club with inside knowledge of his own. There was a breathless hush as he asked why the club had not been informed of the warning which, as he himself knew, had been received several days before, a grave warning of the utmost importance for the future of the state.

The atmosphere in the chamber was close, as though a thunderstorm were imminent. Prälat Hauser found himself in a difficult situation. He admitted that, as president of the club, he had been informed of the warning, but that he had considered the information as not intended to be passed on. A discussion developed in which the deputies demanded the change of the leader of the delegation. That same day Dr. Renner himself agreed to take over the leadership of the Austrian delegation in St. Germain in place of Dr. Klein. I made no subsequent attempt to inquire into what maneuvers behind the scenes could have led to the strange attitude adopted by Prälat Hauser.

The reception accorded the Austrian delegation in St. Germain emphatically confirmed the belief that a critical review of their own position would have been necessary in order to prepare the way for the peace negotiations. The Foreign Ministry in Vienna still cherished its fond illusions to such a degree that even at the very moment when the Austrian delegation was having to resign itself to the bitter facts, Sektionschef Riedel, the most distinguished ministerial advocate of the *Anschluss* plan, together with several other official Austrian delegates, was sent to Berlin with the purpose of furthering the *Anschluss* campaign, *soi disant* incognito.

On May 23 I published the following commentary in plain, straightforward language, on the *Anschluss* issue in a leader in the *Reichspost*:

> Surely nothing can give greater cause for concern than the thought that at this very moment, when in St. Germain the most vital decisions involving the national and economic future of our state, perhaps even our last breath of life, are at stake, the position of our delegation—already burdened by so many political errors—is being made even more difficult or that the confidence in its loyalty and seriousness of purpose could be shaken. The Paris Conference had informed Germany that one of the essential conditions for the conclusion of a peace treaty is Germany's renunciation of a political *Anschluss* with German Austria. If, however, at this very moment when the peace delegation in St. Germain is due to start its delicate task of negotiation, Vienna nevertheless persists in toying about with this critical issue, the consequences are only too clear for every thinking person.

The Austrian delegates found themselves in an unfriendly, not to say hostile, milieu in St. Germain. They were interned in the Villa Reinach and two adjoining buildings. The room assigned to them as a sort of sitting room was cordoned off and they were not permitted to pass beyond these "frontiers." Gendarmes ensured the observance of this strict isolation. The delegates were not even allowed to correspond by letter with the outside world without such private letters being examined by the censor. The delegates were denied the right to take their place with the representatives of the Entente powers at the conference table and so exchange arguments verbally: all contact was restricted to the formal and complicated exchange of written notes. When at one of the rare official occasions in the palace of St. Germain the delegates had to meet the Allied representatives, they were not permitted to use the beautiful

stone staircase of the palace, but were directed to the narrow servants' staircase, the *escalier de services*.

Professor Lammasch had also been assigned by Vienna as a
member of the delegation. Dr. Franz Schumacher, former president
of the District Court of Triente, who represented the interests of
Tyrol in the delegation, comments with tactful reserve on the position accorded to Lammasch in the delegation:

"Every outward consideration and courtesy was shown him by
the leader of the delegation during the stay in St. Germain. Much
less consideration, however, seemed to be given to the weight of his
personality, also in practical affairs. The longer the delegation remained in St. Germain, the less was the importance attached to his
views and his counsel until the point finally came when, having
completed his principal task in preparing the amendments to be
submitted in modification of the stipulations of the League of Nations contained in the peace proposals, he was forced to admit that
his presence was as good as superfluous. Since he had no wish to
stand around to no purpose, he left Paris on June 10, long before
the work of the delegation had come to an end, together with the
representatives of the various Austrian provinces, by no means
satisfied with the way things were looking at the Peace Conference."
("Lammasch in St. Germain" from the book "*Heinrich Lammasch,
seine Aufzeichungen, sein Wirken und seine Politik,*" published in
1922 by Deuticke, Vienna).

The Slovak people's leader, Fr. Andreas Hlinka, visited me in
May on his return to Vienna from Paris where he had sought to
establish contact with the leading statesmen at the Peace Conference. He had always been friendly disposed towards me since the
days when I had championed his cause in the *Reichspost* against the
persecution of the ruthless Magyarization policy of the Hungarian
government to which this fine man had been subjected as leader of
the Slovaks. Our long friendship and the strong desire to pour out
his heart after his experiences in Paris to someone whom he knew to
be a true friend of his people prompted this old warrior from Rosenberg to come to me in the *Reichspost* office. He was deeply concerned by the course which the Peace Conference in Paris was taking under the influence of Beneš and Masaryk in regard to the con-

struction of Central Europe, a course which threatened to thwart the Slovak demands for a constitutional autonomy for Slovakia.

Hlinka stood up in the middle of our conversation, deeply upset. His voice was trembling with suppressed anger. "The Czechs will never beat us down," he declared, "even if we have to sign a pact with the devil against them!" I have often thought of Hlinka's words. He remained a fierce opponent of the Prague advocates of a Czechoslovakian common state to the day of his death, but his own dreams of the presidency of a Slovak national state were only short-lived.

When the terms of the draft peace treaty presented to the Austrian delegation in St. Germain on June 2 were made known in Austria, the whole country rose in shocked protest. Immediately after the text was published Cardinal Piffl turned to the Pope for help in the name of the Austrian Episcopate; he sought the mediation of the Nuncio in Vienna and of Monsignore Maglione, the Vatican representative in Berne. The chairman of the Christian-Social Union drafted a noble manifesto addressed to "the Christians of all nations," a few passages of which are quoted below:

We are not pleading for pity, nor are we threatening a new revolution. Our voices are raised in the name of Christian justice, that justice which is the very foundation of the social and constitutional well-being of all nations. The Peace Treaty of St. Germain threatens to bring about the complete annihilation of German Austria.

A diligent, unassuming and talented people, esteemed for its hospitality and its natural gaiety, is condemned to die as a pauper. What crime have we committed to warrant such a fate? It is true that we loyally defended our native land, the country now faced with destruction; we fought to the last, counting no sacrifice too great, until, weakened by hunger and outnumbered by the enemy, we could fight no more. Our people laid down their lives in the rocky mountains on the borders of the Tyrol, in the gorges of the Isonzo and in the sandy steppes and marshlands of the borders of Russia. We willingly sacrificed our best and our dearest in the defense of our country. Since when has patriotic courage ranked as a crime, a crime, moreover, which divests a people of the right to their home?

We invariably encountered chivalry and honor in our opponents on the field of battle. Why should we be condemned to die like criminals now that the combat is over? The bitter struggle of humanity surely cannot end by setting up a memorial of force and injustice on the mass graves of the fallen? These years of tribulation and distress for the whole human race surely cannot end now with further destruction.

The realization of the cruel fate destined for us German-Austrians under the terms of the Peace Treaty of St. Germain would entail the complete obliteration of a Christian nation. The whole world would be poorer for the loss of a sacred ethnic institution and for the loss of belief in justice and in the inviolability of the Christian civilization. In the name of this threatened Christian civilization we appeal to our fellow Christians in every nation for help for our poor country, already bleeding from a thousand wounds and condemned to a bitter death!

Before the final settlement of the peace treaty Dr. Otto Bauer, the Foreign Secretary, resigned from office. Unable to rectify the grave errors already committed, he was at least honest enough to admit the failure of the extreme policy which he had adopted. The Chancellor, Dr. Renner, who took over his office as Foreign Minister, was forced to declare in his report to the House of Deputies on September 6, 1919: "We have been charged with a gigantic burden, a burden which, despite all our efforts, exceeds every expectation."

The Social Democratic spokesman and deputy, Karl Leuthner, was even sharper in his choice of words in the subsequent debate on the peace negotiations in St. Germain. It is essential to bear in mind these comments on the peace treaty and to realize the position of Austria on September 6, 1919, in order fully to comprehend the magnitude of the fine work of recovery and reconstruction which Dr. Ignaz Seipel was shortly to accomplish in the service of his country.

The coalition government set up on March 15, 1919, after the February elections for the Constituent National Assembly, was a dubious structure composed of Social Democrats and Christian-Socials. It was lacking both in firm internal unity and in an agreed objective. The sole real expression of the coalition was the composition of the government, which included leading figures from both big parties. In this so-called partnership the Social Democrats, stimulated by their considerable gains in the elections, were determined from the start to dominate, confident of further political successes to come. The Social Democratic spokesman, Deputy Eldersch, declared quite unequivocally in the program debate that the success and duration of this political working arrangement depended on the chance provided to begin the work of socialization as quickly as possible, unhampered by capitalist interference. The government must, so he said, be "inspired by a truly Socialist spirit and get to work on the transformation of the democratic republic into a socialist republic."

These words go to illustrate the extent of the Social Democratic partner's claims to leadership in this government coalition, unconditional claims which inevitably forced the Christian-Socials to forego or to modify many of their demands. These same political formulae were to be encountered everywhere in various guise, culminating in the radical Communist demands voiced in tumultuous public meetings and in the streets.

Austrian Social Democracy was visibly under heavy pressure. Up to the summer of 1919 one bloody dictatorship followed another in Germany and the countries of Central Europe: Spartakus in Berlin and Hamburg, Chemnitz and Halle, Kurt Eisner in Bavaria, Karolyi in Hungary, a second revolution in Bavaria, Bela Kun and Tibor Szamuelly. In Austria itself there were workers' and soldiers' councils; illegal force was used; there was terror, house searching, requisitioning in the Vienna margarine factories, in the Grand Hotel and in the bakeries, in private houses and apartments. Looting by gangs of armed "home guards" provided the goods for large-scale black-marketing activities.

In Baden, the spa near Vienna, there were notice boards with proclamations issued by the revolutionary councils. Arbitrary arrests were common and there was wholesale plundering in Neunkirchen and other centers of industry. In Graz bombs exploded during a political meeting held by the Christian-Socials in the Industrial Hall. The state administration all but disintegrated. At the Federal Provincial Conference the Chancellor, Dr. Renner, was already talking about "anarchism" and of "a panic-like state of unrest which had its origins in Hungary." Political agents swarmed over the frontier, subversive political speakers preaching a revolutionary doctrine. A file in the Vienna police headquarters registered no less than fifteen cases of the use of illegal interference on the part of workers' councils in the market regulations. It was only too evident that if these anarchist activities were not brought to a standstill, the administration would collapse completely. These illegal activities undermined official authority.

The attitude of the *Reichspost* during these turbulent months was as straightforward as it was critical. The value of the freedom of the press as a public institution was more than ever evident at this moment when we were concerned with the daily task of confronting the anarchists and those responsible for the use of illegal force. We were concerned to serve truth and justice at a time when many leaders of the people were themselves often unable to speak openly for the very want of facilities. There were, moreover, many honest men who were reduced to silence, overwhelmed and intimidated by the turn of events.

We of the *Reichspost* made ourselves extremely unpopular in various quarters at that time, especially among the various illegal "subsidiary governments." A few weeks after the elections in February, 1919, for the Constituent National Assembly and the new government, the Secretary of State for Finance, Dr. Joseph Schumpeter, asked me to come to see him in his office in the Himmelpfortgasse. On behalf of the government he had taken it upon himself to advise me urgently to move out of my private apartment into the Hotel Imperial where the presence of Italian occupation troops would guarantee my safety. The Austrian authorities themselves felt incapable of undertaking security measures and would be glad to be relieved of the concern for my person. He was sure I would myself understand their point of view.

I understood well enough. I thanked this kind Secretary of State who had left his private scholarly world to serve the state as finance specialist at this critical hour. I did not move my family to the Hotel Imperial, for I could never have afforded what it would have cost me. Upon hearing of the government's good counsel, Dr. Gessmann immediately offered me the use of his apartment in

Vienna, as he himself was going off on vacation for some time. I accepted his offer gratefully and my wife and small son were established in the safety of Dr. Gessmann' apartment for several weeks. It was indeed a highly necessary security measure.

Illegal force and terror were everywhere; house searchings and requisitioning were common occurrences. "Wherever one looks, nothing but terror," as Leopold Kunschak described the situation in a speech on April 16, 1919. The Communists set up great placards urging Austria to "Join the Soviet Republic of Russia and Hungary! Long live the world revolution! Long live the Soviet Republic of German Austria!"

When the Communist Soviet Republic in Hungary collapsed at the beginning of August, 1919, the ringleaders fled to Austria, which naturally led to still further unrest. With the utmost difficulty they ultimately got out of the country by July, 1920, sent off to Moscow via Germany.

Many Christian-Social parliamentarians were understandably none too happy about the sharply critical attitude adopted by the *Reichspost*, not because they in fact disagreed with our point of view, on the contrary, but because they themselves were unjustly charged by the opposition with being responsible for the policy of the *Reichspost*.

One evening in the early summer of 1919 I had a visit from a Christian-Social deputy who had long been a good friend of mine and whom I held in the highest esteem. What he told me that evening as we sat at my desk was no great surprise to me. He was quite frank with me. It seemed that I was proving a nuisance, and by my critical attitude reflected in the *Reichspost* was disturbing the necessary peaceable co-operation between the two big parties.

My convictions were, of course, respected, but it was felt that it would be better if I would exchange my activities as editor of the *Reichspost* with some other, nonpolitical post. The appropriate quarters were fully prepared to fulfill any wish I might have in this direction. I replied laughingly that these gentlemen had certainly no post in their administration sufficiently attractive and lucrative to tempt me. On the other hand I understood their political embarrassment—it was after all still the era of the first coalition government—and their appeal for moderation, and I agreed to consider the matter.

My kind friend came back in a few days to hear what I had decided. "There is only one post which I would wish for if I were to give up my work as a journalist," I told him. "The post of Austrian Ambassador at the Vatican is vacant. This office, combining a service to the Church, is what I would like." A few days later I was duly informed that the Secretary of State, Dr. Otto Bauer, had agreed and that the Council of Ministers had unanimously approved the solution. The Under-Secretary of State, Wilhelm Miklas, who was in charge of cultural affairs, asked me to come to see him. He asked me one or two questions concerning ecclesiastical-political problems, negotiations which would have to be undertaken with the Holy See by the new ambassador. These problems were not new to me. The Under-Secretary declared the interview to have been very satisfactory.

Some time before Dr. Otto Bauer resigned from his office as Foreign Secretary on July 25, the agreement of the Holy See to my appointment was officially requested. Reports of this appeared in the press. It was divulged in journalistic circles that simultaneously with the change in the editorship of the *Reichspost* a change was also to be made on the *Arbeiter Zeitung* whose editor, Friedrich Austerlitz—another disturber of the peace like myself—was also to be promoted to another post.

The gentlemen concerned had, however, reckoned without Dr. Seipel who was, after all, the chairman of the *Herold* concern and as a member of the presiding committee of the Christian-Social Union had every good right to voice his opinion in such a matter. He had, in fact, not been consulted. He made no secret to me of the fact that he wished me to remain with the *Reichspost*.

The reply from Rome took a surprisingly long time to arrive. With evident pleasure Prälat Seipel told me of its receipt and of its contents when we met at the Vienna Christian-Social party congress on Candelmas Day, February 2, 1920. "The Vatican does not desire your appointment," he told me briefly. "The matter is closed." I understood his attitude perfectly. He had no illusions about the task which lay ahead of him and he was not going to allow himself to be deprived of my friendship and counsel in Vienna; above all he had need of the vital reliable support of a large paper like the *Reichspost*. He wanted to be sure that the paper would be in good hands. In making use of his contacts in the appropriate circles in Rome he had backed the editor of the *Reichspost*.

The publication of the news that the appointment of Dr. Funder as ambassador to the Vatican had been declined caused something of a stir, and gave rise to various conjectures. One commentary surmised that the attitude which I had adopted against Italy before the war had influenced the Vatican to consider the sensibilities of various state departments in their decision, an interpretation which caused the leader of the Italian *Fascio* in Austria, Dr. Morreale (a man whose office bore more weight than that of the official ambassador) to assure me that he was authorized to declare that this supposition was groundless. And so I stayed on in my post as editor, and perhaps for this reason Friedrich Austerlitz, my great journalist colleague from the other camp, also remained with his *Arbeiter Zeitung* until he died.

Meanwhile inflation was continuing at full speed. The Austrian economy was faced with disaster. As partner in the coalition government, the Christian-Socials naturally shared to an extent the responsibility for the rapid deterioration of the country's economic position, but for all that the actual government was conducted almost exclusively by the majority party, the Social Democrats. At that time the name of Ignaz Seipel, the man who at countless political meetings had raised the vital questions concerned with the Austrian state and its people, became well known throughout the country.

On October 17 "an agreement on the basic principles of the new coalition" was reached, an agreement which set up as a primary condition that "both parties should share the responsibility together" for the general policy adopted by the government and for government actions mutually agreed upon. This appeared to be a decisive step in the right direction. It was indeed an urgent necessity in view of the rapidly deteriorating situation. On December 11 Chancellor Renner was forced to declare to the representatives of the Supreme Council in Paris:

"Our situation is so desperate that we dare not even return home to Vienna without bread and credit. No government can take it upon itself to continue in office in the knowledge that within a few days millions of people will be faced with ruin. The world would never forgive this government for not having the courage to warn the whole world in time of the catastrophe which threatens our country."

The result was the provision of a credit fund by The Netherlands and the balance of an American dollar credit. The Council moreover firmly declared that the Powers would oppose every attempt to violate the integrity of Austrian territory. Senator Imbert de la Tour furthermore emphasized: "There can be no equilibrium in Central Europe without an independent Austria."

When in 1938 the independence of Austria was brutally destroyed, with disastrous consequences for the whole world, the truth of these words had long since been forgotten in the chancelleries of Europe.

It became evident all too soon that the high hopes which had been set on the renewed coalition, with its formal working contract, were not to be realized. Dr. Seipel, newly-elected chairman of the Christian-Social Union, openly voiced this disillusionment in a sensational speech. He left open the question as to whether the coalition partner had failed to adhere to the conditions laid down in the formal agreement, either because it was unwilling to do so or because it was in fact unable to comply with these points. Whatever the case might be, a change was clearly necessary in the near future, a change which would introduce "new constitutional and economic principles." The decisive year had now come. It would, so Seipel declared, only be a change for the better if the Christian-Socials prevailed in the forthcoming new elections, "for our principles are the right principles and all the more so viewed in contrast to the mistaken policy of the others."

The speech resounded throughout the country, and it became more and more evident that the second coalition was nearing its end. Undeniable facts pronounced its indictment. In July 1919, the budget figures for 1919/20 showed a deficit of four billion kronen. As a result of the appalling inflation and the rise in expenditures, this deficit had increased to 10.6 billion by the spring of 1920.

The coalition received its death-blow from another quarter, however, from the Army Department. Although Paragraph 10 of the Defense Act expressly laid down that "the military service regulations will be issued by the State Government," the Department for the Army took it upon itself to issue a highly important regulation on May 29, without first consulting the Cabinet as a whole, including, of course, the Christian-Social coalition partner. This constituted a flagrant breach of the law, committed by no less a person than a member of the Cabinet itself. Even in this system, perilously near collapse though it was, it was still surprising, and in any case it sufficed as an indictment against the minister.

On June 11 the matter reached its dramatic climax in the National Assembly when the coalition, and with it the government, disintegrated in full session. Two Pan-German deputies questioned the Chancellor personally as to the "unlawful issue" of the service regulation. Dr. Renner met the question with silence and left it to the Secretary of State for the Army to justify the issue of his formal regulation as "merely an internal instruction." Leopold Kunschak, who at once rose as Christian-Social speaker, made the legal position quite clear and declared unequivocally the consequences to be faced as a result of the infringement: the regulation in question was to be withdrawn until the approval of the government as a whole had been obtained.

"We are confronted here with an infringement of the law on the part of the Secretary for the Army," said Kunschak. "It was his duty to present the said regulation to the Cabinet and obtain its sanction beforehand. We are, therefore, not in the position to accept any responsibility for the regulation, regarding it in fact as contrary to the law. It is in our opinion the duty of the Secretary to withdraw the order and to present it to the Cabinet as a whole for approval."

A few tactful words from the side of the Social Democrats, though they would scarcely have prevented the government crisis, might have prevented to some extent the regrettable way in which the matter ended. The radical spokesman chosen by the Social

Democrats to champion their cause only succeeded in ruining their last chances. The same day Dr. Renner and his party friends in the government asked the approval of the Social Democrat Club for their resignation. All subsequent attempts to bridge the gap between the two parties failed.

The end was far from glorious. A mutual working contract, drawn up in all formality, was abandoned with singular lack of formality. The coalition would have parted company in different circumstances had the express wishes of Dr. Seipel been deferred to; Dr. Seipel was himself prevented from being present in Parliament, due to a serious street-car accident.

According to an unwritten law of parliamentary democracy, the task of forming a new government fell to the strongest political party; but Dr. Renner's Social Democrats declined. For all that a "*bourgeois* coalition" was desired by no one, except perhaps its Social Democratic opposition, and so the crisis dragged on.

Before he resigned from office Chancellor Renner had been able to lay the contents of the note received from the Paris Reparations Commission before the Finance Committee. Not only he, but the whole people of Austria had hoped that this note would reward his efforts to bring about some alleviation of the peace terms dictated at St. Germain. He had put all his energy and diplomatic skill into these negotiations. In the note the Reparations Commission freed Austria from the preferential mortgage law which had burdened public property, public revenue, all monopolies, hydroelectric power and transport, forestry and the confiscated agricultural crown lands. A general mortgage was thus removed which had barred the way to public credit. The removal of this control laid the way open for the issuance of Austrian Treasury bills which, with the guarantee of the entire Austrian possessions, would enable Austria to participate in the action of the International Credit Committee for economic recovery in the distressed countries of Central Europe.

Figures were already made known of the foodstuffs which would be made available for the country by this scheme: 200,000 tons of flour from America and other welcome items. But to achieve this Austria was forced to sacrifice to a great extent her independence. The sale of property belonging to the state, the various federal provinces or the cities, was made subject to the approval of the Austrian Section of the Reparations Commission. Public revenue and its uses were similarly controlled and any proposed changes in existing legislation or the introduction of new laws was covered by these regulations.

The Chancellor made no attempt to minimize the significance of the restrictions imposed. He was better equipped than anyone else to judge the position; he had after all seen for himself the elements on the other side and was conscious of the mistakes which Austria herself had made. As he now declared: "With the arrival of the Reparations Commission and the operation of the Peace Treaty we shall be entering a new phase in the life of our state. All those who play a part in public life must come to terms with this new fact and make the fullest use of it, politically, economically and socially. The Reparations Commission will, I hope, prove to be a benevolent guardian, but for all that it is none the less a guardian!"

This new fact with which it was so necessary to "come to terms" was simply that the Allies had taken over the guardianship of Austria. It was an inescapable and compelling fact.

Two years later, if anything in even more desperate straits, Austria was forced to pledge herself to still heavier commitments in connection with the Geneva relief action achieved by Dr. Seipel. It is worthwhile to compare the situation in Austria in 1920 with that of 1922 and to consider in this light the justification of the censure leveled by Dr. Otto Bauer, not in 1920 but in 1922, a censure which dictated the policy of his party.

Chapter 15
A MAN OF COURAGE

The difficulties which obstructed the formation of a new government at the beginning of the summer of 1920 only served to indicate what had been neglected and wasted during the period of co-operation of the two big political parties, despite their formal working agreement. After an interregnum of almost one month, a "proportional government" was set up, a strange creation born of necessity, and a novelty for Austria. It was made up of twelve secretaries of state and four under-secretaries, the ministries were distributed among all the political parties. By no stretch of imagination, however, could it be said to represent a government in which every party contributed its best in a concentrated effort to fulfil the exacting tasks of the moment. The government was in no way a living organism, it had no real program, nor had it a chancellor or a vice-chancellor or any organs of representative character. The chairman of this unique governmental body, Dr. Michael Mayr, was only concerned with presiding over the cabinet meetings and with counter-signing documents upon request of the Cabinet.

The new administration, composed of representatives of the various parties selected according to the number of seats held by these parties in Parliament, was very clearly an emergency structure and was not expected to last long.[1]

The election campaigns of the next few months were accompanied by all the various evils which had overshadowed the life of our country since the collapse of the Empire. We viewed with a sigh of relief the dawn of Election Day on October 17, 1920. Need-

[1] The 1929 Constitution finally brought the election of the government by Parliament to an end by transferring the appointment of the government to the federal President, who now nominates the federal Chancellor of his own accord and the other ministers at the suggestion of the federal Chancellor.

less to say there had been heated political battling during the campaign, but a review of the past three months showed nevertheless that considerable ground had been covered. Above all, the constitution had been drawn up, an achievement which was encouraging and belied the reputation of the proportional system. The credit for this success goes in large measure to Dr. Michael Mayr, the Innsbruck professor of constitutional law. Quietly and diligently, despite many obstacles and in the face of political cross-fire, he completed the preparation of the constitutional legislation as president of this strange governmental body. It now remained to instill life into this constitutional legislation, which became effective as of October 1, and the election results were all the more eagerly awaited.

The Christian-Socials spared neither time nor energy in their work of emphasizing to the people of Austria the vital significance of this election. Never since Lueger's day had the party had a better team of men to lead it, men whose steadfast and courageous outlook inspired real confidence in those stormy days of political unrest.

The elections of October 17 changed the political balance. The Social Democrats polled 1,072,709 votes, whereas the Christian-Socials got a total of 1,245,531. In contrast to the election of 1919 in which the Social Democrats had claimed 1,211,814 votes, this party had now lost some 139,000 of its electorate, thus forfeiting its position as Austria's leading political party. The Christian-Socials, on the other hand, who in the February elections had shown a considerable loss in their total of 1,068,382, had now made up this deficit with the gain of 177,149 votes. The electoral ratio between the two parties was in fact reversed.

From the increased total number of seats in Parliament the Social Democrats now held 66 in place of their former 69. The Christian-Social seats increased from 63 to 82, the German Nationals and the Peasant League gained 26, as compared with their former 25. It was particularly significant in the composition of these figures that in Vienna the Social Democrats polled only 47 per cent of the total vote cast. The party had thus lost the proudest jewel in its political crown.

The German National Democratic parties had polled 617,984

votes in 1919; in the election of October, 1922, the vote dropped to 514,127.[2]

Although the election results had changed the parliamentary position of the two ideological mass parties, the primary political problem—the basic government policy—was by no means solved. The Christian-Socials now ranked as the strongest party in the National Diet, it was true, but they did not in themselves constitute a majority, and certainly not the necessary two-thirds majority which would have secured them the power to settle independently issues of constitutional importance.

Two possibilities now lay open: either the strict application of the majority principle, by which the single strongest party would conclude a political alliance and take over the responsibility for the government of the state, or else the establishment of a non-party government. The Christian-Socials favored the second solution. They advocated the setting up of a Cabinet composed of specialists, believing that such a solution would also make it easier for the Social Democrats to participate in the difficult work confronting the new government in view of the state of the national economy and the general situation in the country. They maintained that a party government as such was an unacceptable solution, considering the balance of political power in the national Diet, the lack of a real majority, not to mention the state of emergency in the state itself.

Seipel declared categorically: "State politics, not party politics! The subordination of party interest in a common endeavor to save our country, which is struggling for its very existence! Above all, a sound economic policy!" His appeal resounded in vain. The Social Democrats firmly rejected any practical participation. The Pan-Germans favored a cabinet made up of civil service men, but at the same time refused to consider those of the leading personalities capable of taking over the exacting governmental functions, notably the proposed premier, the president of the Vienna Police Department, Dr. Johannes Schober.

[2] In the election of national deputies under Seipel's first government in 1923 the Christian-Social vote rose to the unprecedented figure of 1,490,870, whereas the Social Democrat vote remained virtually unchanged with 1,311,-870 votes.

Faced with the accusation that they were seeking to evade their responsibilities as the largest political party, the Christian-Socials resorted to the only possible solution under the given circumstances. On November 21 they nominated Dr. Michael Mayr, a man from their own ranks, as head of a cabinet made up of four Christian-Socials and six high-ranking administrative officials, each a specialist in his own field. The parliamentary principle had been instrumental in this solution, still only a half-measure, however, in the face of the problem confronting the various political parties.

The new cabinet took over an empty exchequer and empty granaries. The national expenditure increased daily in step with the rapid inflation. In Zurich the Austrian krone was worth little more than a centime. The stage was soon reached when even the health of the nation began to suffer.

I was in no way exaggerating when I wrote the following words in New Year 1921:

Usurious profits of almost incredible sums are being amassed every day. Even the classes of society which only a few years ago could be counted upon as reserves of the nation's moral strength have been infected by the pest of rapacity and hardness of heart. Those who can close their eyes to the sight of the poor who are nearing starvation seem to have been caught up in a mad frenzy of pleasure-seeking. Never before have there been so many bars, cabarets and night clubs in Vienna and never have these been so full. Thousands of people are dying in our city, the hospitals are full to overflowing with rickety children. From the depths of this misery comes the hungry cry of the masses, an angry protest against those who can indulge in such irresponsible high living at this time of the people's direst need. Yet this drunken revelery continues, a never-ending carnival danced over the graves of the dead.

No sooner had the new government assumed office than the Social Democratic Trade Union organized a postal strike. Yet another burden was placed upon the unfortunate country at the very moment when the talks on the question of credits to Austria had reached their decisive stage in London. The strike brought the nation to the verge of anarchy.

It was barely over before a new appeal for an *Anschluss* with Germany was suddenly launched from the Pan-German camp. This party had reserved a "free hand" in political affairs, but it had nevertheless been hoped that it would lend its support to the non-Socialist Chancellor. This *Anschluss* action, started in the most critical circumstances and without the remotest chance of success, threatened to seal the fate of Austria. The proposal introduced in the national Diet for a general plebiscite on the *Anschluss* issue resulted in individual plebiscites being held in the various federal provinces. On April 24 such a plebiscite was held in Tyrol in very dubious circumstances, a second followed in Salzburg on May 29. The Styrian Provincial Diet, under Christian-Social leadership, supported a Pan-German motion proposing a plebiscite in Styria with its decision to hold such a plebiscite on July 3.

All through the spring negotiations on the part of the Finance Committee of the League of Nations had dragged on, but a certain amount of progress had nevertheless been made. The finance program of the Austrian government and the guarantees offered for a credit had been accepted. At long last a ray of hope appeared on the horizon for our unfortunate country. At this crucial moment came this *Anschluss* campaign, launched by a political faction which had thereby overstepped its constitutional authorization. Chancellor Mayr gave the only possible answer: the government resigned. Since according to events in Styria the Christian-Social party also seemed to have failed and it was evident that nowhere could the state reckon with the willing support of any one of the political parties in

---

³ The formal Allied veto of the "*Anschluss,*" or union with the German Republic, decided the fate of this political demand. From this moment onward all *Anschluss* propaganda, no matter how well-founded economically, was unrealistic and directed against the vital interests of Austria. As is well known, Hitler occupied Austria by force in March, 1938, after years of systematic propaganda in preparation for this step by a fanatic National Socialist minority. The experiences of the Nazi regime in Austria, and above all the recognition won by the remarkable economic development of the country after World War II, have led to the fact that the vast majority of the people of Austria are convinced of the economic vitality of Austria, with the result that the idea of an *Anschluss* with Germany has vanished completely from the political scene. All the political parties in Austria today support the concept of a free, independent and self-reliant Austria.

Austria, not even with that of the very party which had hitherto formed the core of Austrian state-consciousness, it was small wonder that the political order of the country showed signs of disintegrating. Things indeed looked so bad that there were suspicious-looking troop concentrations in Jugoslavia and south of the Brenner, the purpose of which was clear enough. Was this to be "Finis Austriae"? Was the country about to be parceled out among the other nations?

At this decisive moment the second Christian-Social party congress to be held under the Republic took place on June 7. This congress was significant for the postwar history of the Austrian nation. It was at this congress that Dr. Seipel accomplished a master stroke of party and state politics. From the point of view of party politics this achievement enabled him to form the basis for the great work of economic rehabilitation upon which he was to embark one year later in his capacity as federal Chancellor. The paramount task which confronted him at that moment, however, was the re-establishment of political unity between the two opposing camps within the Christian-Social party itself. His second vital task was finally to integrate the Pan-Germans into a stabilized government system. This political party had hitherto shirked the responsibility of such integration, but it was clear that only by winning its support and participation could a firm and competent government be established. If this could be achieved in the face of the only too evident process of political disintegration, it was possible that the moral credit thus won would provide the necessary basis for the economic assistance from abroad which Austria needed so desperately and on which she was pinning her hopes for the future.

Jodok Fink, the former chairman of the Christian-Social Union, had proposed Dr. Seipel to take his place, a proposal which was unanimously adopted. Dr. Seipel now opened the party congress with a proclamation by the party council in Vienna which revealed the complete unity of the Christian-Social party in Vienna. In this manifesto the party council unanimously approved the action introduced by the former government for the restoration of the Austrian national economy with the assistance of the League of Nations; it further appealed to all parties in the national Diet and in the provinces to refrain from any action which might be detrimental to or hinder such an action. The party council therefore demanded the establishment of a government which would consistently pursue this policy. The press reports on the party congress all stressed the gravity which characterized the proceedings of this congress, which was attended by delegates from all the federal provinces. The Governor of the federal province of Styria was also present.

In his introductory speech as chairman of the Christian-Social Union, Dr. Seipel drew a picture of the general situation in Austria. He sketched the history of the new Republic and indicated the task which now confronted the Christian-Social party, a task which the party assumed fully conscious of its high responsibilities: the preservation of the state of Austria and the avoidance of every action which could stand in the way of the realization of this aim. He spoke openly of the "far from gratifying spectacle" of the downfall of a government led by a member of the Christian-Social party, the most powerful political party in the country, at the very moment when it had at last achieved a measure of success after a long period of hard work in seemingly hopeless circumstances. This downfall had been directly caused by members of the Christian-Social party in the various federal provinces who had sabotaged the foreign policy of the government and of the Christian Social Union in the various federal legislative bodies.

"We must realize here and now that the party cannot and will not withstand such a trial of its strength a second time," he warned. "A crisis like this can befall a party once, and if the party is a vital organism and its various branches and groups are linked together by the strong fundamental bond of common principles, it can overcome the crisis—but only on the condition that the causes of the crisis are removed for the future."

On the second day of the congress Dr. Seipel once again spoke to the party delegates, emphasizing the fact that the unanimous policy of the Christian-Social party as a whole was contained in all the official communiqués of the various party branches, and that the vital task now confronting the party was to secure the existence of the state and people of Austria under the conditions created by the Peace Treaty. This speech met with such a response that the resolution which followed, and which was framed in similar terms, was unanimously adopted. This was indeed a remarkable achievement. The congress had succeeded in putting an end to the crisis which had threatened the disintegration of the Christian-Social party. The re-action which followed in Styria showed that the Christian-Social population of the province were only too glad to be relieved of the tumult of a conflict in which they had had no real part. As a token of the party's confidence in Seipel and his policy the congress elect-ed him chairman of the Christian-Social party in succession to Prince Alois Liechtenstein.

Seipel now turned to his second task. He was faced with the problem of forming a stable government, a prerequisite for which was to obtain the co-operation of the Pan-Germans. This party was now even prepared to accept Schober as Chancellor—thus evading the choice of a man from the ranks of the Christian-Socials—and it was now up to Seipel to win over the Pan-Germans to support a political course based on Christian-Social principles. He therefore sought the authorization of the Christian-Social Union to declare officially to the other parties that if the Pan-Germans did not wish to obstruct the economic aid provided by the League of Nations, and if they seriously aimed for a working Cabinet under Schober, then they would find the Christian-Socials ready to co-operate with them. It was, however, up to the Pan-Germans to help to bury once and for all the affair of the plebiscite in Styria (which had origina-ted from the ranks of the Pan-Germans in that province) and in fact all plebiscite proceedings as such.

Thus agreement was reached. The way was clear for action. The Christian-Socials in Styria eased the situation by their decision in the Styrian Provincial Diet to propose the withdrawal of the mo-tion for a plebiscite. The executive of the Pan-German People's party declared the party's willingness to participate in the election of a specialist Cabinet and to give its support to this government—a hopeful contrast to the "free hand" policy which it had hitherto maintained.

The Christian-Social Union thereupon declared itself prepared to co-operate in this way, on condition that the basic political policy consistently pursued by the Christian-Socials were also accepted by the Pan-German party as the authoritative fundamental policy for the immediate future. The following agreement resulted:

1. The government appointed is to carry through the work of rehabilitation with the assistance of the aid provided by the Finance Commission of the League of Nations. The parties electing this government will give it their support in accordance with the obligations assumed by them toward the delegates of the League of Nations, provided that a decision on the credit aid is reached by the fall of this year at the latest.

2. The parties guarantee that further *Anschluss* plebiscites will not be held as long as this political agreement lasts.

What had been achieved was a working pact conditionally limited by time, an unequivocal political program, and above all a stable government. The program and the political principles on which this was based had been fought for and won by Dr. Ignaz Seipel. He had retrieved Austria from a perilous situation which had seemed almost hopeless and had set up a new order for the country, the first vital step toward establishing the national well-being.

On June 21, 1921, the Schober "specialist government" was elected by 98 votes against the 67 of the Social Democrats. In addition to the specialist ministers, two Christian-Socials were included in the Cabinet. Seipel's achievement, the result of patient and tenacious hard work and no less brilliant diplomacy, is all the more to be appreciated in the light of the crisis which had threatened to disintegrate the political life of the country.

The new government was faced with no easy task. Concern for the foreign credits so desperately needed increased as the issue dragged on endlessly in England, for either the Allies failed to realize the urgency of the Austrian problem or the matter was half-strangled in bureaucratic red tape. The promised financial aid committed the government to fulfill certain conditions involving far-reaching tax and administrative measures. Behind all this, moreover, hovered the profiteers and speculators, a constant danger to the precarious economy, not to mention the activities of the terrorists and law-breakers. The ominous events of December 1, 1921, in which rioters reduced the main shopping streets in the center of Vienna and in various other districts to ruins in protest against the growing inflation, were proof enough of the unrest in the country. The situation was dangerous. The tide of popular feeling rose and broke all the dams in the capital in a flood of angry tumult. These large-scale riots were clearly organized by a powerful but invisible hand.

The mass protest was the natural product of a very real misery. Even good salaries and new scales of wages were practically worthless in the face of the inflation which increased almost hourly. Thousands saw their wage-packets and incomes disappear before their eyes in the vortex of rising prices, knowing that at the same time profiteers were lining their pockets without raising a finger in honest work.

The instigators of the demonstrations in the streets with their anarchist slogans were the Communist opponents of the Social Democrats. However the censorious speeches of the Social Democratic leaders themselves and the line taken by their press had very decidedly influenced the opinion of the masses and so paved the way for this Communist action. There was, however, no sequel to the events of December 1. The demonstrators themselves were, so it seemed, overcome by the sight next day of the devastation which they had created. Only the plunderers came away the better.

It was a troubled Christmas. The state administration had imposed severe restrictions upon the national resources. The Christian-Social Finance Minister, Dr. Gürtler, applied all his energy and wits to master the economy, but the necessary comprehensive financial reform could not be achieved by national means alone. Foreign aid was, however, as yet unable to keep pace with internal measures, and meanwhile the economic situation in the country itself was growing more perilous daily. In his Christmas article in the *Reichspost* Dr. Seipel spoke of the "gigantic threat," but as a priest he also wrote of the eternal truth, never to be forgotten:

> All our reform work will be worthless unless we are determined at the same time to strive for the reform of our own souls and work toward this end. Our nation has need both now and in the future of great spiritual resources. It has need of a real confidence in the future which can only find its deepest roots in belief and confidence in God. It has need of a sense of

personal sacrifice which can only be instilled by a deep inner love of God. There is much which we are forced to concede to those upon whose comradeship we are still dependent on our political road. There is, however, one concession which may never be made, no matter how powerful the spirit of the age may be: we must never allow our Christian ideals to be shattered, nor sacrifice the religious integrity of our nation to the trend of the times. We know well that we are rendering the best service to our people and our country in maintaining a firm stand on this point.

Austria had a great debt of gratitude for the help afforded to the country in her hour of need after World War I, especially by the neutral states. The wonderful help of Pope Benedict XV, of the Catholics of Switzerland and Holland and of the population of Denmark, Sweden and of the United States, particularly for the Austrian children, will never be forgotten. Help from American Catholics, organized by the National Welfare Conference in Washington, continued right up to the mid-'twenties.

The *Reichspost* too found itself in need of extra assistance, for the newspaper had neither wealthy men, foreign capital nor gilt-edged securities behind it to help it to weather the economic storm. The value of Austrian currency fell so rapidly that by the time the monthly subscriptions came in, this sum represented only a tiny fraction of the cost of the newspaper as calculated at the beginning of the payment period. The day finally came, as come it must, when the paper was faced with financial ruin.

One morning when my telephone rang I picked up the receiver and could scarcely believe the words I heard: Archbishop Mundelein of Chicago, whose name I knew only from the Catholic News Service in Washington and with whom neither I nor the newspaper had ever had any personal contact, had sent me one thousand dollars for the *Reichspost*—one thousand heaven-sent dollars to save our life at this critical moment! I was unashamed of the tears in my eyes. . . .

Differences of opinion in matters of foreign policy had led to the fact that many Pan-German deputies had gone over to the side of the Social Democratic party, as bitter opponents as ever of the government, with the result that the government soon found itself with a dangerously small majority. This state of affairs could obviously not continue. During the preceding weeks, England, France and Italy had agreed to the provision of credits for Austria, with the promise of further aid in the future. The suspension of the preferential mortage law was being considered, but all financial help from abroad was useless as long as it was being poured into a bottomless sack. As the law for the use of these credits introduced in mid-March in the National Assembly demanded, this financial assistance must serve to establish a fund destined "to regulate the market for foreign currencies, not for household purposes" or other such ends. This plan was carried through on the initiative of the Christian-Social Union which, already at the beginning of March, invited the other parties to form a working majority and a government based on such a concrete plan.

All the previous unplanned assistance from abroad had been ineffectual in regulating the national economy and had not succeeded in preventing the rapid drop in the Austrian currency. On December 31, 1920, Austrian foreign bills in Zurich still stood at least at 1.572; one year later they were quoted at 0.19, and two months later at 0.1, that is to say that one Austrian krone was worth only one-tenth of a Swiss centime. The dollar was worth 654 kronen in Vienna on December 31, 1920, whereas one year later, on January 2, 1922, the official price had soared to 5,273 kronen. Two and a half months later, on March 14, the day on which the draft bill for the use of foreign credits was presented to the National Assembly, the official rate of 8,048 kronen showed no signs of remaining static. It was, therefore, understandable that the British finance delegate, Young, declared both in an open letter to the press and in a private note to Chancellor Schober that he could not undertake to provide credits for Austria before the necessary legislation for the appropriate use of these credits had been put through Parliament. This declaration was interpreted all too rigorously by the Pan-Germans, with the result that the Chancellor felt obliged to hand in his resignation.

Though the Pan-German party declared itself ready to co-operate "in the formation of a working majority and a government based on a concrete working plan," the party felt that it could not consider proposals for the formation of such a government since, as it knew, "influence from abroad" played a considerable role in the formation of this government. Negotiations for the setting up of a parliamentary working body were therefore abortive.

Nevertheless the man who was responsible for the policy of the Christian-Social party and led the other parties as well at the conference table withstood this test of strength. He came forward with a new proposal. Without effecting any change in the existing government, he said, agreement should be reached on all financial measures designed to guarantee the strict appropriation of foreign credits. His courage was rewarded. On March 16 a "parliamentary truce" was concluded with the participation of all parties, even the Social Democrats, which provided for the settlement of the various items of vital legislative business on the parliamentary agenda within limited periods of time.

Public opinion had in no small measure directed this course. People were tired of fruitless party doctrine, and in those turbulent days the moderate, decisive policy of Dr. Seipel, firmly directed toward its ultimate goal, won the approbation of many who had formerly by no means supported the Christian-Social program. It was significant that the leading Graz newspaper in Styria and Carinthia, most of the readers of which had pan-German leanings, applied Abraham Lincoln's famous words to the Pan-German party when it wrote: "You can fool all the people for some time, some of the people all the time, but not all the people all the time."

In the midst of all this political unrest there was still somehow time to celebrate an unusual occasion. The Christian-Social Deputies' Club held a special ceremony with Mass in the Votive Church and an extraordinary meeting in Parliament to honor six members of the party who had been deputies in the House for twenty-five years. The club included me among these members, for although I was not a deputy, I had been a journalist in Parliament for a quarter of a century and by my unique position was closely connected with the Christian-Social Club and its most intimate members. As chairman of the club, Dr. Seipel defined this unusual position in his speech addressed to the honored jubilee members:

"We regard Dr. Funder as our fellow combatant, our companion in arms in the true sense. His relationship to the party is different from that of the editor of the Social Democrat *Arbeiter Zeitung*. As is well known we have no party press[4] in this sense. As editor of the *Reichspost* Dr. Funder is not an employee of the party: he runs his newspaper concern independently. If in this work he stands one hundred per cent on our side, this is not because he is a party employee but because he is our ally.

"Our jubilee members come from the various provinces. We have Fink from Vorarlberg, Weiskirchner from Vienna, Schoiswohl from Styria, Schöpfer from Tyrol, Mayer from Lower Austria and Loser, another deputy from Vorarlberg. As for our Dr. Funder, I hardly know where to assign him—whether to Styria where he was born, or to Vienna, the place where he has worked for so long. I think the best solution is to call him an Austrian through and through, a man who can represent the Viennese point of view just as well and with the same understanding and warmth of feeling as that of the provinces."

In my speech in reply I expressed my thanks to this club which had been a sort of school and at the same time a home to me for so many years.

The cordial relations between the Christian-Social Club and the *Reichspost* had never been marred by the slightest disharmony, even when on certain important issues the newspaper was not afraid to make use of its own freedom of judgment and even of criticism. Both sides were aware that this very freedom of opinion gave the public the confidence which was essential before they could help to further the aims of the party. It was not the function of this paper to act as a narrow party organ, a sort of extension of the party or-

---

[4] This passage can be fully understood by the American reader only if it is remembered that on the Continent the link between some (but by no means all) newspapers with a political party is often very close. For this reason it is in fact quite feasible to talk of the journalists (especially those of left-wing papers) as employees or even "yes-men" of the party executives. This development of the press as an exclusively party organ has tended to increase if anything within the last few years. It is, however, a fact that the non-party papers have for the most part considerably larger circulations than the party papers.

ganization, but rather, as Seipel so aptly described it, as an ally. The Christian political party need never fear a truly Christian journalist who is really aware of the responsibilities involved in his profession and views his work not as a mere trade but a true vocation, a vital duty.

But the political pact between the parties lasted only a bare two months. Dr. Otto Bauer openly voiced his censure of the Finance Minister, Dr. Gürtler, in the Finance Committee by introducing a "lack of confidence" motion holding him responsible for the increasingly high prices and for "arbitrary" increases in certain customs tariffs already foreseen by the Minister in March. The motion was supported by the Pan-Germans and was subsequently carried by 14 votes to 10, resulting in Dr. Gürtler's resignation. The Pan-Germans supported this action, influenced by a personal feud with the Minister of Finance.

A new crisis had now been provoked for the ministry, with demands for new men from the ranks of those who had caused the Minister's downfall. The democratic rules of the game would normally have required that the victors on the ramparts take over the leadership. Neither Dr. Bauer's Social Democrats nor the Pan-German party were, however, prepared to do this. In spite of Kunschak's declaration that the Christian-Socials would put no obstacles in the way of such a government, they firmly declined to take this step. The more adamant their refusal, the louder grew the cries for the new man, for the chairman of the Christian-Social club. On May 20 the foremost Social-Democratic newspaper appealed to the people in its leading article to "Vote for Seipel!"

This was indeed something quite unprecedented, indeed almost unbelievable. The people seriously desired to see a priest take over the government of the country. Never before in the constitutional history of Austria had anyone dreamed of such a thing, neither the countless anti-clericals nor even the Catholics themselves. Perhaps the Social Democrats were secretly reckoning that their troublesome opponent might break his neck on the hazardous mission on which they so urgently desired to send him.

The perilous political territory which he would have to cross gave good grounds for such a speculation. The situation at the time was such that there were even grave doubts as to whether Austria could herself hope to avoid disaster. It was true that reports of the financial negotiations in London were not unfavorable, but promises had after all been dangled for over a year without realization and even the most courageous optimists had begun to lose hope. Dr. Richard Weiskirchner, for instance, a man with understanding and experience in overcoming difficult administrative problems, a close associate of Dr. Lueger and mayor of Vienna with its two million inhabitants during the critical war years, had never been a pessimist. Even he, however, declared at a political meeting in Vienna on May 22:

"The victorious powers have created a cripple state in their Treaty of St. Germain. It is now up to them to provide for its existence. If these next few weeks are to pass fruitlessly and new credits do not reach us to enable us to establish a new issuing bank with a newly-founded, stable currency, then we can only say that all our devoted efforts to save this fragment of a state were useless. The Entente Powers can then take over this state, the product of their own hands, and do what they like with it. We have come to the end of our patience!"

It seemed as though the reconstruction program which Dr. Seipel presented on May 24 had been prepared expressly to counter this wave of pessimism and hopelessness, for it was greeted with open scorn by Seipel's apparently irreconcilable opponent, Dr. Otto Bauer, and his party friends. Seipel's program made no claim to be a philosophers' stone, but it nevertheless signified something of infinite value in itself: it proved that there was still one man in Austria who was not prepared to give in. It was his example which brought about a change of heart among the Pan-Germans who under Schober's chancellorship had been the reed blown by the wind. Now at their party congress in Graz they found the courage to overcome their former resentment, and by 307 votes to 58 they empowered their party leaders to lend their support to Seipel in the formation of a stable working government majority. Before the end of May the government was set up, based on these parties. Seipel's Cabinet was significant. The new Chancellor had picked Richard Schmitz as his Minister for Social Affairs.

The new government appeared in the House for the first time on May 31. The galleries were filled to overflowing. The atmosphere was almost electric as Chancellor Seipel began his government declaration:

"Rarely has a government been called for so long and so insistently as the government elected today. What is more, the very party which has not today given us its vote was the most clamorous in this demand. I am, of course, quite aware that it was not only trust and affection for me personally which urged Social Democratic speakers to demand again and again that Professor Seipel should at last take over the government. Most of these merely cherished the hope that the leader of the Christian-Social party would perish among the hazards of a hopeless situation. Or perhaps they reckoned that in this way they would gain new weapons in their agitation campaign against him and his party? Others among them perhaps regarded it as a real demand of democracy in the Western sense that the leader of the most powerful political party should personally assume the constitutional responsibility for the government. However this may be, I wish to stress here and now that the opposition of today is nevertheless also responsible for this government to which they did not give their vote. I do not altogether care for the phrase, since the person concerned is myself, but it is none the less true that they in fact talked so long of the devil until he finally did appear."

Seipel then followed with those fine words which revealed the depths of his own soul:

"There are certainly others more competent to take the place which I fill today, but God has led me to this place. My trust is in Him that, together with my fellow ministers, I may be enabled to give of my best in the service of my country."

This moving *de profundis* in the hour of the country's direst need was an expression of unbroken trust in God and confidence in the vitality of Austria and in her salvation. The words were significant of the fine character of this priest who was fully conscious of the great mission entrusted to him. Seipel knew well what this mission meant, he was prepared to accept his task, aware of the obstacles, disillusionment, lack of understanding, hatred and personal sacrifice which would be involved. He had no illusions. No sooner had he assumed office than the nation was shattered by the repercussions of yet another financial earthquake. There were renewed currency fluctuations and a new storm of speculations on the stock exchange. Large-scale strikes broke out. Every day increasing numbers of unemployed, disabled soldiers and other unfortunate victims of the economic crisis found themselves on the streets.

So began the Way of the Cross which Seipel had to follow with his ministers. But he remained upright and unbroken. The historic moment finally came on Wednesday, September 6, when the Chancellor stood up before the League of Nations in Geneva and told these lords of the world what would happen to Europe if a vacuum were created in its center, a vacuum which would inexorably draw everything down into its bottomless abyss.

Geneva intervened with success, but the psychological problems reflected in the relief action deserve wider attention than that hitherto accorded to them, for these problems have a political significance the influence of which played a decisive part in European affairs right up to World War II.

"At this moment, more than ever before, it is for the whole nation to take an active part in the formation of public opinion in matters which concern the well-being of Austria." This was the appeal, unmistakably addressed to all Austrians, irrespective of their political creed, with which Chancellor Seipel arrived at the Westbahnhof in Vienna on his return from his victorious mission in Geneva. The appeal was answered with sharp criticism from the ranks of his political opponents, particularly Dr. Otto Bauer, who voiced in Parliament his condemnation of the attitude adopted by both the Federal Chancellor and the Foreign Secretary at Geneva. It was scarcely surprising, therefore, that Seipel did not renew his invitation for co-operation. Dr. Renner, who had apparently already forgotten St. Germain, refrained for obvious reasons from any comparison of Dr. Seipel's achievements with the peace treaty which he himself had been forced to bring home to Austria. In a passionate speech in Parliament Dr. Renner fiercely repudiated the terms of the Geneva agreement by which Austria accepted obligations not to the victorious powers and for an unlimited number of years, but to the League of Nations, and then only on the acceptance of a two-year financial control.

When Ignaz Seipel died in 1932 the leading Austrian Social Democratic newspaper paid a fitting tribute to the memory of their political opponent, describing him as "by far the most outstanding man of the Austrian bourgeoisie" and declaring: "the only statesman of true European stature produced by the bourgeois parties ... we too salute our great political opponent with three salvos of honor over his bier." This was the man whom they had attacked so bitterly ever since he assumed public office, even when they came to realize his true greatness, even when they recognized the outstanding qualities of the "only statesman of true European stature."

Yet Ignaz Seipel was more than just a great statesman. His personal example shone like a beacon at this dark time when the whole social order was suddenly changed, when fortunes were made overnight at the expense of the masses, when principles were thrown to the wind in an irresponsible urge for gain. He was the leader at this time of moral and economic insecurity. Himself a professor of moral theology at the University of Vienna, Seipel followed in the footsteps of his master, Dr. Franz Martin Schindler. He too preferred to proclaim his moral teaching by the practical example of his own daily life.

Even when he assumed the high office of Chancellor, he continued to live in his small scholar's apartment consisting of a study and a bedroom furnished with monastic simplicity. He never employed a private secretary. From no other great figure in Austrian public life have so many hand-written letters been preserved as from Seipel. With the exception of routine official documents he always answered all his correspondence himself, by hand. Among the countless letters which I myself received from him, many of which contained detailed political information, surveys of the current situation, draft plans and the like, not one was dictated or typewritten. No other Federal Chancellor ever ran his office more economically. Seipel was extraordinarily exact, even puritanical, in all financial affairs.

His private life was so simple and spartan that it was almost impossible to discover a single need or wish which could be fulfilled. When his friends and admirers brought him gifts at Christmas and other occasions he would accept these with gratitude, only to give them away again at once himself. As far as I know Seipel never had a bank account or any form of savings in his life, nor did he hold any state bonds or shares, apart from the few ten kronen *Herold* shares which he was obliged by law to hold as a member of the board of the *Herold* concern; neither he nor any of the other members ever accepted a penny for their services to the company. He was all the richer in the number of his "clients," people who came to seek his assistance and whom he always helped behind the scenes.

Toward the end of his life, already a very sick man, he undertook a pilgrimage to the Holy Land, but he made the journey in such discomfort and so quickly that he came home quite worn out from the hardships he had endured. Only by chance through a brief comment did I learn that he had not had sufficient funds to enable him to travel more comfortably, as his state of health at that time would have demanded. It was not mere chance that he was one of the founders of the Caritas Socialis, the organization which he so dearly loved and which he inspired by his devotion toward helping the poor and needy. It was this same impulse which had driven him to take over the chancellorship of Austria, an office which no other man dared to embark upon at this perilous juncture. Seipel recognized the need for moral and social reform and stepped into the breach.

This same spiritual approach to the problems of the time led this great priest to devote himself to the problem of peace for mankind. One of the most outstanding literary tributes to Ignaz Seipel appeared in 1946 in a little book published in a series produced by the Austrian Catholic Action. Here one of his closest friends, Richard Schmitz, writes:

"He viewed the whole social problem essentially as a question of peace between the conflicting classes. He was true to this conviction to the day of his death, for he sacrificed the last of his dwindling strength toward winning the support and recognition of Catholic Austria for the great truths contained in the Papal encyclical *Quadragesimo Anno*. He examined over and over again the tension between party and state, nation and fatherland, state and religion, and between the peoples of the world in the light of the idea of peace.

"He was one of the first to advocate an organization for humanity which he visualized as a composite unit, each member conforming to make up a perfect whole. His own book *Nation und Staat*, although small, was a valuable contribution toward the work for peace. Another of his short works contained proposals for a Catholic movement for peace, and in the midst of the tumult of the war he was active, together with like-minded friends at home and abroad, in his efforts to achieve peace. This work, which he began as a scholar, was continued as a politician and a statesman. Not only in Austria, but also on the various journeys he undertook throughout Europe and in America, his public speeches in the cause of peace were greeted with heart-felt applause. Seipel spoke in the cause of peace, both for his own native Austria and between the other nations of the world.

"It was he who proposed that the League of Nations should be expanded to provide for the autonomic settlement of national problems, and the sermon which he preached from the pulpit of Notre Dame church in Geneva to the Catholic delegates to the League of Nations re-echoed all over the world. He pursued this tireless work in the interests of peace right up to the end of his life and his sole concern was that his work should be continued after his death.

"The ideal of peace, the establishment of a new and better social order inspired his whole life. One day shortly after Seipel's first term of office as Chancellor I received a message from Cardinal Piffl: he wished to see me concerning a confidential matter. I learned that the Prince Bishop of Sekau, Dr. Schuster, was far from well and that the Cardinal was concerned to find a successor to be appointed as suffragan bishop. Dr. Seipel ranked first on the list, in fact his appointment to this high clerical office depended only upon the decision of Seipel himself. Upon leaving the Cardinal I went straight to Dr. Kienböck, who had been Minister of Finance in Seipel's first cabinet and as such was best qualified to judge the situation and assess the manifold economic problems with which Austria was confronted at this precarious juncture. I told him of my conversation with Cardinal Piffl. We lost no time in going to Dr.

Seipel. Kienböck shared my own dread at the prospect of Seipel's retirement from political life. Were Seipel to go before the Geneva relief action had been fully secured, now, at this critical point when the currency had only just been stabilized, this would inevitably bring about a severe setback for Austria. The situation was indeed serious. Everything hung in the balance and Seipel was still needed. We laid the facts before him.

"Dr. Seipel gave us plenty of time and he listened attentively to all we had to say. Then he sat there for several minutes without answering. When he at last spoke his voice was grave. He was a priest, he said, and as such he felt that if he were called upon to assume the pastoral responsibility of a diocese then this must be regarded as his primary duty. Dr. Kienböck reminded him that the dangers which threatened Austria were not of a political nature only—if the work of reconstruction so successfully begun were to collapse, the country would be plunged back into the disastrous situation of 1922. Austria could scarcely hope to recover a second time from such a blow.

"Seipel sat there before us, sunk in meditation. It was only too clear what an inner struggle this decision was costing him. At long last he raised his head, with a deep sigh. 'I'll stay,' he said. We rose and left him sitting there, both deeply moved. On October 20, 1926, Prälat Ignaz Seipel became Chancellor of Austria for the second time, and on May 19, 1927, he began his third term of office. Austria had need of him.

"During the last years of his public life Seipel devoted a great deal of time to propagating the idea of a corporative state, the idea upon which his great master, Dr. Schindler, had concentrated for so long. Seipel was a true disciple of Schindler: he regarded the realization of the ideal of a state based on such corporative principles as a real mission.

"It was this concept which had in fact influenced the early Christian-Social reform program so profoundly, already in the 'eighties, with Franz Martin Schindler and Prince Alois Liechtenstein as its most convinced exponents. As early as 1889 a resolution proposed by Schindler at the second Austrian *Katholikentag* was unanimously adopted by the Social Section. This declared the corporative organization of society on the basis of trades and professions to be 'the most effective weapon against the social evils of the present day,' and proclaimed that 'corporative organization represents the first of all our aims, the first of all our demands for the solution of the social question. . . .' The resolution further asserted that such a corporative system would put an end to the chaos caused by the sudden collapse of the old social order and the ruthless exploitation of the masses in the selfish urge for material gain.

"Now, after forty-two years, these same reform principles were evident in the encyclical *Quadragesimo Anno,* the solemn declaration of Pope Pius XI which examined every fundamental principle of the social question in detail. The encyclical had made a deep impression upon Ignaz Seipel. As August Knoll commented in the *Schweizerischen Rundschau* of March 1, 1933, in an article on Seipel's reaction to the contents of the encyclical, Seipel's concept for the ordering of the classes of society prepared in 1929 'coincided exactly with that of the encyclical of May 15, 1931.'

"The system of universal equal suffrage which had replaced the old electoral system of Liberal days designed only for the privileged classes had disappointed the high hopes cherished for it in the early days of the Christian-Social movement. It had been hailed as the prelude to a better state of affairs in public life. In effect the system had become rigid, deprived of all vitality by the calculated and artificial side-effects of proportional representation. These developments were to be observed not in Austria alone, and not only in Austria were political thinkers concerned with seeking a solution to the problems involved.

"Seipel was once again led to consider the introduction of the corporative form of society, the concrete realization of which he felt would not be possible without the planned co-operation of the state. He dedicated his last ounce of energy toward this reform. He was invited to speak on this subject at the Styrian Christian-Social provincial party congress in Graz in the fall of 1931. He spoke as a sick man, with a high temperature. His speech, which lasted over one hour and in which he dealt exhaustively with every aspect of the corporative order, was greeted with tremendous enthusiasm. He convinced his vast audience of the significance of this great idea,

and the meeting developed into a demonstration of loyalty to this
outstanding Christian statesman and sociologist.

"Seipel left for Vienna late that afternoon. I was traveling back
to the capital myself by the same train and I took good care that
Seipel should not see me on the station at Graz. I felt he should
travel alone so as to be able to get some sleep. But he sent a railway
official to look for me and I shared his compartment on the journey
back. Seipel did not sleep for as much as a quarter of an hour, and
our conversation consisted of a long discourse on democracy, a
monologue conducted by Seipel, the great European statesman. I
confined my remarks to a few brief comments and sat in admiration
and astonishment, fascinated by the words of the man who sat
opposite me, his face flushed by fever.

"Seipel analyzed the great fundamental democratic principle.
He discussed the advantages of such a system, the progress which
had been made, but he spoke also of the deviations, of the pitfalls
for the unwary, of the dangers of democracy if once reduced to a
purely mechanical form. This 'formal democracy,' so he insisted,
must be further developed into a 'constructive democracy' the authenticity and strength of which lay in overcoming the class differences of contemporary society.

"As Seipel continued to speak, at times as though he were thinking aloud, it was as though the blueprint of a great plan for social
and political reform were unfolded before my eyes. I was full of
concern for this man who was wearing himself out in his dedication
to a grandiose concept which he regarded as the final mission of his
life. For him there existed no more worthy task than 'to work for
the recognition and acceptance in Austria of the Holy Father's great
social concept as set out in *Quadragesimo Anno.*' He died, content
in the thought that he had worked to the very end, until he could
work no more, toward the realization of this aim.

"With Ignaz Seipel's death many lights went out in Austria."

No other European nation has had to face so many vicissitudes
during the course of the last twenty-five years or so as Austria.
Wrenched out of her ancient setting at the end of World War I,
her historical, economic and political ties severed overnight, the new

little nation between the Danube and Lake Constance had a hard struggle to secure her existence. The face of Europe had been changed, ravaged by war and its grim aftermath, but the people of Austria had to be given new hope, they had to be inspired with a new confidence, to be made to believe in the viability of the new state built up so laboriously out of the ruins of the old Empire.

It was a bitter struggle; at one point the Austrian state was forced to spend as much as one-third of its budget on food for the starving population. The currency was on the point of collapse and the nationl economy was faced with ruin. It was Ignaz Seipel and Victor Kienböck who mastered this perilous situation with the aid of Geneva. No sooner had Austria begun to recover from this crisis, however, than the effects of the world economic slump made themselves felt. Great banking houses collapsed and the savings banks and similar institutions closed their doors one after another. The unrest which resulted was naturally reflected in political life, and the state had to weather a new storm.

People were embittered, disillusioned, discontented. The moment was ripe for political adventure, for the past masters of high-sounding political slogans proclaiming a new salvation, exponents of a new "nationalism" ready to exploit the masses for their own ends. It was easy enough for them to find followers among the malcontents with empty stomachs. In fact they found quite a swarm of followers. Thus the illegal National Socialist organizations grew, swelled by the ranks of the opportunists and those driven into their arms by sheer desperation. The newspapers already referred to "a political movement."

The struggle over the Lausanne Loan took on a new political significance. The 300 million schilling League of Nations loan was urgently needed by the Austrian government. But propaganda had succeeded in undermining the government majority. The pan-German faction of this majority succumbed to the force of the slogans and went over to the opposition, with the result that this new bloc almost ranked in strength with the government majority. The resulting situation in Parliament was so absurd that some chance issue would have been enough to split the precarious majority. As it was, the motion introduced by the pan-Germans expressing lack of confidence in the government and urging the dissolution of Parliament and the holding of new general elections produced a state crisis.

The Reichstag elections in Germany on March 5, 1933 resulted in a complete victory for the Nationalists, and the now entirely Nationalist opposition in the Austrian parliament had good grounds to hope for new blood among the electorate. In the Vienna municipal elections held in April the National Socialists did in fact succeed in gaining access to the hitherto closed doors of the Rathaus. New general elections did not, however, take place, and in the face of various threats and difficulties the Lausanne Protocol was eventually put through the House in 1932 by the narrow margin of 82 votes to 80.

The fifteen National Socialists who had penetrated into the sacred precincts of the Vienna Rathaus, that proud citadel of Austria, might flaunt their victory, but their success had more of an optical than a practical view. It was nevertheless only to be expected that the National Socialists should be encouraged by the successes of their party and their activities increased accordingly. The current economic situation provided a fitting background and their numbers swelled in proportion to the dissatisfaction of the people. It took a fearless champion like young Dr. Dollfuss, who had now taken over the chancellorship, to step into the breach in the ensuing political conflicts. He sacrificed his own life in this heroic stand. Not the question of Parliament or of democracy as such was important at that moment, but, as Schuschnigg declares in his book *Dreimal Österreich*, "Austria herself was at stake."

It was a hard road and there were points on the way where democracy swayed perilously, like a reed bent by the storm. There were rumors of a civil war. The Heimwehr leaders were faced with grave responsibilities at that hour. The forces of the revolutionary National Socialist camp grouped around Tavs, Leopold and Schattenfroh were only too ready for action at any moment. At this juncture the parliamentary mechanism was brought to a standstill.

Hitler's propaganda increased. The slogans advocated *Anschluss*, a break with Austria, the abolition of the Austrian state. The National Socialists should take over control of the country as soon as possible, using every available means to achieve this end.

But Austria weathered the storm. Men were there at the right moment ready to stake everything in the struggle for their country's freedom and independence, men who counted no labor, no combat too hard, no sacrifice too great.

The Austrian people will long remember with gratitude the significant words of the Chancellor of the German Federal Republic Dr. Adenauer, words which constitute an open manifestation of the restoration of Austria's independence and freedom.

For seven long years Austria was robbed of her freedom, degraded and humiliated, and she can hope for no more noble testimonial to her national honor than the following words of the historical speech delivered by Dr. Adenauer on his state visit to Austria in June, 1957:

"We can never lose sight of the great principles of our common Christian Western civilization, for they return again and again to warn us and to help us. An essential part of this heritage is our love of freedom and independence and of those eternal human values which no system of totalitarian oppression can destroy. You in Austria and we in Germany know the truth of this. I believe that it is this unbroken will for freedom and independence which, after all the dark years of degradation, war and hardship, has made Austria what she is today."

INDEX OF NAMES